IMAGERY

30°E 60° 90° 120° 150°

EUROPE

ASIA

AFRICA

AUSTRALIA

ANTARCTICA

EUROPE-ASIA
BOUNDARY

NATIONAL GEOGRAPHIC

SATELLITE ATLAS OF THE WORLD

Washington, D.C.

NATIONAL GEOGRAPHIC
SATELLITE ATLAS OF THE WORLD

Imaging satellites are the silent sentinels of the space age. They are another incredible example of how the space program benefits us here on Earth in a way that we could never have imagined when our space journey began 40 years ago."

SENATOR JOHN GLENN

NATIONAL GEOGRAPHIC

SATELLITE ATLAS
OF THE WORLD

Published by THE NATIONAL GEOGRAPHIC SOCIETY
JOHN M. FAHEY, JR. *President and Chief Executive Officer*
GILBERT M. GROSVENOR *Chairman of the Board*
NINA D. HOFFMAN *Senior Vice President*

Prepared by THE BOOK DIVISION *and* NATIONAL GEOGRAPHIC MAPS

THE BOOK DIVISION
WILLIAM R. GRAY *Vice President and Director*
CHARLES KOGOD *Assistant Director*
BARBARA A. PAYNE *Editorial Director and Managing Editor*
DAVID GRIFFIN *Design Director*

BOOK DIVISION STAFF FOR THIS BOOK
CARL MEHLER *Project Editor and Director of Maps*
CAROLINDA E. HILL *Text Editor*
STUDIO A *Design*
LESLIE ALLEN, ELISABETH BOOZ, PATRICK BOOZ,
    JOHN E. ESTES, KIM HEACOX, K. M. KOSTYAL, ROBIN T. REID *Writers*
ANTONIO J. BUSALACCHI, JR., RALPH FERRARO,
    CARL HAUB, CAROLINDA E. HILL, THOMAS R. LOVELAND,
    CARL MEHLER, PEYTON H. MOSS, JR., JOHN T. NEER,
    WALTER H. F. SMITH *Contributing Writers*
MARTHA C. CHRISTIAN *Contributing Editor*
KIMBERLY A. KOSTYAL *Senior Researcher*
KAREN D. KLINE, KEITH R. MOORE, ROBIN T. REID *Researchers*
THOMAS L. GRAY *Map Editor*
JOSEPH F. OCHLAK, SCOTT ZILLMER *Map Researchers*
JEHAN AZIZ *Map Production Manager*
JOHN S. BALLAY, JAMES HUCKENPAHLER, MAPPING SPECIALISTS, LTD.,
    BETH N. WEISENBORN, SCOTT ZILLMER *Map Production*
STUART ARMSTRONG *Illustrator*
R. GARY COLBERT *Production Director*
CLAYTON BURNESTON *Senior Image Technician*
GEORGE BOUNELIS, STEPHEN T. GOLDMAN *Image Technicians*
PEGGY CANDORE *Staff Assistant*

NATIONAL GEOGRAPHIC MAPS
ALLEN CARROLL *Managing Director*
DANIEL J. ORTIZ *Director of Map Ventures*
DIERDRE BEVINGTON-ATTARDI *Project Manager*
LISA R. RITTER *Senior Remote Sensing Researcher-Editor*
SUSAN A. CARNEY, KARLA TUCKER *Researchers*
ERIC A. LINDSTROM, DAVID B. MILLER, GUS PLATIS *Map Editors*
A. RUSSELL LITTLE, KEN A. MARLOW, *GIS Analysts*
SEAN MOHN, STEPHEN P. WELLS *Map Production*
MICHAEL J. HORNER *Map Librarian*
PATRICIA A. HEALY *Staff Assistant*

MANUFACTURING AND QUALITY CONTROL
GEORGE V. WHITE *Director*
JOHN T. DUNN *Associate Director*
CLIFTON BROWN *Manager*

MARK A. WENTLING *Indexer*

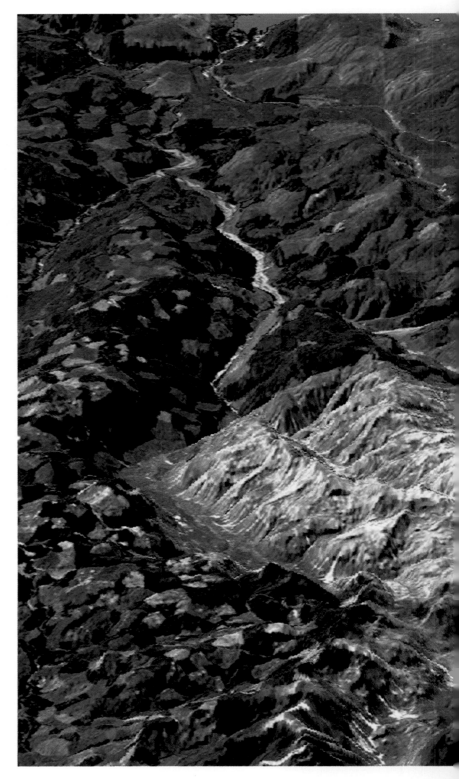

Previous Pages: EASTERN MEDITERRANEAN

MOUNT ST. HELENS, 1996 · *Sixteen years after its violent eruption*

TABLE OF CONTENTS

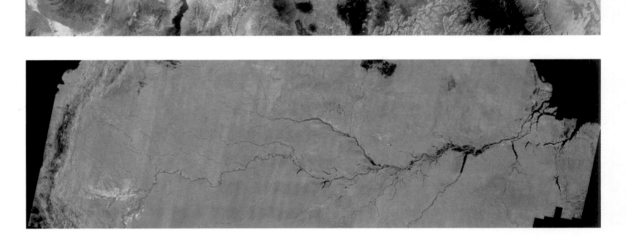

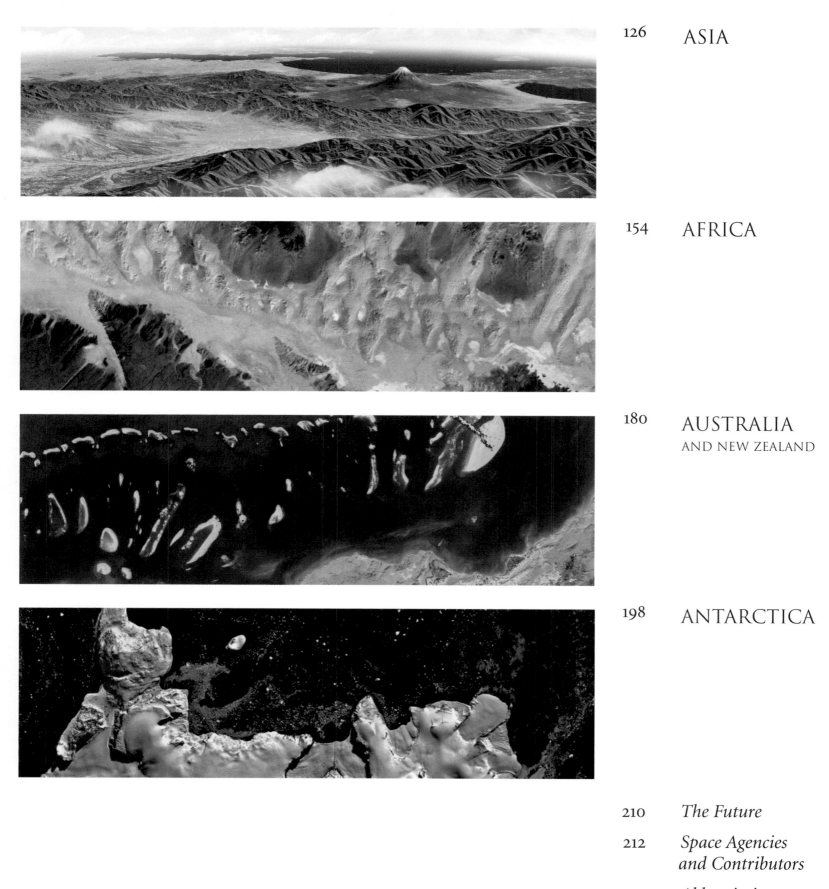

INTRODUCTION

By John E. Estes

Maps are important tools for recording the locations of features or objects. Even early humans probably made crude maplike diagrams in soft sand or dirt to show where game could be found. The earliest known maps, drawn on clay tablets around 2300 B.C., depict watercourses and settlements in the Middle East. Carefully drawn maps, dating from a later time, show parts of the Nile Valley and may have been used to reestablish property boundaries after the Nile's yearly flood.

In the fourth century B.C. Plato and his followers, through their works, began to establish the idea that the Earth is a sphere. Around 225 B.C. Eratosthenes estimated the circumference of the Earth by measuring the shadow cast at the same time of day in both Aswan and Alexandria, Egypt. Although he was not the first to do so, he was perhaps the most accurate, coming within some 200 miles of the correct figure.

Maps and mapmaking have changed over the centuries. Yet, it has only been in the last 40 years that Earth-orbiting satellites have provided a practical way of gathering consistent global data that we can use to measure, map, monitor, and model our dynamic Earth system. Governments have employed such data during international crises; industries have used the information to discover and manage natural resources; and academics have studied the data to increase their understanding of the Earth.

As we move into the next millennium, the world population is growing by about 250,000 each day. Cities spread over prime agricultural lands, energy consumption increases, and wildlife habitats shrink and break into patches that cannot sustain migratory species. Forests continue to be cleared for agriculture and wood products, threatening biological diversity.

Concern began to rise in the early 1970s that planned fleets of supersonic jets might affect the stratospheric ozone layer that protects us from harmful ultraviolet radiation. The jets were never built, but by the mid-1970s scientists worried that chlorofluorocarbons from refrigerators, air conditioners, and aerosol sprays might be depleting the ozone layer. Their fears were realized in the mid-1980s, when ground data from Halley Bay, Antarctica, revealed decreases in stratospheric ozone over a period of several years. The presence and extent of the so-called ozone hole were quickly confirmed when satellite data were examined. Scientists monitoring the phenomenon almost immediately began working with medical experts and policymakers to educate people about health problems that might result from it, and in 1987 an international agreement was reached on reducing the production of ozone-depleting chemicals.

Covering about 70 percent of the Earth, oceans interact with the atmosphere in complex ways. They release water into the atmosphere in a process that is vital for life; provide habitats for hundreds of thousands of species; and transport large quantities of heat from low to high latitudes, acting as a stabilizing factor for many of the world's climatic regimes. The interaction of the oceans and the atmosphere can have global consequences, as illustrated by the 1997-98 El Niño, one of the largest such events on record.

In normal years, easterly trade winds push warm water from the eastern Pacific into the western Pacific, where it generates abundant rainfall. In turn, nutrient-rich cold water wells up along South America's west coast. During El Niño, however, the easterlies weaken and can reverse, letting warm water flow back and pile up off South America. The upwelling of cold water slows or stops, fisheries disappear, and rainfall patterns shift. Responsible for doubling average precipitation in southern California, implicated in fires in Florida and Indonesia, and thought to be a reason for fewer Atlantic hurricanes, El Niño has had a major impact on our lives.

In 1997 scientists used satellites to measure sea surface temperatures and to map and monitor the growing pool of warm water in the equatorial eastern Pacific. As we continue to employ more advanced systems, we will become even more skillful at taking measurements, making maps, monitoring developments, and creating climate models. We will also improve our ability to help people prepare for the next El Niño and for other shifts in weather patterns. By gathering and interpreting satellite data, we are increasing our understanding and appreciation of the complex interactions of our global system, confirming what Socrates said long ago: "If we could rise above the Earth, then would we ... understand the world in which we live."

THE EARTH

Hundreds of NOAA satellite images make up this cloud-free composite of Earth as viewed from space. Except for a small portion in the visible red, the data used to create the mosaic cannot be seen by human eyes. Data processed for the top and bottom sections of the composite show the Earth in natural color. The isolated central swath illustrates how selected energy bands can identify water (gray), vegetation (red), desert (yellow), and bare rock (blue).

HISTORY OF SATELLITES

On July 25, 1891, some 65 years after the first photograph was taken and 33 years after the first aerial photograph was made from a captive balloon, a patent was granted for an apparatus to take pictures from a rocket. About 15 years later, Albert Maul was credited with taking the first such photographs. The first photographs from an airplane were taken by Wilbur Wright while he was flying over Italy in 1909. And in 1946, a captured German V-2 rocket from World War II , equipped with a camera and launched from White Sands, New Mexico, made the first photographs of Earth from space.

The first artificial satellite to orbit the Earth, Sputnik 1, was launched in 1957. Within four years the first systematic observations of the planet began with the Television and Infrared Observation Satellite (TIROS-1), whose primary mission was to monitor the weather; since that time an unbroken series of weather satellites has helped us improve our understanding of local and global weather patterns. Also put into orbit were remote sensor systems used by the intelligence community and the civil sector, and previously classified images from those systems are becoming available. The material here, however, focuses on other satellite systems that are representative of many that have orbited and several that are still in the planning stage.

In July 1972 the first satellite dedicated to imaging land areas was placed in orbit, and the seventh satellite in this series—known as the Landsats—is scheduled for launch in early 1999. The TIROS and Landsat remote sensor

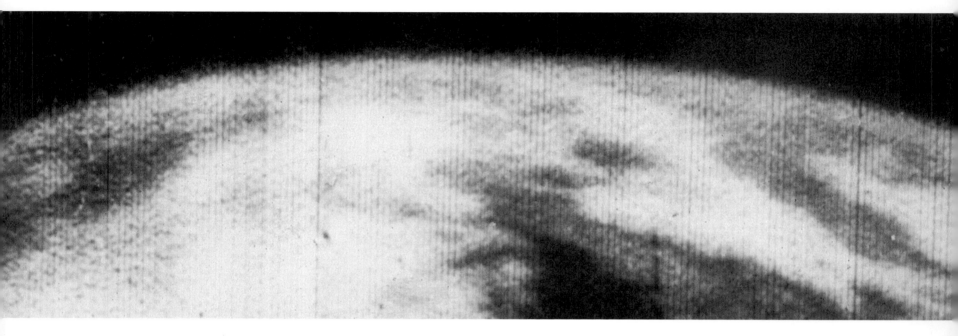

FIRST TELEVISION IMAGE

Taken on April 1, 1960, the first television image from the first meteorological satellite—the Television and Infrared Observation Satellite (TIROS-1)—depicts cloud patterns over eastern Canada and New England. Images were recorded on tape as an analog signal for later transmission to the ground.

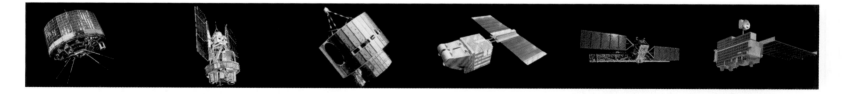

TIROS
1960–PRESENT

The U.S. launched the latest satellite in this series, NOAA-15, in spring 1998. The sun-synchronous meteorological satellite has a near-polar orbit 833 to 870 km (518 to 541 miles) high.

LANDSAT
1972–PRESENT

The U.S.'s Landsat 7 is scheduled for launch in early 1999. From 705 km (438 miles) up, the near-polar, sun-synchronous satellite provides data used in agriculture, forestry, water resources, and urban analysis.

GOES
1974–PRESENT

The Geostationary Operational Environmental Satellite (1-10) is in geostationary orbit 35,800 km (22,243 miles) up. This U.S. satellite's observations help in meteorology and climatology.

SPOT
1986–PRESENT

France's Satellite Pour l'Observation de la Terre (1-4) are sun-synchronous satellites with near-polar orbits 822 km (511 miles) high. Observations aid in land use, water resources research, and coastal studies.

RADARSAT
1995–PRESENT

Canada's Earth-observing satellite has a circular, sun-synchronous orbit 798 km (496 miles) high. The satellite collects data day and night and sees through nearly all kinds of weather.

EOS AM-1
UPCOMING

The U.S.'s Earth Observing System AM-1 will help study land, oceans, atmosphere, ice, and life as an integrated system. Its polar, sun-synchronous orbit will be 705 km (438 miles) above Earth.

systems are in orbits that take them over the Poles, while satellites in the Geostationary Operational Environmental Satellite (GOES) series, begun in 1974, sit in the same location above the Equator and take images of weather patterns below them. Although the spatial resolution of GOES is lower than that of Landsat, the system offers frequent observations of the same area, helping meteorologists make more accurate weather forecasts. In March 1998, operational tests of GOES-10 began by imaging the continental U.S. at five-minute intervals.

Another important system for mapping and monitoring land resources is the Satellite Pour l'Observation de la Terre (SPOT), a French satellite series that has provided images of the Earth's surface since 1986. SPOT 4, with an

improved sensor for monitoring global vegetation, was put into orbit in early 1998. In 1995, Canada launched RADARSAT, the first operationally oriented radar satellite system to provide timely delivery of large volumes of data. The active microwave (radar) sensor on RADARSAT can acquire imagery day and night and is able to collect data through clouds, rain, dust, haze, and smoke. The system can monitor surface conditions in the far north and south and in areas of high cloud cover, such as the tropics.

Current plans call for the launch of satellites having multiple advanced sensors that provide global core resolution data. One such satellite, EOS AM-1, will give us yet another important tool for understanding what may be the only planet capable of sustaining life as we know it.

COLD WAR

Beginning in the early 1960s, the United States and the Soviet Union employed satellites to gather intelligence about each other, and many knowledgeable people have since written that those satellites did much to prevent conflict during the Cold War. Intelligence satellites in the early 1960s allowed each

superpower to track the military and industrial developments of the other, confirming that a missile gap did not exist. Now scientists use images such as the ones shown above to study global change: At left, the U.S. Capitol in Washington, D.C., as it appeared to the former Soviet Union's Cosmos; at right, the Kremlin in Moscow, as seen by the U.S.'s Corona.

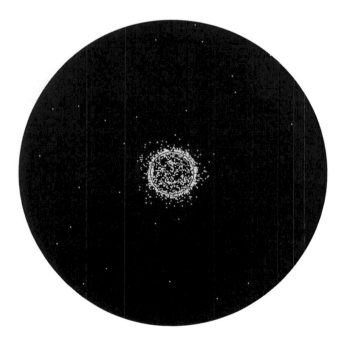

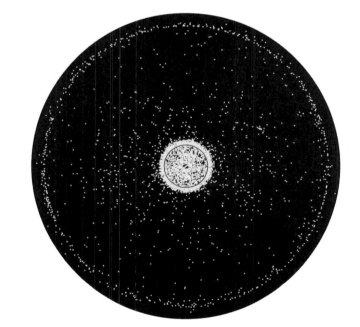

SPACE JUNK

Tracked since 1961 by the Naval Space Command (NSC) in Dahlgren, Virginia, the number of detectable Earth-orbiting objects—sometimes called space junk—tripled in three decades, from 3,058 in 1965 to more than 9,000 in July 1998. The number includes both operational and nonoperating Earth-

observing and communications satellites, as well as debris. The illustrations above depict objects around Earth (red circle) in the NSC space catalog for 1965 (left) and 1998 (right). In 1965, the NSC kept track of 576 objects categorized as spacecraft, including satellites, and 2,482 objects classified as debris. The partial 1998 tally includes 2,437 spacecraft and 6,697 debris objects.

HOW SATELLITES WORK

For a child who climbs a tree to get a better look at the neighborhood, the tree is the platform, the eye is the sensor system, and the brain is the recording device. For researchers, resource managers, and policy-makers who use remote sensing to get a better look at our planet, the platform is a satellite orbiting the Earth. The sensor is a camera; a multispectral-linear or an area-array scanner; a passive or thermal infrared system; or an active microwave (radar) system. The recording device is film or a digital medium.

The pictures in this atlas come from many sources, from astronaut-acquired photography to unmanned spacecraft in low-Earth, polar, and geostationary orbits. Thermal emissions show us the nighttime lights of the world or let us look through smoke to see areas where fires are still burning. We can also use radar—active microwave sensor systems that provide their own source of illumination—to see in the dark and to look through clouds. Most Earth-resource satellites record image data in digital formats. These data are then telemetered and processed to provide pictures such as the ones in this atlas. The diagram below represents a simplified explanation of how satellite data are processed into images.

ELECTROMAGNETIC SPECTRUM

Wavelengths and frequencies of electromagnetic radiation extending from gamma rays to radio waves define the electromagnetic spectrum (opposite). If the entire length of the spectrum wrapped around the world three times, the portion visible to humans would reach about the length of a pencil.

Landsat 5

Earth
Receiving
Station

Orbital Paths
of Satellite

185 X 185 Kilometers

Black-and-White
Images

False-Color
Composite
Scene

Filters

HOW DATA BECOME IMAGES

In the diagram above, the Thematic Mapper (TM) aboard Landsat 5 images a wide swath containing Cape Cod, Massachusetts. TM's scanning mirror records surface radiation in 7 bands of the electromagnetic spectrum. Sensors digitally record this information as 256 levels of brightness and send it to a receiving station where data for each band are processed into separate black-and-white images. Users select the desired band combinations and add colors with a computer or filter array to make the final image easier to interpret. A combination of brightness levels from bands 2 (green region of the spectrum), 3 (red), and 4 (near infrared) formed this false-color composite (upper right).

SATELLITE ORBITS

Remote sensing satellites image the Earth from various altitudes and orbits. In a geostationary orbit more than 35,000 kilometers (22,000 miles) in space, a satellite can hover over a specific location. A sun-synchronous, polar-orbiting satellite covers each location at the same time, typically from about 650 kilometers (400 miles) up. Other orbits may be as low as 160 kilometers (100 miles) and only cover the same location on the ground with the same sun angle once in a three-month period.

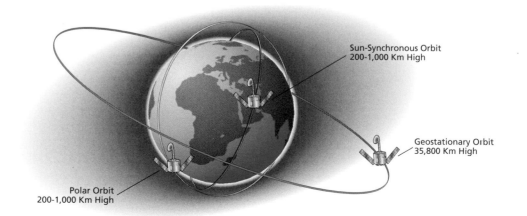

Sun-Synchronous Orbit
200-1,000 Km High

Geostationary Orbit
35,800 Km High

Polar Orbit
200-1,000 Km High

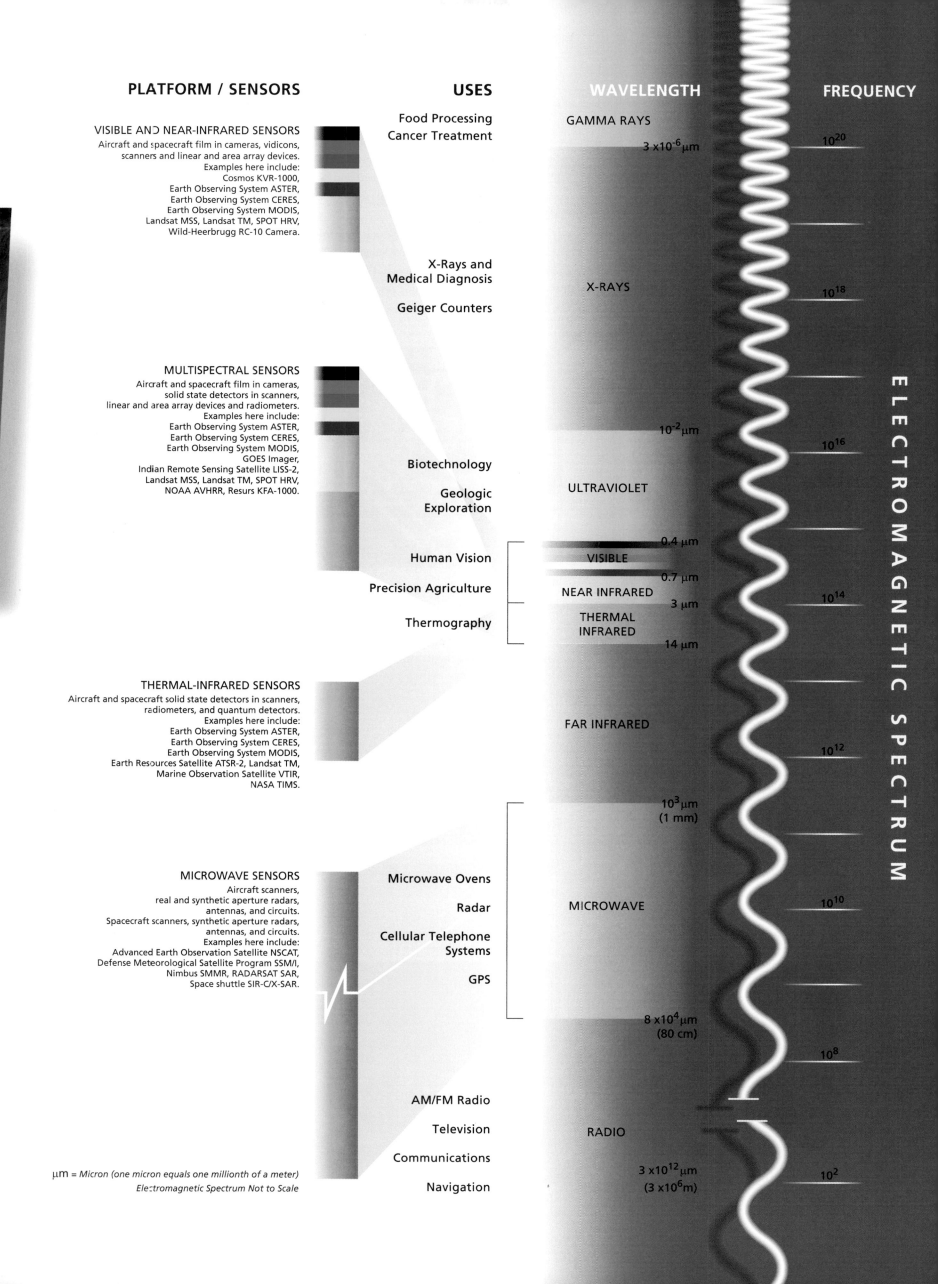

PLATFORM / SENSORS

VISIBLE AND NEAR-INFRARED SENSORS
Aircraft and spacecraft film in cameras, vidicons,
scanners and linear and area array devices.
Examples here include:
Cosmos KVR-1000,
Earth Observing System ASTER,
Earth Observing System CERES,
Earth Observing System MODIS,
Landsat MSS, Landsat TM, SPOT HRV,
Wild-Heerbrugg RC-10 Camera.

MULTISPECTRAL SENSORS
Aircraft and spacecraft film in cameras,
solid state detectors in scanners,
linear and area array devices and radiometers.
Examples here include:
Earth Observing System ASTER,
Earth Observing System CERES,
Earth Observing System MODIS,
GOES Imager,
Indian Remote Sensing Satellite LISS-2,
Landsat MSS, Landsat TM, SPOT HRV,
NOAA AVHRR, Resurs KFA-1000.

THERMAL-INFRARED SENSORS
Aircraft and spacecraft solid state detectors in scanners,
radiometers, and quantum detectors.
Examples here include:
Earth Observing System ASTER,
Earth Observing System CERES,
Earth Observing System MODIS,
Earth Resources Satellite ATSR-2, Landsat TM,
Marine Observation Satellite VTIR,
NASA TIMS.

MICROWAVE SENSORS
Aircraft scanners,
real and synthetic aperture radars,
antennas, and circuits.
Spacecraft scanners, synthetic aperture radars,
antennas, and circuits.
Examples here include:
Advanced Earth Observation Satellite NSCAT,
Defense Meteorological Satellite Program SSM/I,
Nimbus SMMR, RADARSAT SAR,
Space shuttle SIR-C/X-SAR.

μm = Micron (one micron equals one millionth of a meter)
Electromagnetic Spectrum Not to Scale

USES

Food Processing
Cancer Treatment

X-Rays and
Medical Diagnosis

Geiger Counters

Biotechnology

Geologic
Exploration

Human Vision

Precision Agriculture

Thermography

Microwave Ovens

Radar

Cellular Telephone
Systems

GPS

AM/FM Radio

Television

Communications

Navigation

WAVELENGTH

GAMMA RAYS

$3 \times 10^{-6} \mu m$

X-RAYS

$10^{-2} \mu m$

ULTRAVIOLET

0.4 μm
VISIBLE
0.7 μm
NEAR INFRARED
3 μm
THERMAL
INFRARED
14 μm

FAR INFRARED

$10^{3} \mu m$
(1 mm)

MICROWAVE

$8 \times 10^{4} \mu m$
(80 cm)

RADIO

$3 \times 10^{12} \mu m$
$(3 \times 10^{6} m)$

FREQUENCY

10^{20}

10^{18}

10^{16}

10^{14}

10^{12}

10^{10}

10^{8}

10^{2}

ELECTROMAGNETIC SPECTRUM

HOW SATELLITES WORK

According to an old saying, some people can't see the forest for the trees. In remote sensing, people frequently want to see individual trees, while others want to look at whole forests. Practitioners of remote sensing always try to maximize the contrast between an object they are interested in and the object's background. Seeing a golf ball on a green is one thing; seeing a golf ball in a sand trap is another. In winter, a golf ball on a snow-covered green will be almost impossible to see unless it is, say, orange.

To deal with such difficulties, analysts of remotely sensed data select images at various spatial, spectral, and temporal resolutions. Spatial essentially relates to the size of things that can be identified. Spectral describes the different wavelengths of energy used, and temporal refers to how often (the time of day or season) data are acquired. Today's sensor systems can provide coarse to fine spatial resolution, from 1 kilometer (.62 miles) and greater to 1 meter (3.28 ft) and smaller. They also provide data acquired in various spectral bands, from the visible to active microwave at different times of year. Natural-color and false-color infrared, for example, help identify tree species.

We can see the Pentagon (below, top) more clearly at 1-meter resolution than at 10- or 30-meter resolution. The natural-color, near-infrared, and thermal-infrared images of Cape Canaveral, Florida (middle), show the NASA launch facility in the upper right near the Atlantic coast. And the scenes of Point Barrow, Alaska (bottom), show the opening of leads in the ice pack, important information for shipping in the Arctic.

SPATIAL

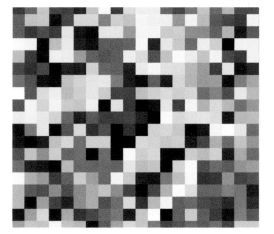

30 METER

10 METER

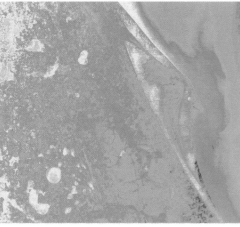

1 METER   *The Pentagon, Arlington, Virginia*

SPECTRAL

NATURAL

NEAR INFRARED

THERMAL INFRARED   *Cape Canaveral, Florida*

TEMPORAL

FEBRUARY 4, 1992

FEBRUARY 7, 1992

FEBRUARY 10, 1992   *Point Barrow, Alaska*

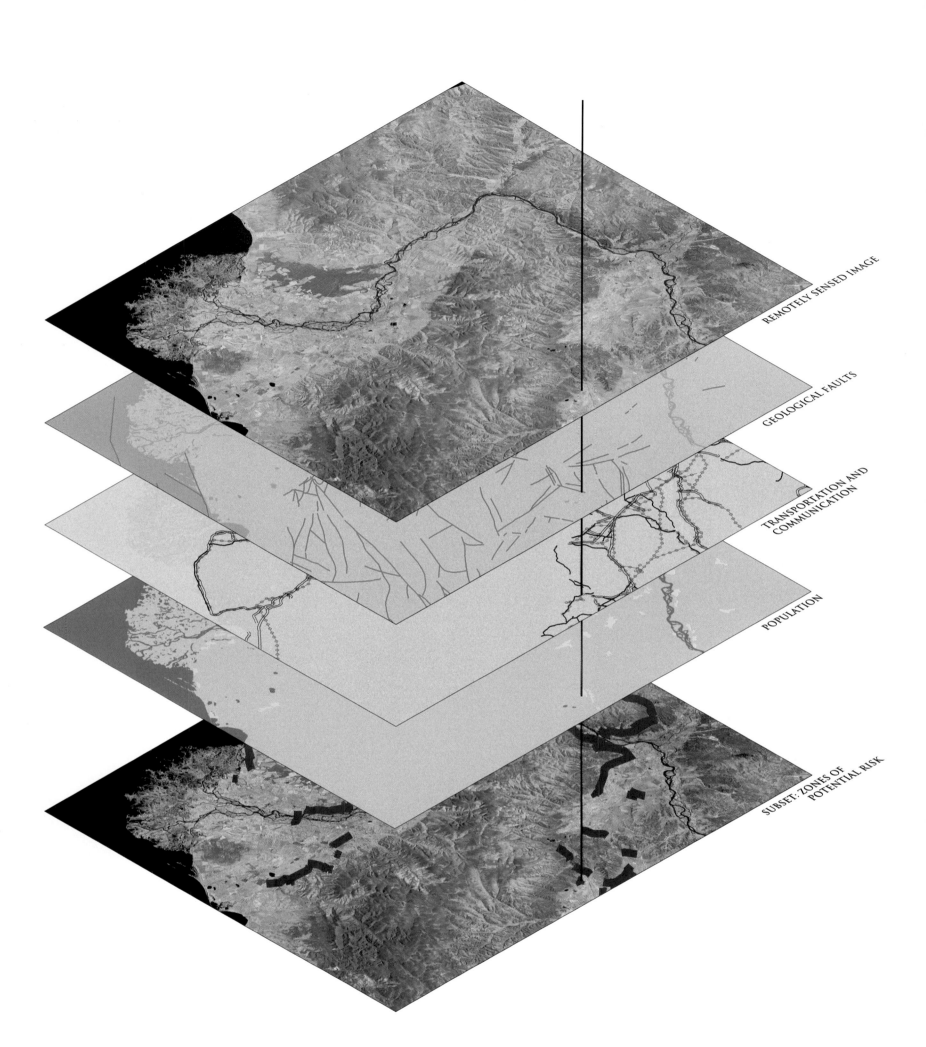

REMOTELY SENSED IMAGE

GEOLOGICAL FAULTS

TRANSPORTATION AND COMMUNICATION

POPULATION

SUBSET: ZONES OF POTENTIAL RISK

GEOGRAPHIC INFORMATION SYSTEM (GIS)

Remotely sensed imagery and other layers of data (as shown here) combined within a GIS and referenced by space or geographic coordinates, can improve our ability to measure, map, monitor, and model planetary resources. GIS allows imagery, topographic and geologic maps, environmental information, and other data to be combined and quickly analyzed to provide managers, planners, and public officials with timely, accurate data. The figure above shows data from a joint USGS–Russian GIS project developed for the Selenga Delta region, on Russia's Lake Baikal. This is the first publicly available GIS product to use recently declassified Russian geologic and topographic maps. In this example, the locations of known faults are coregistered with data on the area's transportation and communication lines and its population. In the lowest layer, the combined data highlight zones of potential risk (red).

WORLD

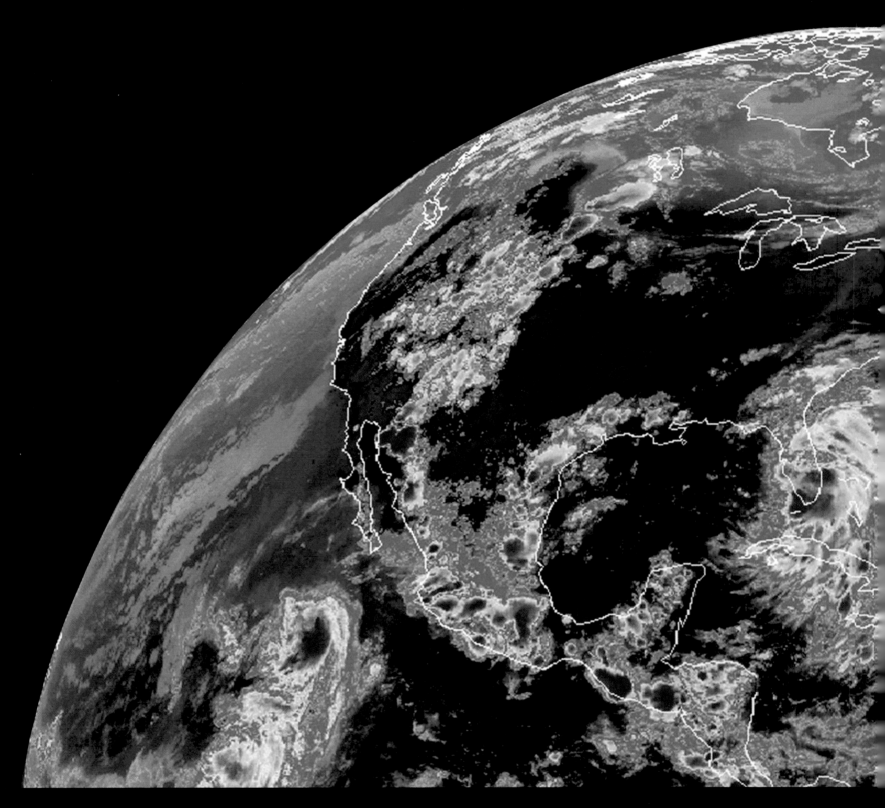

Some 93 million miles from the Sun, the blue planet Earth whirls in space, its origins shrouded in time and controversy. Geological evidence indicates that the Earth is between 4.5 and 4.6 billion years old.

The fifth largest planet in our solar system, Earth is the only one known to support life. Although uncertain when living creatures first appeared, scientists have found fossils of thread-like bacteria that are 3.5 billion years old. As the Earth's oxygen levels rose between 2 billion and 600 million years ago, more biologically complex animals evolved.

Man, a relative newcomer to Earth, arrived roughly 150,000 to 200,000 years ago. Today, close to six billion people inhabit the Earth. The continent of Eurasia is the most populous with 4.3 billion. Africa is second (763 million), followed by North America (470 million, including Central America and the

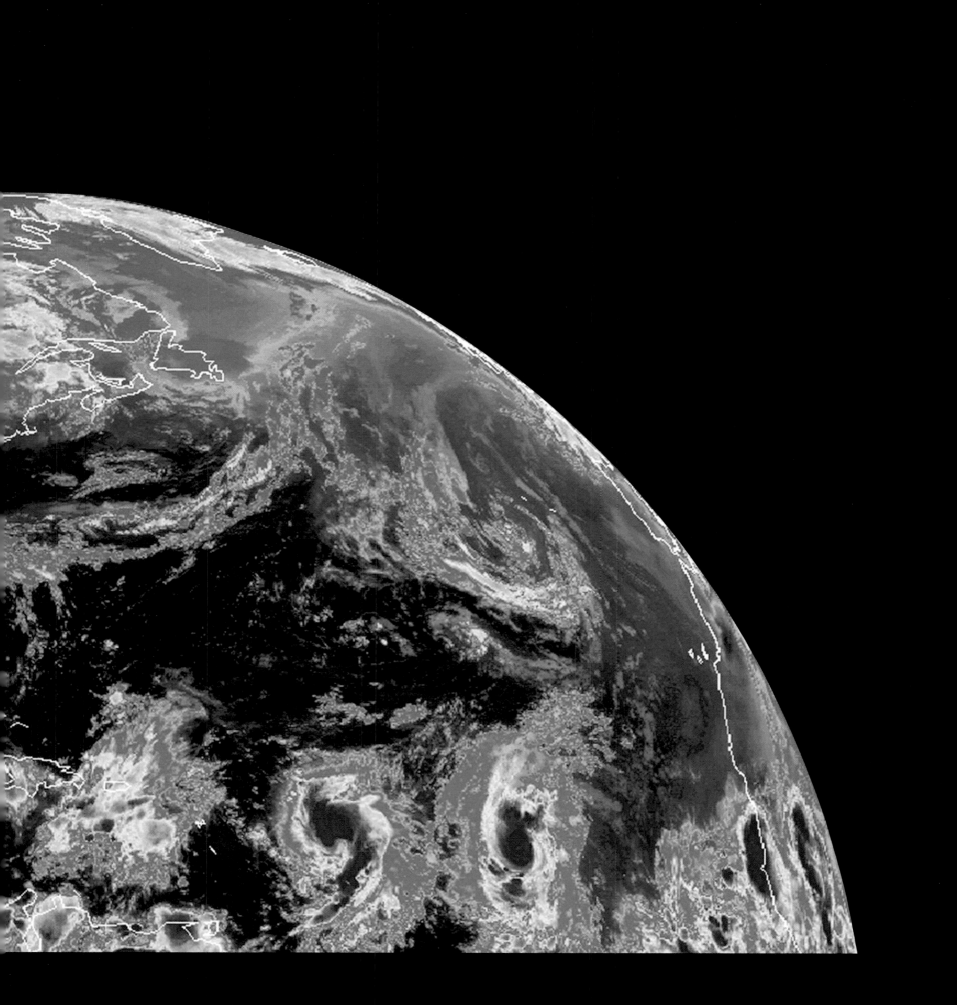

Caribbean islands), South America (331 million), and Australia (30 million, including New Zealand and Oceania).

Satellite technology enables us to see our home base as never before. Acting as eyes in the sky, satellites peer down from the heavens and beam back to Earth images as informative as they are beautiful. Through them, we observe geologic landforms, track weather systems, and monitor the impacts of humans on the planet.

PARADE OF STORMS

This nearly half-disk view at 22,300 miles high by the GOES-8 satellite detected a series of five storms in the North Atlantic Ocean in August 1995. They were (from left to right) Tropical Storm Jerry, a tropical wave, Hurricane Iris, Hurricane Humberto, and what was to become Tropical Storm Karen. Tropical Storm Gil looms in the Pacific.

WORLD · PHYSICAL

T he beauty and complexity of Earth's landscapes—above and below the oceans—are revealed by the Global Satellite Mosaic, produced for the National Geographic by NASA's Jet Propulsion Laboratory, using more than 500 satellite images from the National Oceanic and Atmospheric Administration. The cloud-free images show Earth in its natural colors, with major glaciers, deserts, mountain ranges, and rain forests easily recognizable. For example, follow the ribbon of vegetation along the Nile into the stark, dry Sahara. Notice that the mountain ranges, created with elevation databases from the Department of Defense, seem to rise off the map. The deepest areas of the ocean are dark blue; light blue areas highlight continental shelves, submarine ridges, and underwater mountains.

WINKEL TRIPEL
PROJECTION

WORLD MAP PROJECTIONS

Earth's spherical surface model, the globe, represents the only undistorted view of the exterior of our planet. Transferring mapped data, in this case, satellite imagery, from a globe to a plane (flat) surface results in a map projection. No single projection can avoid all the properties of distortion: distance, direction, shape, and area. As displayed here, using satellite-captured data in combination with existing geo-referenced data systems gives cartographers the versatility to produce one theme in many different projections.

Aleutian Trench

NORTH

PACIFIC

OCEAN

Hawaiian Islands

P
O
L
Y
N
E
S
I
A

Line Islands

Tuamotu Archipelago

Tonga Trench

Louisville Ridge

SOUTH

PACIFIC

OCEAN

Hudson
Bay

NORTH

AMERICA

ROCKY MOUNTAINS

Gulf of
Mexico

West Indies

Caribbean
Sea

Central
America

Amazon
Basin

SOUTH
AMERICA

ANDES

Peru-Chile Trench

Drake P

Ellsworth L

Marie Byrd Land

NATIONAL BOUNDARIES

While man's impact is quite evident, and even striking, on many remotely sensed scenes, sometimes, as in the case with most political boundaries, it is invisible. State, provincial, and national boundaries can follow natural features, such as mountain ridges, rivers, or coastlines. Artificial constructs that possess no physical reality—for example, lines of latitude and longitude—can also determine political borders. The world political map (right) represents man's imaginary lines as they slice and divide Earth.

The National Geographic Society recognizes 192 independent states in the world as represented here. Of those nations, 185 are members of the United Nations.

Both of Earth's physical Poles (far right) are projected using the same Global Satellite Mosaic data as used on the opposite side of the gatefold.

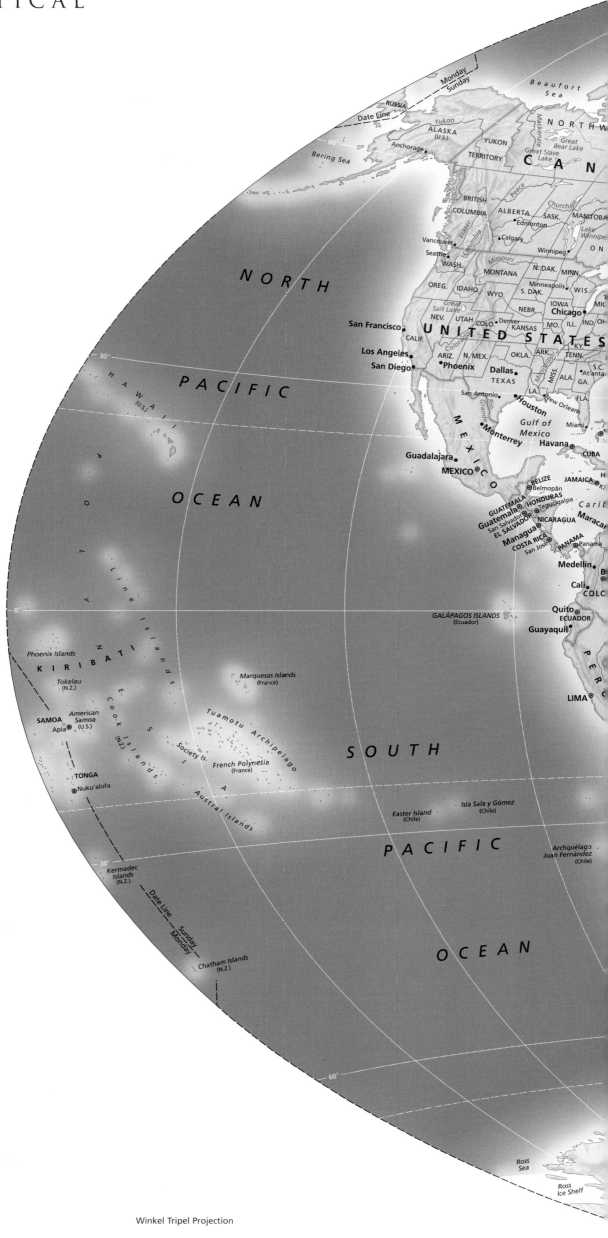

NORTH
AMERICA

ASIA

North Pole

EUROPE

Meridian of 0° Greenwich (London)

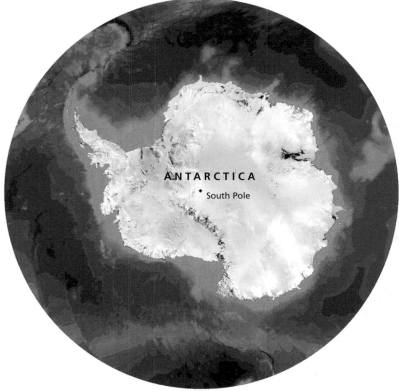

ANTARCTICA

South Pole

Azimuthal
Equidistant Projections

Continuing to evolve after four billion years, Earth balances itself on the sciences of physics, chemistry, biology, and geology. All nine of the peripheral world mosaics (opposite right and wrapped below) feed into and affect the delicate equilibrium of the larger **biosphere** image. For instance, as winds whisk across the open fetch of the ocean in the Southern Hemisphere, where the interruption of continental mass is less than in the Northern Hemisphere, and **wind speed** increases, ocean **surface waves** are driven to greater heights. This wind-wave correlation—coupled with ocean surface relief caused by underlying gravitational fields where submarine mountains and trenches exist—creates circulation and current systems. These systems, such as the Agulhas Current, off the southern tip of Africa,

then produce regions where **sea level variability** occurs and, thus, mixing. These turbulent areas, shown in red, are associated with high productivity of important microscopic phytoplankton—the base of the oceanic food web. Like plants on land, phytoplankton require light, water, appropriate temperature, nutrients, and carbon dioxide. Measuring, monitoring, and modeling these myriad elements—and their effects on the biosphere—from space with regularity and certainty enable scientists to better understand and quantify systems interrelationships and the role of ocean biology in the global carbon cycle, key to the Earth's survivability. Far from static, these global pictures are constantly changing. As CAT scans to the human body, they represent a new vision of the planet's vital data as it lives and breathes.

BIOSPHERE

LIVING PLANET

Tens of thousands of mosaiced satellite images represent ocean and land processes that result in life. The biosphere (above) depicts Earth's productivity. In the oceans, red, yellow, and green indicate water rich in phytoplankton. On land, green areas portray high-potential plant productivity; tan areas suffer from productivity limitations due to aridity and temperature.

TOPOGRAPHY / BATHYMETRY

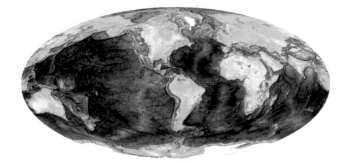

CLOUD AMOUNT

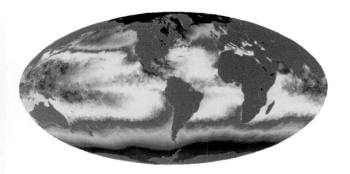

SEA SURFACE TEMPERATURE

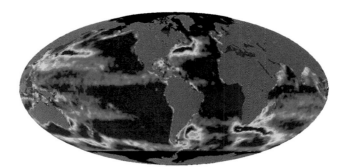

SEA LEVEL VARIABILITY

SURFACE WAVES

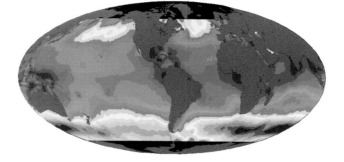

WIND SPEED

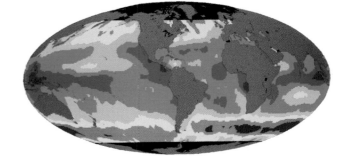

DAY / NIGHT SURFACE
TEMPERATURE DIFFERENCE

SNOW DEPTH AND SEA ICE

PRECIPITATION

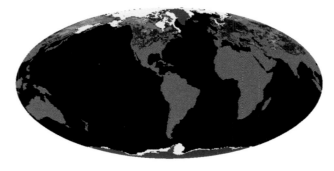

TOPOGRAPHY / BATHYMETRY

The elevation of Earth's surface reflects the variety of geological processes that continually renew its shape. Orbiting spacecraft can measure the shape of the moon and the other planets more easily than that of Earth, because Earth is covered by a variety of materials. Rocks and soils, vegetation, water and ice all reflect energy differently, so that an instrument that performs well in one environment may fail in another. Space-based observations must be verified with "ground truth" measurements collected in the field, under logistical and political limitations.

Winkel Tripel Projection

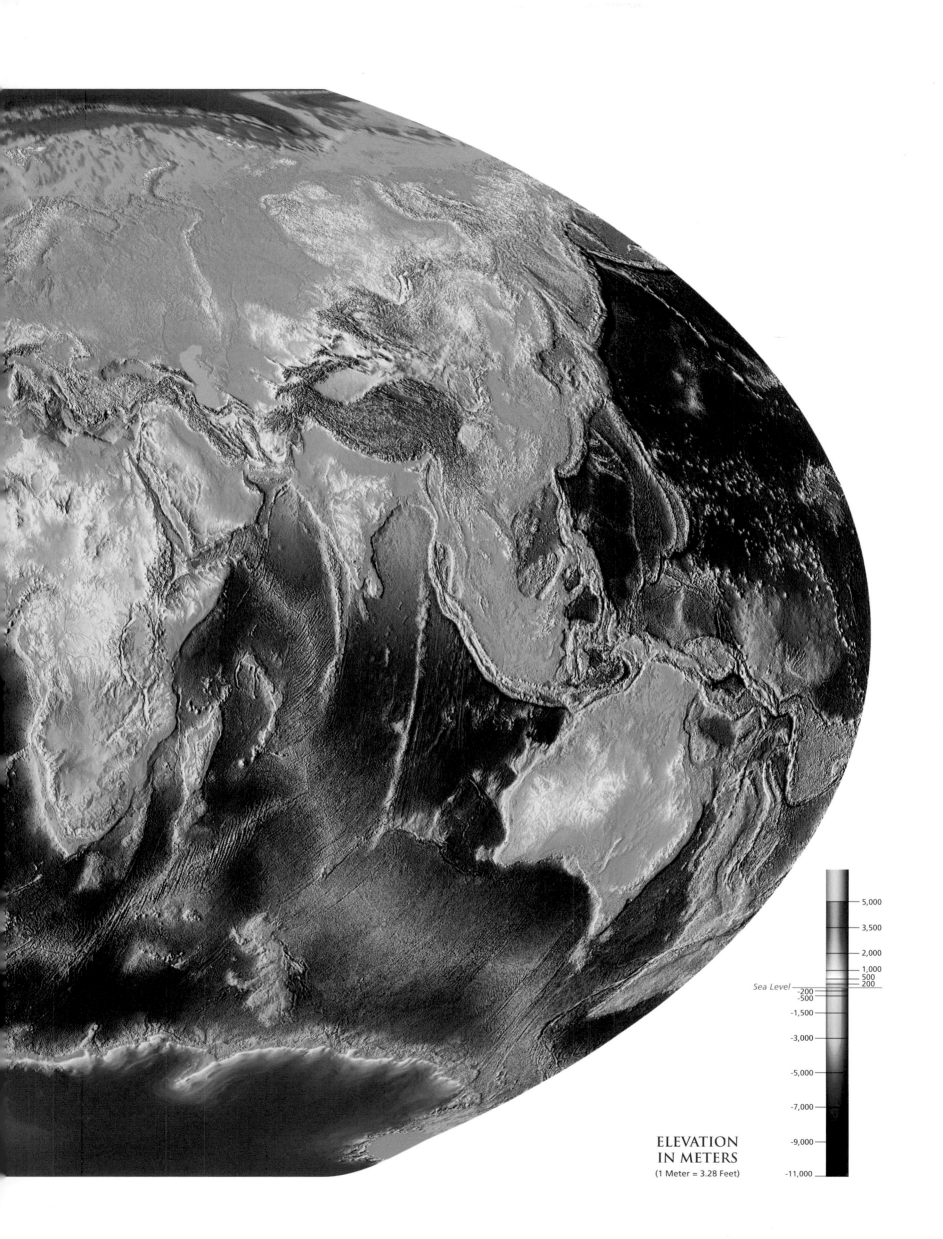

ELEVATION
IN METERS
(1 Meter = 3.28 Feet)

5,000

3,500

2,000

1,000
500
200
Sea Level —200
—500

—1,500

—3,000

—5,000

—7,000

—9,000

—11,000

PHYSICAL EARTH

Chains of volcanoes mark the present-day boundaries of 16 rocky slabs, or plates, that make up the Earth's crust. These plates move apart along diverging boundaries, or spreading centers, as new crust emerges. Hot magma rises from Earth's interior and spills out as basalt onto the seafloor along 40,000 miles of mid-oceanic ridges, including the spreading center that bisects the Atlantic. Where plates converge along boundaries, or subduction zones, old, dense crust sinks into ocean trenches and melts in the mantle below to fuel volcanoes and earthquakes, like those in the Pacific's Ring of Fire.

ARCTIC

GREENLAND

Baffin
Bay

Iceland
Grímsey
Iceland
Surtsey, Iceland

Bering
Sea

Bering
Strait

Mt. McKinley
20,320 ft
6,194 m

Great Bear
Lake

Great Slave
Lake

Westerlies

Katmai/Novarupta, Alaska

Southern Alaska

Hudson
Bay

Lake
Winnipeg

ROCKY MOUNTAINS

Kodiak-
Bowie

NORTH
AMERICA

L. Superior
L. Huron
Gulf of
St. Lawrence

Subarctic Current

Cobb

Mount St. Helens, Washington

Yellowstone

L. Michigan

L. Ontario
L. Erie

Westerlies

Azores

North Pacific Drift

Lassen Peak, California

San Francisco, California
Loma Prieta, California
San Andreas Fault

Baton

NORTH
ATLANTIC
OCEAN

MID-ATLANTIC RIDGE

NORTH
PACIFIC
OCEAN

San Fernando, California
Northridge, California

Landers,
California

Gulf Stream

New England

Guadalupe-
Baja

Gulf of
Mexico

Hawaii-
Emperor

Hawaii

Paricutín,
Mexico

Cape
Verde

Northeast
Trade Winds

Michoacán,
Mexico

El Chichón,
Mexico

Caribbean
Sea

Edge of diffuse
plate boundary

Soufrière Hills, Montserrat
Montagne Pelée, Martinique
Southern St. Vincent

North Equatorial Current

Santa María,
Guatemala

Guatemala

Northeast Trade Winds

Nevado del Ruiz, Colombia

EQUATOR

Galápagos

Amazon

SOUTH
AMERICA

Southeast Trade Winds

Southeast Trade Winds

South Equatorial Current

Marquesas

Northern Perú

ANDES

EAST PACIFIC RISE

Northern Bolivia

Samoa

Tahiti
Tahiti-
Society

Peru Current

Trindade

Gambier

Easter

Juan
Fernández

Cerro Aconcagua
22,834 ft, 6,960 m

SOUTH
ATLANTIC
OCEAN

Austral-
Cooks

Quizapú,
Chile

Río de la Plata

Walvis
Ridge

Falkland Current

MID-ATLANTIC RIDGE

Southern Chile

Westerlies

SOUTH
PACIFIC
OCEAN

Cerro
Hudson, Chile

Louisville

Cape Horn

Drake Passage

Westerlies

Weddell
Sea

Ross
Ice Shelf

ANTA

Winkel Tripel Projection

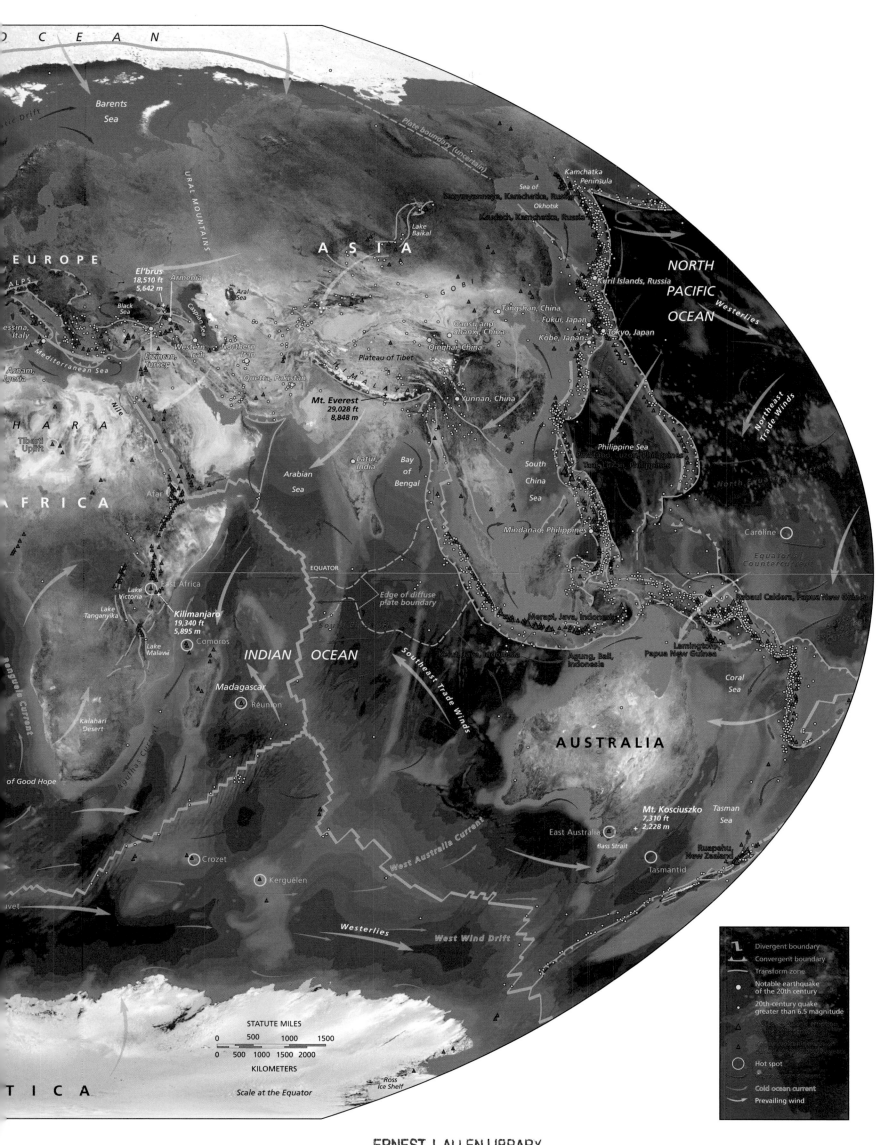

OCEAN

Barents
Sea

Arctic Drift

EUROPE

ALPS

El'brus
18,510 ft
5,642 m

Armenia

Black
Sea

Messina,
Italy

Mediterranean Sea

Erzincan,
Turkey

Asnam,
Algeria

SAHARA

Nile

Tibesti
Uplift

AFRICA

Benguela
Current

Afar

East Africa

Lake
Victoria

Kilimanjaro
19,340 ft
5,895 m

Lake
Tanganyika

Lake
Malawi

Comoros

Agulhas Current

Kalahari
Desert

of Good Hope

ivet

Crozet

Kerguélen

ASIA

URAL MOUNTAINS

Lake
Baikal

Aral
Sea

Caspian Sea

Western
Iran

Northern
Iran

Quetta, Pakistan

Plateau of Tibet

GOBI

HIMALAYA

Mt. Everest
29,028 ft
8,848 m

Arabian
Sea

Latur,
India

Bay of
Bengal

EQUATOR

Edge of diffuse
plate boundary

INDIAN   OCEAN

Madagascar

Réunion

Southeast Trade Winds

West Australia Current

Westerlies

Kamchatka
Peninsula

Sea of
Okhotsk

Bezymyannaya, Kamchatka, Russia

Kronotsk, Kamchatka, Russia

Kuril Islands, Russia

Tangshan, China

Gansu and
Shanxi, China

Qinghai, China

Fukui, Japan

Kobe, Japan

Tokyo, Japan

NORTH
PACIFIC
OCEAN

Westerlies

Northeast Trade Winds

Yunnan, China

Philippine Sea

Pinatubo, Luzon, Philippines

Taal, Luzon, Philippines

South
China
Sea

North Equatorial Current

Mindanao, Philippines

Caroline

Equatorial
Countercurrent

Merapi, Java, Indonesia

Kelut, Java, Indonesia

Agung, Bali,
Indonesia

Rabaul Caldera, Papua New Guinea

Lamington,
Papua New Guinea

Coral
Sea

AUSTRALIA

Mt. Kosciuszko
7,310 ft
2,228 m

East Australia
Current

Bass Strait

Tasmantid

Tasman
Sea

Ruapehu,
New Zealand

West Wind Drift

Plate boundary (uncertain)

STATUTE MILES

0   500   1000   1500

0   500   1000   1500   2000

KILOMETERS

Scale at the Equator

Ross
Ice Shelf

TICA

Divergent boundary

Convergent boundary

Transform zone

Notable earthquake
of the 20th century

20th-century quake
greater than 6.5 magnitude

Hot spot

Cold ocean current

Prevailing wind

WORLD · VEGETATION

Earth's vegetation plays crucial roles in shaping future climate and in influencing daily weather. Vegetation also harbors the biodiversity of the Earth, affects the risk of wildfires, and modifies air quality. By absorbing the important greenhouse gas, carbon dioxide, vegetation also acts as a deterrent to global warming. The large map below provides an unprecedented view of the Earth's vegetation. For the first time, images taken from orbiting satellites have been used to map and inventory vegetation, providing an objective assessment of its composition, including modifications of its natural state by urbanization, agricultural development, and other human pursuits. For example, this map shows that forests and woods

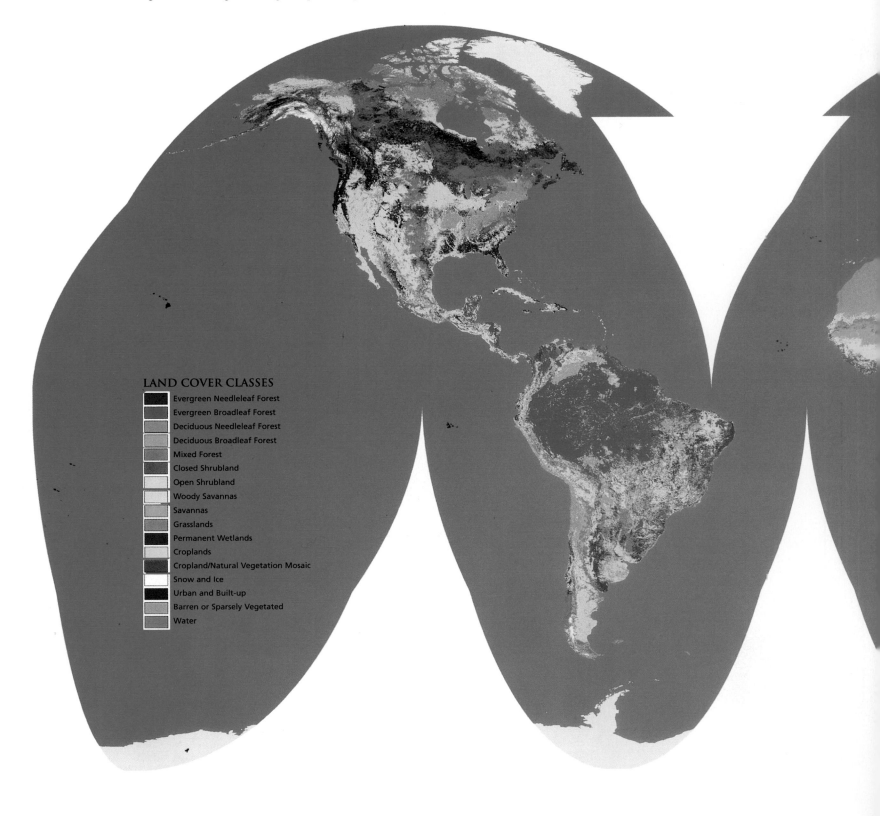

LAND COVER CLASSES

- Evergreen Needleleaf Forest
- Evergreen Broadleaf Forest
- Deciduous Needleleaf Forest
- Deciduous Broadleaf Forest
- Mixed Forest
- Closed Shrubland
- Open Shrubland
- Woody Savannas
- Savannas
- Grasslands
- Permanent Wetlands
- Croplands
- Cropland/Natural Vegetation Mosaic
- Snow and Ice
- Urban and Built-up
- Barren or Sparsely Vegetated
- Water

January	March	May	July	September	Nov.
February	April	June	August	October	Dec.

SEASONALITY

The maps at right show the month of the onset, peak, and end of a region's growing season, respectively. For example, to find out when the Pacific Northwest is at its greenest, match the region's color in the second map to the color-keyed months. Regions not changing seasonally are shown as follows: dark green is always green, gray is barren, blue is water, and white is snow.

ONSET

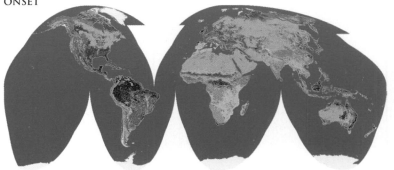

are still the commonly found vegetation type, covering nearly 28 percent of the planet. About 18 percent of the Earth is covered by cropland and mosaics of cropland and natural vegetation. Perhaps this map's most important value is to provide a baseline in the early 1990s, from which future assessments of global environmental change can be made.

LAND COVER

Using satellite images taken between April 1992 and March 1993, this map shows 17 types of Earth's land cover (keyed by color). With a resolution of one kilometer, the equal-area projection map provides means to measure, manage, monitor, and model a wide range of Earth's environmental characteristics.

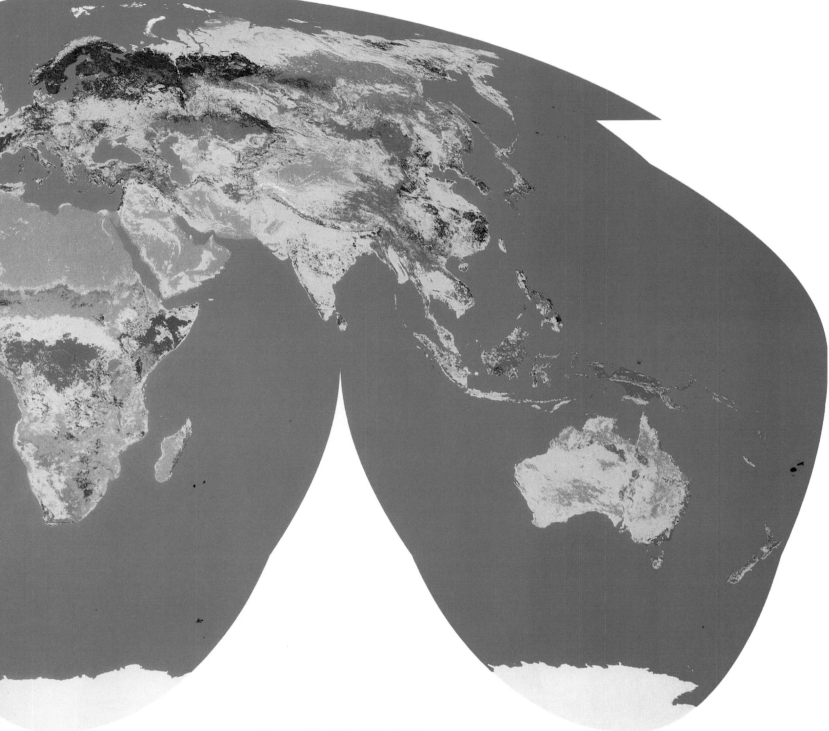

Interrupted Goode Homolosine Projection

PEAK

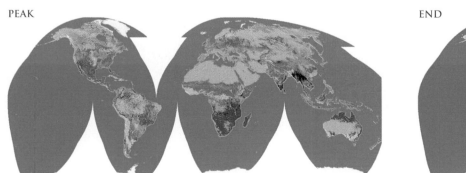

END

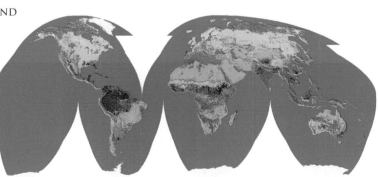

Weather satellites maintained by the National Oceanic and Atmospheric Administration (NOAA), as well as by other international remote sensing agencies, take measurements 24 hours a day, continuously collecting data that scientists use in their study of weather patterns around the globe.

The TIROS satellites were the first series of weather satellites placed in operation, in the 1960s. Now they have been joined by a host of low-altitude (e.g., 500-mile-high) polar-orbiting and high-altitude (e.g., 22,000-mile-high) geosynchronous orbiting satellites. These spacecraft are equipped with instruments that measure energy emitted from or reflected by the

CLOUDS

One of the first variables obtained from weather satellites was information on the cloud patterns associated with large-scale weather systems. Clouds affect climate by interacting with incoming solar radiation and outgoing emitted radiation. As part of the International Satellite Cloud Climatology Project,

this global composite of the Earth's cloud cover on October 15, 1983, was assembled from data transmitted within a single hour by multiple NOAA and internationally operated geosynchronous satellites as well as by NOAA polar-orbiting satellites. Scientists use such composites of information to develop long-term climate models that are also used by weather forecasters.

PRECIPITATION

Patterns of global precipitation are important to scientists studying the Earth's hydrological cycle and water balance. Since nearly two-thirds of the Earth's surface is covered by ocean and since ground-based rainfall measurements are made only in populated land regions, satellites offer perhaps the only way in which global rainfall patterns can be determined. Microwave-based sensors, originally flown on U.S. Department of Defense meteorological satellites and now operated by NOAA, provide global rainfall information. The image at right shows the global annual mean rainfall as determined by 11 years of measurements from the Special Sensor Micro-wave Imager (SSM/I). The areas of heaviest rain show up in the tropical regions known as the Inter Tropical Convergence Zone (ITCZ), where as much as 4,000 mm (157+ in) falls annually.

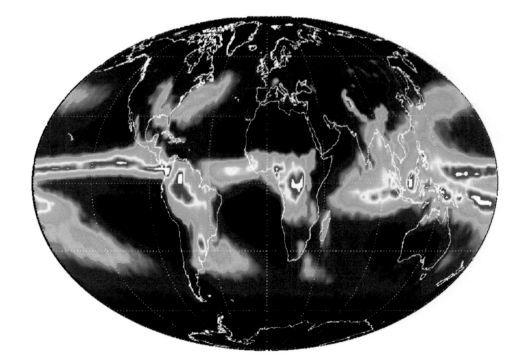

Earth's surface and atmosphere in the visible, infrared, and microwave portions of the electromagnetic spectrum.

Each of these portions of the spectrum offers uniquely valuable information to meteorologists and research scientists. The polar-orbiting satellites provide near-global coverage twice a day, while the geosynchronous satellites provide regional data as frequently as every five minutes over a fixed geographical region.

Such a combined suite of satellite sensors provides information useful for making short-term weather forecasts as well as for understanding long-term variations in the Earth's climates.

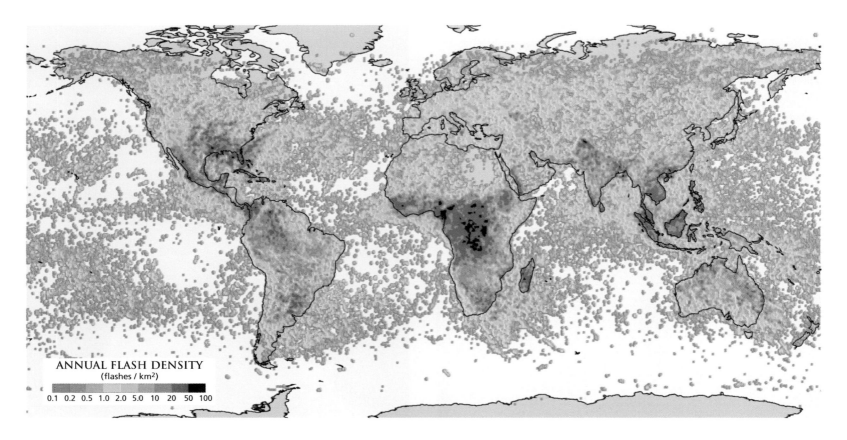

ANNUAL FLASH DENSITY
(flashes / km²)

0.1 0.2 0.5 1.0 2.0 5.0 10 20 50 100

LIGHTNING

Scientists have become increasingly aware of the key role of lightning in the dynamic interplay of forces occurring in Earth's atmosphere. For example, lightning may be a reliable indicator of the strength of large-scale summer storm systems. To better understand the physical connections between lightning and rainfall, a new satellite technology was developed at the NASA/ Marshall Space Flight Center. The above image shows the number of lightning flashes detected from space in 1997, more than 90 percent over land. A correlation exists between the number of flashes and the areas of greatest rainfall. Deserts are the exception, with considerable lightning but little rain.

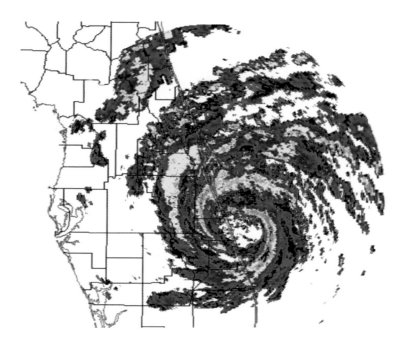

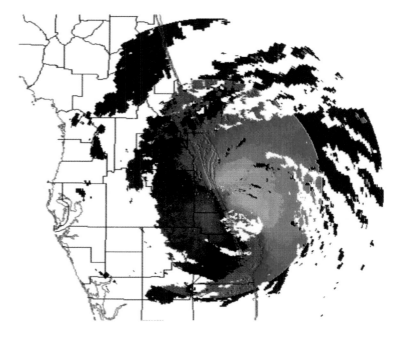

HURRICANES

Tropical cyclones, called hurricanes in the U.S., originate in warm tropical oceans and rank among the most devastating of meteorological phenomena. Before weather satellites, ships reported information on these storms. Now satellites serve as key monitors of hurricanes. As the storms move close to land, forecasters also use ground-based NOAA Doppler radar systems. As depicted in the images above, Doppler radar pinpoints storm centers, locations of heaviest rainfall (highest reflectivity), and strongest wind (highest velocity). Additionally, NASA's Tropical Rainfall Measuring Mission satellite has radar onboard, providing information on storm structure from space.

pproximately 70 percent of the Earth's surface is covered by oceans, and ocean environments hold much of the life and biodiversity of our planet. As the salty taste of our own tears reminds us, oceans are the original incubators of life on Earth. Land-dwelling animals and plants benefit from the ocean's moderating effects on climate; ocean currents distribute the sun's energy (and—to the degradation of the entire Earth—human waste) over the globe.

Scientists and explorers continue to be challenged by the logistics of investigating the deep oceans. These areas were once considered featureless and lifeless, as their depths were out of reach of the instruments and vehicles available to explore them. But today, new tools have enabled scientists to find bizarre life-forms at the bottom of the sea and to discover that deep ocean currents play vital roles in modulating global climate change. They also know that the ocean floor contains the flattest plains and tallest mountains on Earth. The study of these features will test the hypotheses of the plate tectonic theory, leading to a better understanding of the causes of earthquakes, volcanic eruptions, and tsunamis (catastrophic tidal waves).

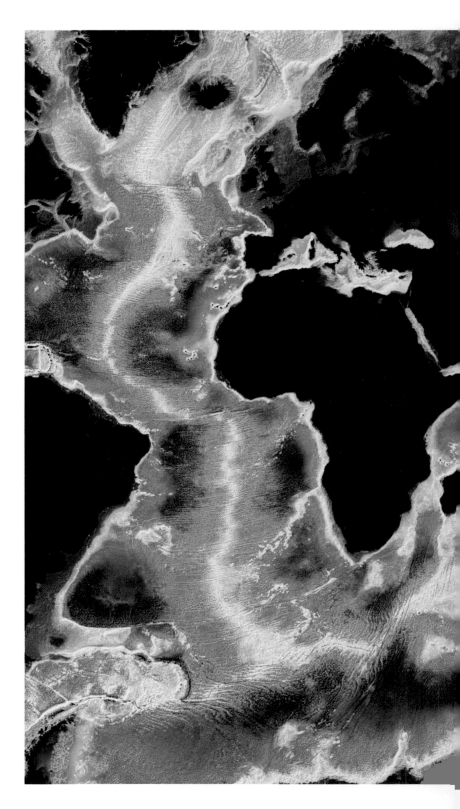

DEPTH IN KILOMETERS
(1 kilometer = 0.62 miles)

0
-1
-2
-3
-4
-5
-6
-7

OCEAN FLOOR

This computer-generated image (right) portrays ocean depths as revealed in maps that combine satellite measurements of the geoid with conventional echo-sounding depth measurements by ships. A rainbow of hues indicates a range of depths from shallow continental shelves [less than 0.2 km (0.1 mi) deep] to mid-ocean ridges [2.5 km (1.5 mi) deep] to abyssal plains [5 km (3 mi) deep] to trenches [greater than 6 km (3.7 mi) deep]. This globally uniform view of the topography of the ocean floor can be obtained only with satellites. A uniformly detailed view helps answer questions about the distribution of mid-ocean ridges, trenches, volcanoes, fish habitats, areas of possible seabed resources, and obstacles to flow that steer ocean currents. This view provides spectacular confirmation of the basic tenets of plate tectonic theory.

GEOID

Scientists refer elevations on Earth to a hypothetical level surface called the geoid (left), or mean sea level. Over oceans, the geoid is the shape the ocean surface would have if waves, currents, and tides ceased to move. By studying Earth's gravity field, scientists define where mean sea level would be in land-covered areas as well. The non-uniformity of Earth's materials causes irregularities in gravity's pull, producing small hills and hollows (shown at left, greatly exaggerated). A spacecraft orbiting Earth can measure the geoid's variations to an accuracy of a few centimeters (about 1 inch) in a year's time at a cost of about 60 million dollars (U.S.). Because mountains and valleys on the ocean floor add to and subtract from the Earth's gravitational field, their presence is revealed in the highs and lows of geoid data.

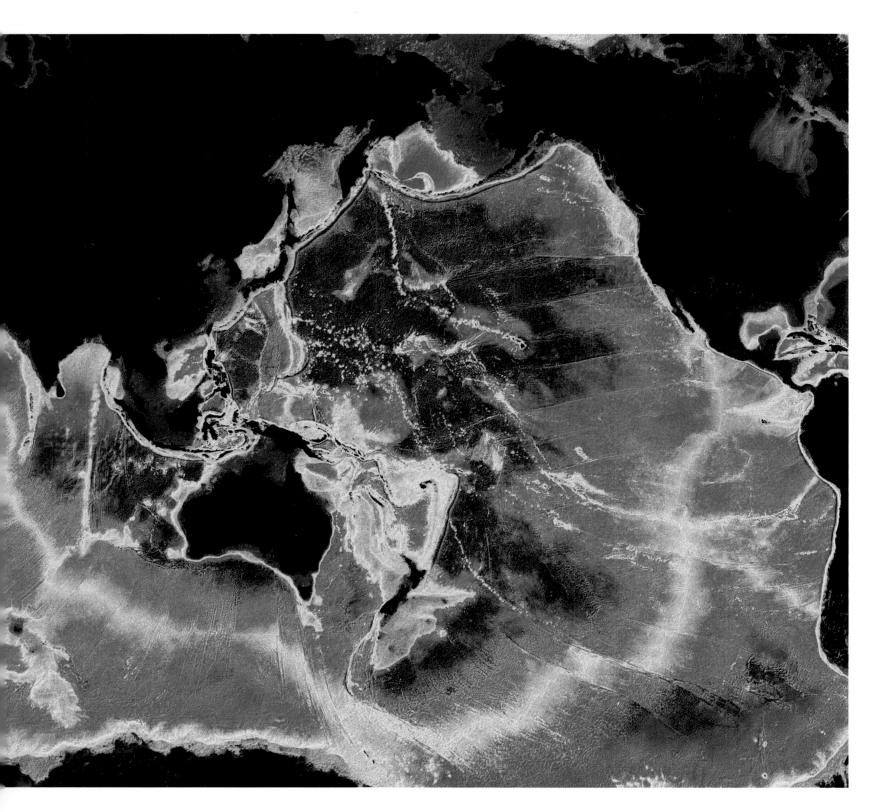

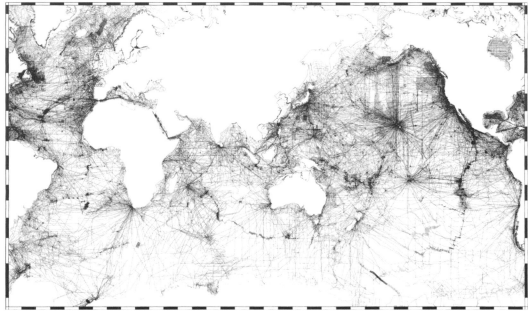

SHIP TRACKS

Although seafarers have explored the oceans for centuries, accurate measurement of the full range of their depths became possible only after World War II, with the development of the echo sounder. Shown at left, and shared scientifically in unclassified databases, are the locations of all soundings made since the 1950s. Measurements are clustered near major ports and in the territorial waters of developed nations, leaving large gaps in the remote oceans. Unsurveyed areas can be as large as some of the midwestern states of the U.S. Using current echo-sounder technology, a complete survey of the oceans would require more than a hundred ship-years at a prohibitive cost of more than a billion dollars (U.S.). Instead, scientists use satellite geoid measurements and the imaging technique shown above to pinpoint places to test their hypotheses by new surveys.

The largest interannual signal of the Earth's coupled climate system is the El Niño/Southern Oscillation (ENSO) phenomenon. A prerequisite to understanding the effects of human activities on climate requires us to distinguish between natural variability, such as that caused by El Niño, and that due to human influence, such as global warming. El Niño has its origin in the equatorial Pacific Ocean, but its effects have worldwide implications. El Niño appears every four to seven years as a result of coupled interactions between the tropical Pacific Ocean and the atmosphere above it. Simply put, anomalous changes in the equatorial Pacific trade winds cause changes in the equatorial Pacific Ocean circulation. The resultant perturbations in the ocean give rise to changes in sea surface temperatures (SST). These fluctuations, in turn, induce changes in the surface wind field, and the cyclical atmosphere-ocean interaction begins anew. An indicator of El Niño is the shift of the warmest water of the global ocean from the dateline in the Pacific Ocean eastward by about 5,000 km (3,107 mi), inducing SST anomalies of 2–4°C (4–7°F). This eastward migration of a critical atmospheric heat source changes global weather patterns (precipitation and temperature) far beyond the equatorial Pacific. The 1982–83 El Niño negatively affected global economies by more than 13 billion dollars. Since then, an ocean observation system has been deployed to predict and monitor future ENSOs. Moreover, a series of remote sensing satellites has been launched to supplement and enhance the in situ observations. The 1997–98 "El Niño Event of the Century" will be the first major El Niño to be measured from start to fi-

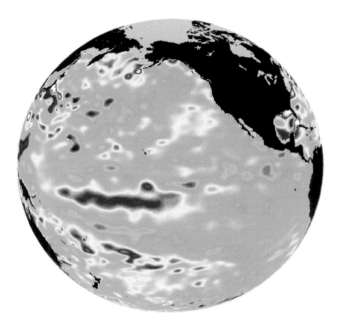

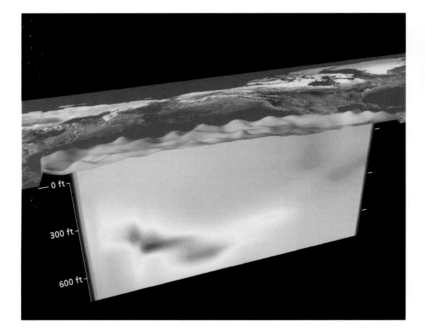

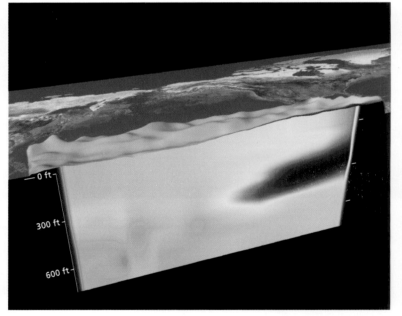

JANUARY 1997

Prior to the onset phase of El Niño, sea level is higher in the western tropical Pacific and lower in the eastern tropical Pacific in response to the normal trade winds blowing from east to west. Sea surface ocean temperatures were cooler in the upper ocean to the east and warmer at greater depths in the west. During this time the trade winds started to weaken (not shown) in the far western tropical Pacific.

JUNE 1997

In response to the relaxation of the trade winds, sea level has decreased in the west and has increased in the east, by way of an eastward propagating sea level signal along the Equator— known as an equatorially trapped Kelvin Wave. In relation with this propagating feature, there is a west-to-east increase in temperature at depth in the ocean.

nish by space-based observations of sea surface temperature, sea surface topography, sea surface winds, and precipitation.

The strongest and most direct of ENSO climate variations occur in the tropical belt. Along the coast of Ecuador and Peru, El Niño brings torrential rains to a region that is normally semiarid. In other areas, such as Australia, Indonesia, northeast Brazil, and South Africa, an El Niño event implies drought. Over the continental United States the impact is less direct, but El Niño remains a significant factor in climate variations. For example, along the West Coast changes in sea surface temperatures and ocean circulation perturbations are of interest to U.S. fisheries. ENSO also has an impact on the jet stream, causing precipitation on the West Coast, followed by drought and increased incidence of forest fires.

TOP ROW (GLOBES):

Departures from normal sea surface height, as measured from the TOPEX/Poseidon radar altimeter satellite, are reflected in the colors on the globes below: red indicates high, with white being the highest; blue indicates low, with purple being the lowest.

BOTTOM ROW (CUTAWAYS):

These depth-versus-longitude sections along the Equator in the Pacific Ocean depict a combination of the actual sea surface topography, as measured from the TOPEX/Poseidon altimeter, and ocean temperature departures from normal, as measured by a series of NOAA moored oceanic buoys. Blue represents cooler temperatures; red indicates warmer temperatures.

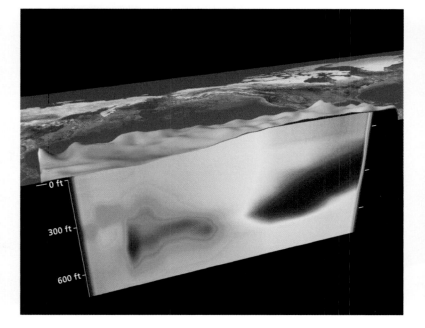

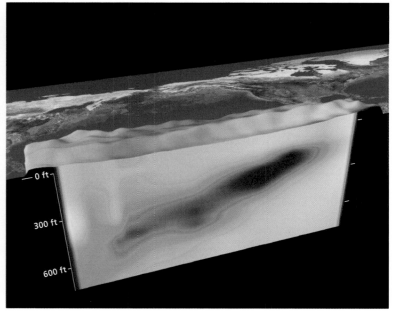

NOVEMBER 1997

By late 1997 the El Niño event has reached a mature phase. Sea level is 20 to 30 cm (8 to 12 in) higher than normal in the east and depressed by a similar amount in the west, resulting in a complete reversal of the normal sea level gradient along the Equator. This reversal is reflected at depth with colder than normal temperatures in the western equatorial Pacific and warmer than normal temperatures in the eastern equatorial Pacific. In turn, these anomalies at depth manifested in surface anomalies of 4 to 5 °C warmer-than-normal water.

MAY 1998

The El Niño event is nearly over, and there are signs that the opposite phase of the El Niño/ Southern Oscillation, known as La Niña, may be forthcoming. By May 1998 sea level and sea surface temperatures had returned to close to normal values in the eastern equatorial Pacific Ocean. Colder than normal temperatures at depth from west to east in the equatorial Pacific Ocean signal the potential for a rapid reversal from El Niño to La Niña conditions for the latter part of 1998.

WORLD · POPULATION

The 20th century has seen a population explosion unlike any other. Now humankind has spread throughout the inhabitable Earth, as illustrated by the maps below. Reaching a population of one billion—achieved about 1800—took all of prehistory and most of history. Since then, the billions have come faster and faster: two billion in 1930, three in 1960, four in 1975, and five in 1987. In 1999, human numbers will total six billion. Demographers have a reasonable expectation that the rate of growth will slow and the global population will reach some unknown final size. But that size will depend on the future birthrates of today's developing countries, where virtually all population growth now occurs.

LIGHTS AT NIGHT

- Human Settlement Lights
- Natural Gas Flares
- Fishing Fleets
- Fires

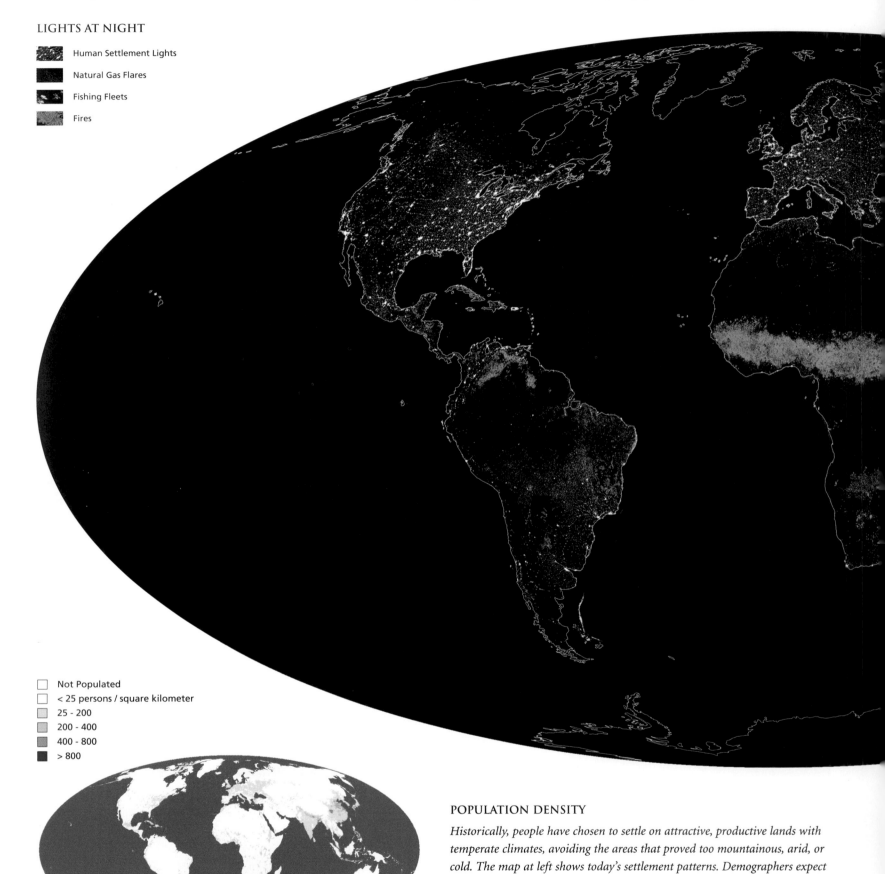

- Not Populated
- < 25 persons / square kilometer
- 25 - 200
- 200 - 400
- 400 - 800
- > 800

POPULATION DENSITY

Historically, people have chosen to settle on attractive, productive lands with temperate climates, avoiding the areas that proved too mountainous, arid, or cold. The map at left shows today's settlement patterns. Demographers expect future maps to reflect enormous population growth in Africa and Asia.

1750   1800   1850   1900

POPULATION PYRAMIDS

The sharp difference between the age structures of developing countries and developed countries foretells future population profiles. For example, Nigeria's young population means an ever increasing number of new parents. In Italy, a low birthrate virtually assures the opposite scenario—population decline.

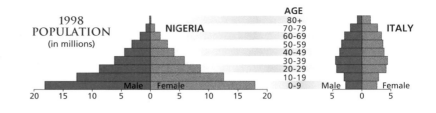

1998
POPULATION
(in millions)

NIGERIA

AGE
80+
70-79
60-69
50-59
40-49
30-39
20-29
10-19
0-9

ITALY

Male   Female

20   15   10   5   0   5   10   15   20   5   0   5
Male   Female

POPULATION PORTRAIT

Nighttime satellite imagery, available since the 1970s, can tell demographers a great deal about population density and energy use around the world. The images, however, require careful interpretation. On the whole, light emissions correspond quite well with actual population density: Note the bright lights clustered along the coasts of North America, Europe, and Asia (left). But dark areas can deceive: The densely populated areas of poor nations with low rates of energy consumption have less light output.

POPULATION GROWTH

High birthrates and rising life expectancies have caused a population explosion during the 20th century, and while many couples now seek to limit the size of their families, today's potential for growth remains staggering. In the diagram below, United Nations projections show possible paths for the future. With a low global birthrate, about 1.7 children per woman, the population at the end of the next century could drop below that of today. But a high birthrate could push the total to 25 billion and higher.

STATUTE MILES
800   1600   2400   3200
800   1600   2400   3200   4000   4800
KILOMETERS

Mollweide Projection

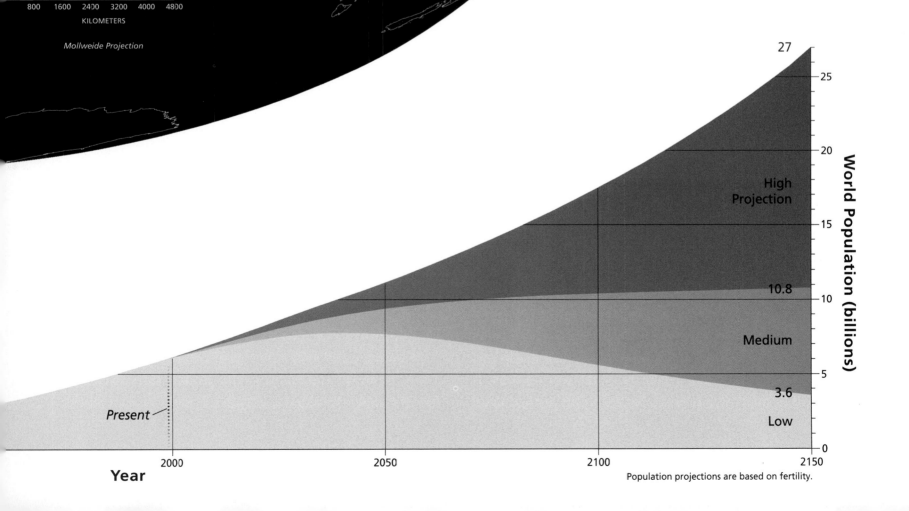

27

25

20

High
Projection

15

10.8

10

Medium

5

3.6

Low

Present

0

Year   2000   2050   2100   2150

World Population (billions)

Population projections are based on fertility.

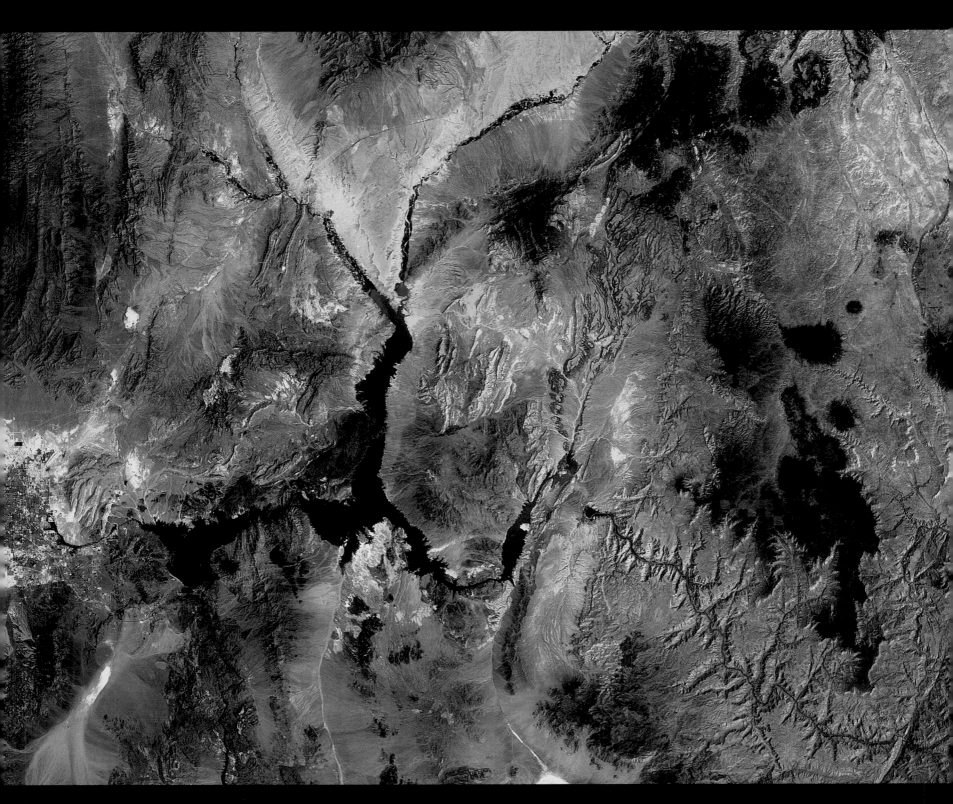

NORTH AMERICA

N orth America is a diverse realm, reaching from the Arctic to the Caribbean, from the Atlantic to the Pacific. The third largest continent, with just over 16 percent of Earth's land, it was a world full of new possibilities for the Europeans who came here in the 15th century. Even now, its potential remains vast and its population, some 7 percent of the world's total, is manageably small. Relatively stable politically, its mainland

holds only 10 countries, with the United States, Mexico, and Canada—the world's second largest nation, after Russia—claiming most of its 9,360,000 square miles. Also falling within the continent's bounds are the West Indies and Danish-owned Greenland, Earth's largest island.

In geologic and geographic terms, North America boasts a host of world superlatives: The greatest tides sweep the Bay of Fundy; the oldest rocks anchor the Canadian Shield;

and the largest canyon is called, naturally, the Grand Canyon. The second deepest ocean trench lies off Puerto Rico; only the Pacific's Mariana Trench is deeper. The weather is also extreme: Hurricanes torment tropical and temperate areas alike; frigid winters beset Canada and the northern U.S.; droughts and downpours plague the Pacific and parts of Central America. Despite such vicissitudes, immigrants still flock to North America's shores,

GRAND CANYON

For millions of years the Colorado River cut into the multihued rock of the Colorado Plateau, carving a canyon that now ranks as a wonder of the world. From Lake Mead in the west, the mile-deep Grand Canyon zigzags 280 miles across northwest Arizona, widening to as much as 18 miles across. The view above zooms in on 9 of the 432 Landsat TM images used to create a mosaic of the lower 48 states (see pages 46-47).

Grand
• Canyon

EUROPE

ICELAND

Greenland Sea

Denmark Strait

Wandel Sea

G R E E N L A N D

Cape Morris Jesup

Lincoln Sea

Baffin Bay

Hayes Peninsula

Ellesmere Island

QUEEN ELIZABETH ISLANDS

Axel Heiberg Island

Devon Island

Davis Strait

Baffin Island

Labrador Sea

NORTH

Island of Newfoundland

Cape Breton Island

Anticosti I.

Gulf of St. Lawrence

Nova Scotia

Bay of Fundy

Gulf of Maine

Cape Cod

Cape Farewell

Hudson Strait

Ungava Bay

Labrador

Melville Peninsula

Foxe Basin

Southampton Island

James Bay

A P P A L A C H I A N   M O U N T A I N S

L. Ontario

Lake Erie

Prince Patrick Island

M'Clure Strait

Melville Island

Parry Channel

Somerset Island

Prince of Wales Island

Boothia Peninsula

Thelon

Hudson Bay

Lake Huron

Lake Superior

Lake Michigan

ARCTIC OCEAN

Banks Island

Amundsen Gulf

Victoria Island

C a n a d i a n   S h i e l d

Lake Winnipeg

Beaufort Sea

Great Bear Lake

Great Slave Lake

G R E A T   P L A I N S

Missouri

Chukchi Sea

Point Barrow

North Slope

Brooks Range

Mackenzie

Mackenzie Mountains

Peace

R O C K Y   M O U N T A I N S

Great Salt Lake

Snake River Plain

GREAT

ASIA

Bering Strait

Seward Peninsula

Yukon

A L A S K A

Alaska Range

Mt. McKinley (Denali) 20,320 ft; 6,194 m Highest point in North America

Coast Mountains

Cascade Range

Sierra

St. Lawrence Island

Bering Sea

Kenai Pen.

Gulf of Alaska

Alexander Archipelago

Queen Charlotte Islands

Vancouver Island

Mt. Rainier 14,410 ft; 4,392 m

Alaska Peninsula

Kodiak I.

Cape Mendocino

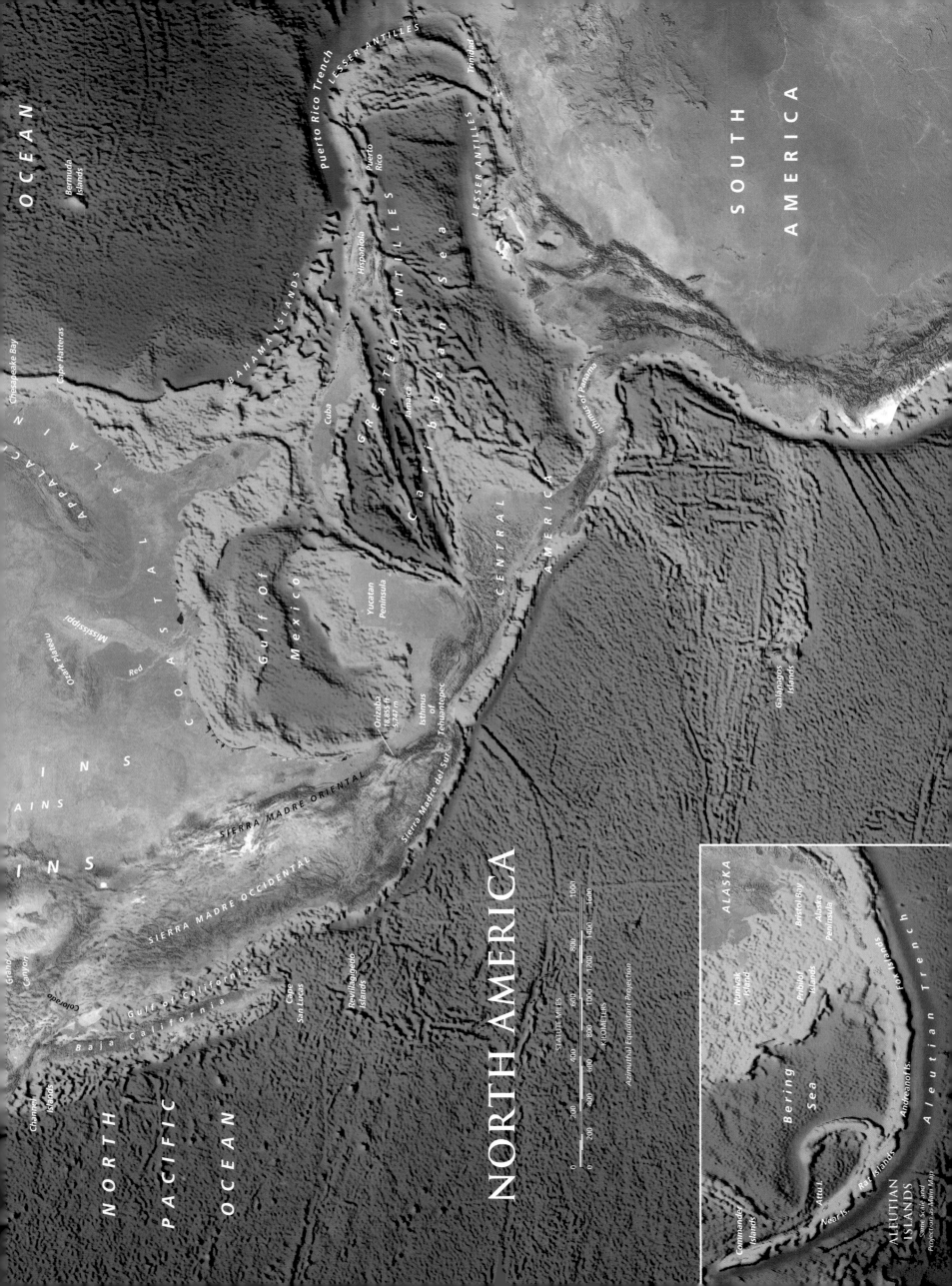

ATLANTIC
OCEAN

Bermuda
Islands

Chesapeake Bay
Cape Hatteras

A P P A L A C H I A N

COASTAL PLAIN

Ozark Plateau
Mississippi
Red

BAHAMA ISLANDS

Puerto Rico Trench

LESSER ANTILLES

Trinidad

Puerto
Rico

Hispaniola

Cuba

G R E A T E R   A N T I L L E S

Jamaica

LESSER ANTILLES

C a r i b b e a n   S e a

Isthmus of Panama

SOUTH

AMERICA

Gulf
Of
Mexico

Yucatan
Peninsula

C E N T R A L

A M E R I C A

Orizaba
18,855 ft
5,747 m

Isthmus
of
Tehuantepec

Galápagos
Islands

SIERRA MADRE ORIENTAL

Sierra Madre del Sur

SIERRA MADRE OCCIDENTAL

M O U N T A I N S
A I N S
I N S

Grand
Canyon

Colorado

Gulf of California

Cape
San Lucas

Revillagigedo
Islands

B a j a   C a l i f o r n i a

Channel
Islands

NORTH AMERICA

NORTH

PACIFIC

OCEAN

STATUTE MILES
0   200   400   600   800   1000
KILOMETERS
0   200   400   600   800   1000   1200   1400   1600
Azimuthal Equidistant Projection

ALASKA

Bristol Bay

Nunivak
Island

Pribilof
Islands

Alaska
Peninsula

Fox Islands

Aleutian Trench

Bering
Sea

Andreanof Is.
Rat Islands

Attu I.
Near Is.

Commander
Islands

ALEUTIAN ISLANDS
Same Scale and
Projection as Main Map

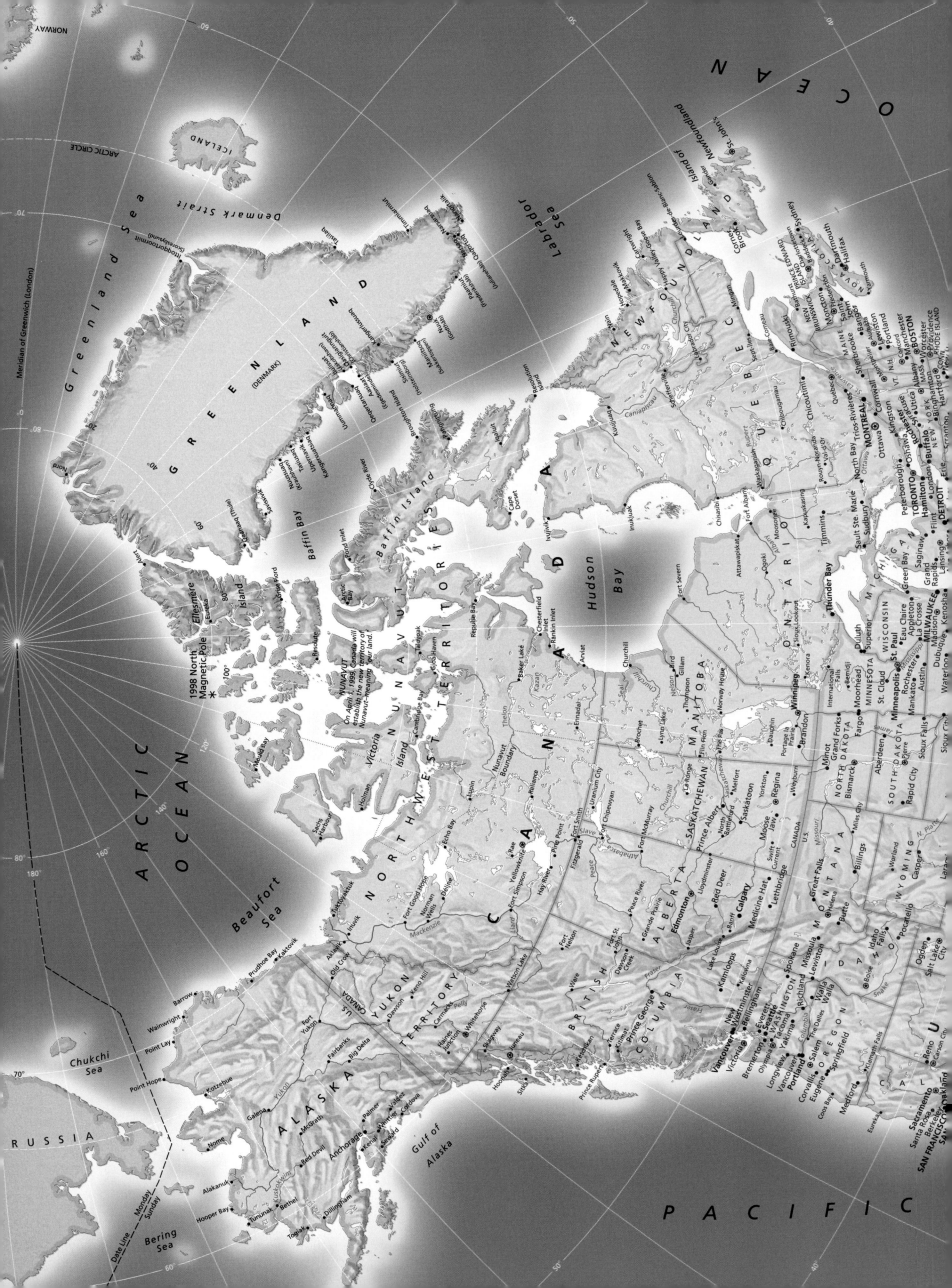

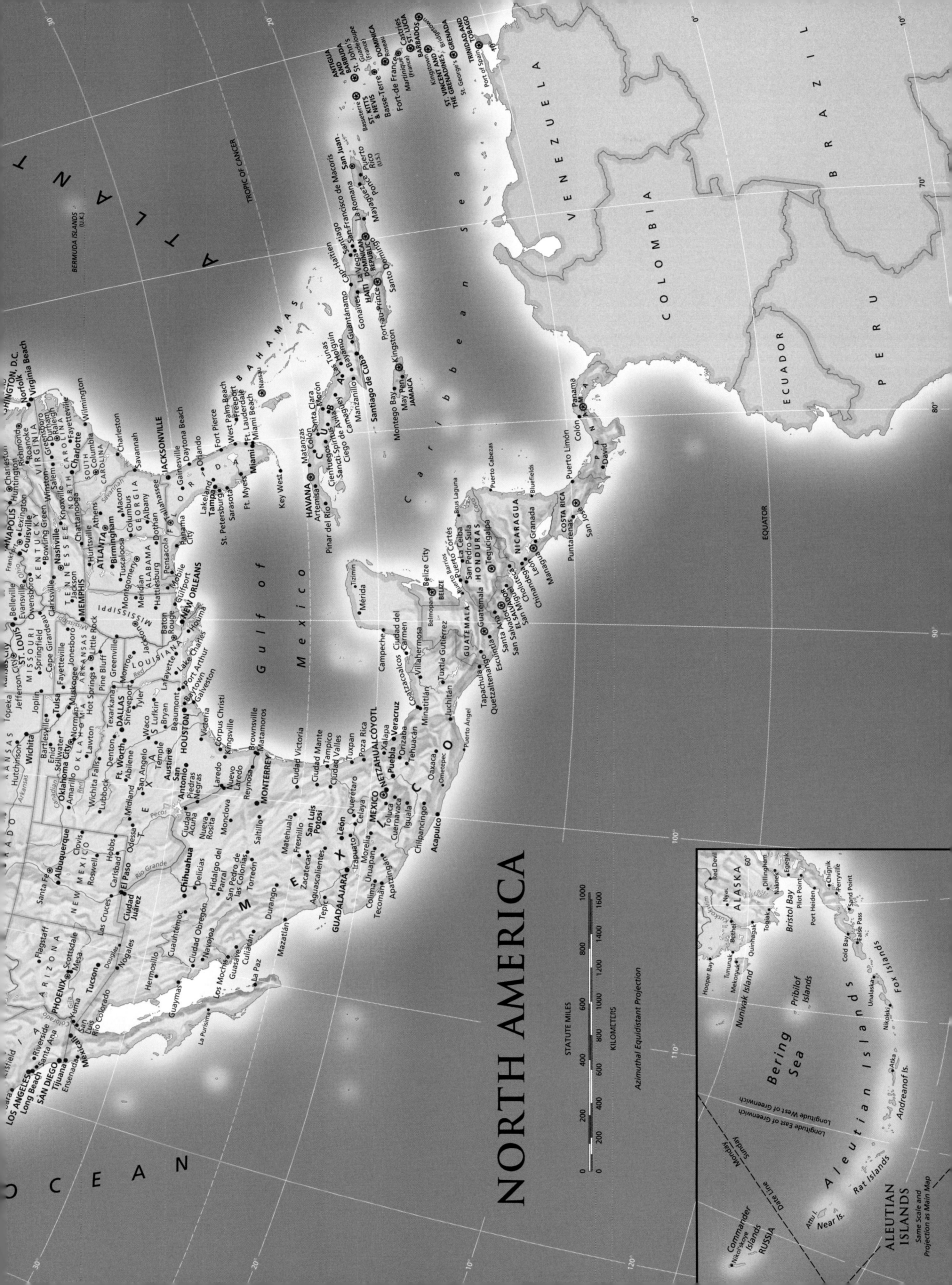

NORTH AMERICA

Azimuthal Equidistant Projection

STATUTE MILES
0   200   400   600   800   1000

KILOMETERS
0   200   400   600   800   1000   1200   1400   1600

ATLANTIC OCEAN

BERMUDA ISLANDS (U.K.)

TROPIC OF CANCER

BAHAMAS

Gulf of Mexico

M E X I C O

C u b a

Caribbean Sea

Greater Antilles

HAITI
DOMINICAN REPUBLIC
JAMAICA
Puerto Rico (U.S.)

ANTIGUA AND BARBUDA
ST. KITTS AND NEVIS
DOMINICA
ST. LUCIA
BARBADOS
ST. VINCENT AND THE GRENADINES
GRENADA
TRINIDAD AND TOBAGO

Basse-Terre (France)
Fort-de-France (France)
Castries
Roseau
Kingstown
St. George's
Bridgetown
Port of Spain

VENEZUELA

COLOMBIA

ECUADOR

PERU

BRAZIL

EQUATOR

BELIZE
Belmopan
GUATEMALA
HONDURAS
EL SALVADOR
NICARAGUA
COSTA RICA
PANAMA

Guatemala
Tegucigalpa
San Salvador
Managua
San José
Panama

WASHINGTON, D.C.
VIRGINIA
NORTH CAROLINA
SOUTH CAROLINA
GEORGIA
FLORIDA
TENNESSEE
KENTUCKY
ALABAMA
MISSISSIPPI
LOUISIANA
ARKANSAS
MISSOURI
KANSAS
OKLAHOMA
TEXAS
NEW MEXICO
ARIZONA
COLORADO

ATLANTA
MEMPHIS
NEW ORLEANS
DALLAS
HOUSTON
SAN ANTONIO
MONTERREY
GUADALAJARA
MEXICO
NETZAHUALCOYOTL
PHOENIX
LOS ANGELES
SAN DIEGO

HAVANA
Santiago de Cuba

Key West

Miami

Jacksonville

Charlotte

OCEAN

ALEUTIAN ISLANDS

ALASKA

Bering Sea

Pribilof Islands

Nunivak Island

Bristol Bay

Aleutian Islands

Fox Islands

Andreanof Is.

Rat Islands

Near Is.

Commander Islands

RUSSIA

Date Line

Longitude West of Greenwich
Longitude East of Greenwich

Monday
Sunday

Same Scale and
Projection as Main Map

From sea to shining sea, the lower 48 states of the United States encompass about 32 percent of North America's total land area. Stretching across the continent's midsection, these states are blessed with almost every landform Earth offers—mighty mountains and rivers, vast fertile plains, immense lakes, mineral-rich deserts, and well-watered coastal plains. The distinctive personalities of the two sides of the country, as well as its interior, show clearly in the satellite mosaic at right.

The western terrain is rumpled by mountains, plateaus, and basins that begin with the Coast Ranges and end with the Front Range of the Rocky Mountains to the east. A continent-long system, the Rockies extend well beyond the 48 states, angling north into Canada and south to the Mexican frontier.

Where the Rocky Mountains end, the country's seemingly endless plains begin. Part of the continent's central platform, the Great Plains to the west and the Central Lowland to the east extend across several states and stretch northward to the five Great Lakes.

The immense Mississippi River system drains the plains and plateaus that lie west of the Appalachian Mountains, an ancient, well-worn system having North Carolina's 6,684-foot Mount Mitchell as its highest peak. The Piedmont that gently rolls eastward from the Appalachians gives way to the capacious Coastal Plain seamed by navigable rivers.

Natural features are not the only objects visible in this mosaic of satellite images. The urban areas of the United States are linked together by a complex network of highways and railways, and many of them can be seen at right.

THE LOWER 48 STATES

As complex as the nation it pictures, this natural-color mosaic pieces together 432 different images to achieve its cloud-free clarity. Each pixel in the original mosaic shows 100 feet of terrain.

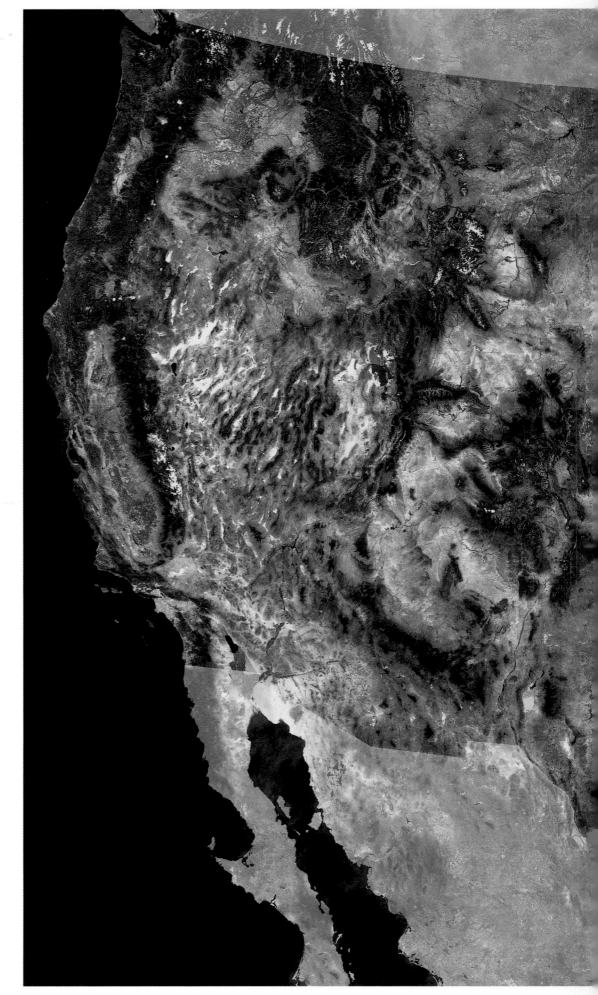

An inhospitable landscape often locked in ice, North America's far northern reaches have a primal wildness reminiscent of the ice ages that shaped them. Ironically, ice itself led to the peopling of the continent, perhaps as early as 30,000 years ago. Because more water was locked in ice then, less of it reached the ocean. As a result, the world sea level dropped, exposing a land bridge that linked Asia to Alaska. Asian hunters eventually followed woolly mammoths and other prey animals across the bridge into North America.

Even now, glaciers cover 29,000 square miles of Alaska, and Greenland is trapped beneath an ice sheet covering five-sixths of the island's landmass. But global warming is forcing much of the continent's ice into retreat, with potentially drastic consequences. According to scientists, if a large portion of Greenland's ice sheet melted, the meltwater could raise ocean levels significantly. To monitor glacial retreat on the island, researchers are increasingly relying on data obtained by satellites.

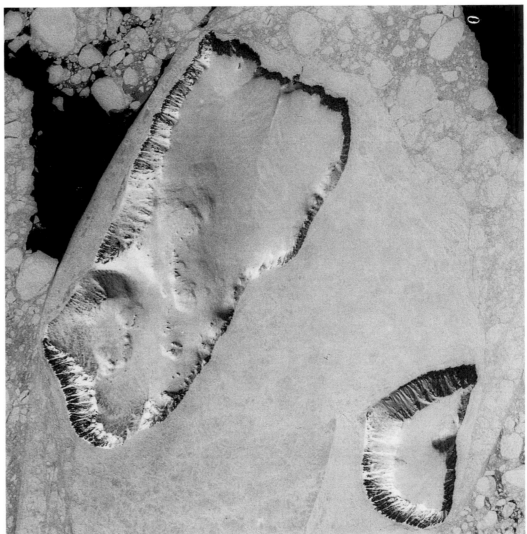

DIOMEDE ISLANDS

Stepping-stones between countries and continents, Russia's Big Diomede Island and the U.S.'s Little Diomede lie only 2.5 miles apart in the Bering Strait, a body of water separating Asia from the North American mainland. In winter, ice forms in the 50-mile-wide strait, making it possible to walk from one island to the other. An orbiting U.S. spacecraft made this recently declassified photograph during the Cold War era.

MOUNT McKINLEY, ALASKA

Created by merging Landsat data with digitized terrain elevations and then tilting the scene, the image above simulates an oblique view of the Alaska Range from 15,000 feet over the Tokositna River. The continent's highest peak, 20,320-foot Mount McKinley, or Denali—"high one"—crowns the range.

GREENLAND

Earth's largest island, Greenland encompasses an area of more than 840,000 square miles, most of it hidden beneath a vast ice sheet as much as 11,100 feet thick. Traditionally, scientists have monitored the shrinking of the sheet by measuring the icebergs calved by its glaciers. Satellite interferometry can help them mark the position of a glacier's grounding line, or junction with the sea, and follow the retreat or advance of the glacier. To monitor the Petermann Glacier (right), scientists used three radar images taken a day apart. Recent research shows that melting from beneath the ice sheet, rather than calving icebergs along its edges, actually causes greater ice loss. Using radar altimetry, scientists created a 3-D topographic model (above) that allows them to monitor the changing contours of the ice sheet.

Grounding Line

California's Death Valley is the continent's hottest, driest spot. Baking in a heat-trapping pocket between the Panamint and Amargosa Ranges, this 140-mile-long basin reaches 282 feet below sea level—the hemisphere's lowest point on land. Geologic processes that began three million years ago led to the crustal sagging that created the basin, and over time lakes filled its depressions, then evaporated, leaving thick deposits of sediment. A 200-square-mile salt pan, the remains of one such lake, now occupies much of the valley.

Death Valley averages only 1.71 inches of rainfall a year, and in summer the ground can reach temperatures of 200°F. Surprisingly, a number of hardy plants live along the edges of the valley: Creosote and mesquite bushes, for example, use roots that grow as long as 60 feet to find moisture.

The landforms here hold other surprises. At the Racetrack, a 2.8-mile-long playa of dried mud, rocks mysteriously leave long tracks on the ground. One theory says that when winter rains fall on the former lake bed and temperatures drop precipitously, thin ice sheets form on the shallow waters, with the rocks locked into them. Strong winds send the ice sheets and rocks skimming along the surface of the impermanent lake.

People have also left tracks here: A century ago, 20-mule teams hauled out borax, a naturally occurring compound used in cleansers. In 1933 Congress recognized the uniqueness of Death Valley by making it a national monument, and in 1994, the California Desert Protection Act elevated its status to national park.

Death Valley

MAPPING DEATH VALLEY

Data obtained by the Thermal Infrared Multispectral Scanner (TIMS) helped scientists create this image of Death Valley (above). Still in the experimental stage, this system can use several thermal bands—Landsat has only one—to obtain valuable information about a region. Aircraft currently obtain the data, but satellites will have the capability before too long. The Advanced Spaceborne Thermal Emission Reflection Radiometer (ASTER), for example, will soon fly aboard the EOS AM-1 satellite.

VALLEY OF EXTREMES

Death Valley's extensive central salt pan shows in this intricate TM image as a long streak of bright red (opposite). Badwater Basin, lowest point in the Western Hemisphere, lies here, its shallow pool fed from the south by the Amargosa River. In contrast to the deep basement of the basin, nearly 300 feet below sea level, the 11,049-foot-high Telescope Peak and the rest of the Panamint Range rise only a dozen miles to the west. Magenta at higher elevations denotes substantial plant life in this seemingly inhospitable realm.

Enormous river systems water North America's lands. Flowing north, south, east, and west, rivers course down from mountainous divides and vein the land as they make their way toward the three oceans that touch the continent. As the great rivers near the coasts, they fan out into fertile deltas or empty their waters into bountiful, scenic bays.

The ecosystem formed by the Chesapeake Bay and its tributaries (opposite) has long supported the fishing and shellfish industry. In recent years, however, toxins entering the water from nearby industrial sites have threatened fish populations and watermen's livelihoods.

In the center of the U.S., the Mississippi and its tributaries, the continent's largest river system, drain 1,291,341 square miles. This river has long been contested, alternately claimed by rival Native Americans; French, English, and Spanish forces; and Civil War armies. Disputes between people have done little to disrupt the river's flow, but levee-building, dredging, and pollution have had a major impact in recent years.

MACKENZIE RIVER, CANADA

Draining the northern reaches of the continent, the Mackenzie splays out through a vast lake-pocked delta before flowing into the Beaufort Sea. Canada's longest and North America's second longest river, the 2,635-mile-long Mackenzie flows through a region of permafrost and slows when it nears its mouth. Releasing tons of sediment picked up on its long journey, the river continues to build its delta at the edge of the icy sea.

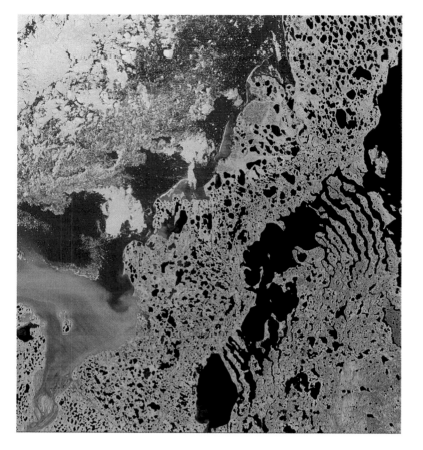

MISSISSIPPI RIVER, LOUISIANA

Moving in the opposite direction from the Mackenzie, the Mississippi forms a web of several channels, creating a "bird-foot" delta at the Gulf of Mexico. The world's fourth longest river system, the Mississippi and its tributaries flow 3,710 miles, depositing roughly 200 million tons of sediment a year on the delta.

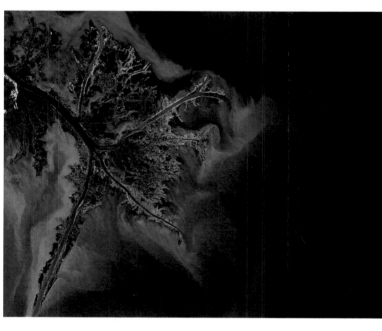

CHESAPEAKE BAY

"Heaven and earth never agreed better to frame a place for man's habitation," English adventurer John Smith wrote of the Chesapeake Bay in 1608 (opposite). One of the world's largest estuaries—covering 64,000 square miles but averaging only 20 feet deep—the bay formed from the drowned southern end of the Susquehanna River, its biggest tributary. Other tributaries gave rise to the notable cities visible from north to south in the image: Baltimore, Maryland, a major East Coast port on the Patapsco River; Annapolis, capital of Maryland, on the Severn; Washington, D.C., capital of the U.S., on the Potomac; and Richmond, capital of Virginia, on the James River. Separating the bay from the Atlantic Ocean, the broad Delmarva Peninsula derives its name from the states that share its fertile lands—Delaware, Maryland, and Virginia.

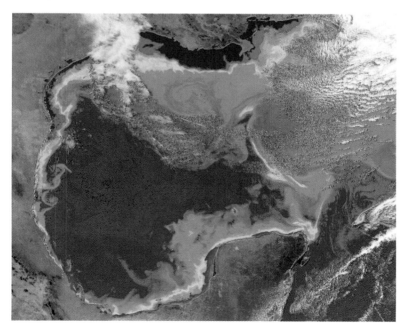

GULF OF MEXICO "DEAD ZONE"

The most turbid, plankton-rich part of the Gulf of Mexico appears red in this SeaWiFS image. Huge numbers of phytoplankton feed on nutrients carried by rivers. When they die, decomposition of all this organic matter causes oxygen-depleted waters and one of the world's largest "dead zones." This seasonal phenomenon peaks during the summer.

Weathering and tectonic movement are constantly reshaping the face of the planet. Even astral debris plays a part: More than 200 scars caused by the impact of comets, asteroids, and meteorites have been found around the world. Throughout Earth's long history, numerous collisions with space rocks have occurred, but many of the scars left by long-ago impacts later were obscured by erosion and tectonic activity or were buried by ice, sediment, or water.

What happened before can happen again, so scientists want to find out how devastating the past impacts were. Fortunately, encounters with large chunks of space debris are quite rare; collisions on a much smaller scale occur every day, however. Scientists estimate that 50 tons of meteor mass bombard the atmosphere each day, but friction causes 90 percent to disintegrate. Although most of the remaining 10 percent plunge into the oceans, the small percentage that strike land can have deadly results: An asteroid that struck North America 65 million years ago, for example, may have caused the extinction of the dinosaurs.

What would happen today if a large object struck the planet? If it landed in an ocean, tsunami-like waves could inundate nearby coasts, and localized climates would be temporarily altered. But if it hit land? A dust cloud could rise into the atmosphere and remain for weeks, even months, possibly causing global cooling and certainly producing acid rain and wildfires. Like the doomed dinosaurs, people might find Earth a far less hospitable planet.

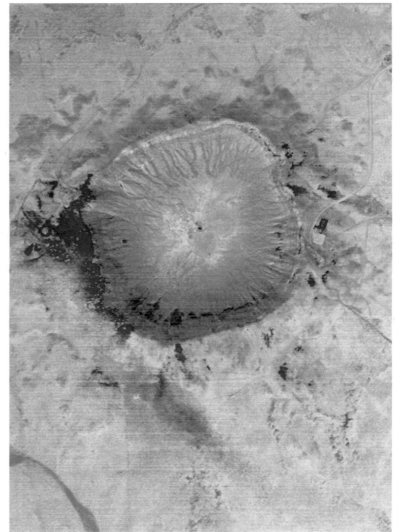

MANICOUAGAN CRATER, QUEBEC

About 40 miles in diameter, this "astrobleme," or eroded crater, in eastern Canada (above) reveals its full face to high-flying satellites, but its shape remains barely noticeable to observers on the ground. Satellite imagery lets scientists detect well-worn surface patterns caused by meteorites that struck the planet in the distant past—in the case of Manicouagan, 210 million years ago. Ranging from quite small to thousands of feet in diameter, impact craters show up on every continent except ice-covered Antarctica.

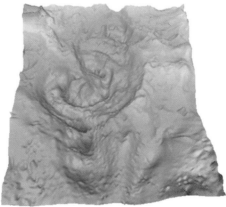

CHICXULUB CRATER, YUCATÁN

Partially covered by the Gulf of Mexico, but visible in a 3-D model using gravity field data, the 120-mile-wide Chicxulub crater dates from an asteroid impact that may have ended the dinosaur age.

METEOR CRATER, ARIZONA

Leaving a lasting impression, a meteorite about 150 feet across struck the Earth about 50,000 years ago, sending up a cloud of debris visible in a large part of North America. Meteor Crater, near the city of Winslow, Arizona, measures three-quarters of a mile wide and 575 feet deep (above). Windblown, silica-rich sands make red swirls in and near the crater in this TIMS image made from the air. Scientists believe most Earth-striking meteorites wander from the asteroid belt that arcs between the orbits of Mars and Jupiter.

Ice has also shaped Earth's surface. About 16,000 years ago, Ice Age glaciers began receding from several enormous basins in North America. By roughly 10,500 years ago, debris from the glaciers had trapped water in the depressions, and the five Great Lakes had begun to assume their present form. The lakes now cover 95,000 square miles, hold one-fifth of the world's aboveground fresh water, and have 8,000 miles of shoreline—almost as much as the continent's oceanic coastlines combined. They reach their greatest depth, 2,400 feet, in Lake Superior. The Great Lakes have long been exploited for their natural resources and transportation potential. Connected to one another and to the Atlantic, via the St. Lawrence Seaway, they form an inland sea accessible by large oceangoing vessels.

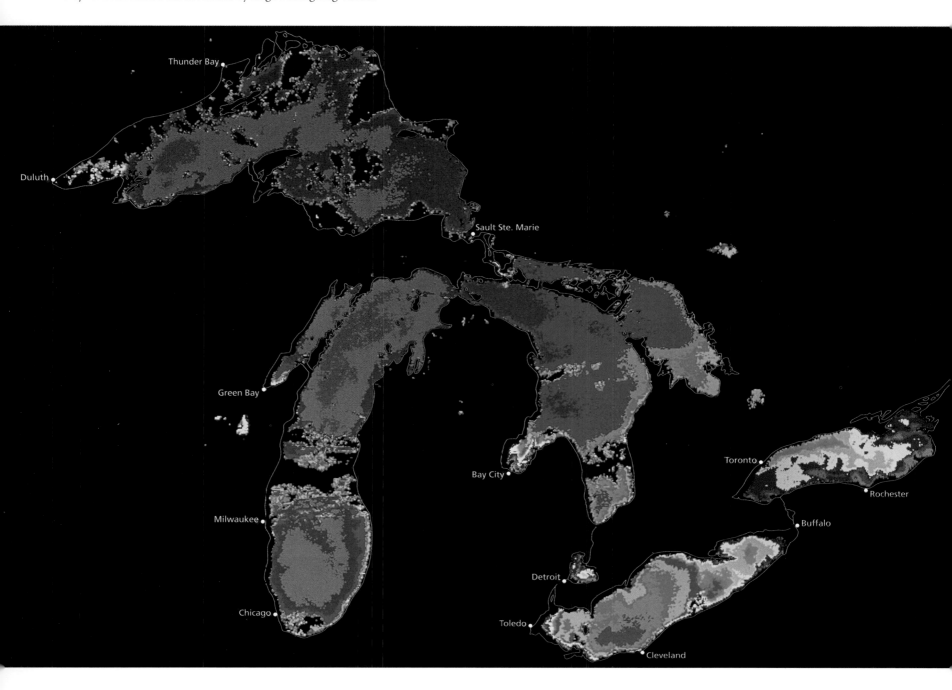

GREAT LAKES

For all their immensity, Lakes Superior, Michigan, Huron, Erie, and Ontario (west to east) suffer from the runoff of municipal and agricultural wastes. Because the lakes drain through narrow channels, natural cleansing takes time. Lake Superior needs 180 years to turn over its entire volume—much too long to deal with sediment buildup, algal growth, and river deposits. Erie replaces its water in three years, but the smaller volume of this shallower lake makes pollution easier here. The lakes' increasing turbidity levels, monitored by satellites, accelerate oxygen loss in a process called eutrophication. In this image, cool colors reflect low turbidity and hot colors, high.

Extending from the polar regions to the tropics, North America spans a remarkable range of climates and biosystems, from ice fields to plains to coral reefs. The vast Columbia Icefield (below), in Canada, occupies rugged Rockies terrain so high and formidable that, despite the size of the ice field, it apparently remained unknown to people until the end of the 19th century. Its glaciers spill down from 10,000-foot summits along the Continental Divide, their meltwaters eventually feeding into three different oceans—the Atlantic, the Pacific, and the Arctic.

In the tropics, the small Central American country of Belize claims the most extensive coral reef system in Atlantic waters. The tiny coral polyps that build such reefs thrive in this area of the western Caribbean, an arm of the Atlantic Ocean. By secreting a material that cements their hard external skeletons to one another, coral colonies gradually form reefs that, in turn, support thousands of other animal species.

COLUMBIA ICEFIELD, CANADA

North America's largest subpolar ice field, which sprawls along the border between the Canadian provinces of Alberta and British Columbia, holds 126 square miles of the Rocky Mountains in its frozen maw (above). Meltwaters from the glaciers that creep slowly down from the ice field feed into a number of rivers. To create this 3-D view looking from the northeast, WorldSat merged TM imagery, for color, and SPOT panchromatic imagery, for sharpness, and then draped the result over a digital elevation model.

CORAL REEF, BELIZE

In this SPOT image (opposite), the coral reef near Belize appears as a turquoise shadow in coastal waters. Longest continuous coral reef system in Atlantic waters—geographers consider the Caribbean Sea an arm of the ocean—the reef rests atop the edge of the continental shelf, which drops off sharply into ink-black waters. Near the coast, eroded coral atolls known as the Turneffe Islands enclose a protected lagoon. Belize City sits on the peninsula just left of center; at left, popcorn-like clouds drift over lush forests.

Orbiting far above the weather, satellites have revolutionized meteorology, often spotting potentially dangerous weather conditions such as hurricanes and tornadoes in time for life-saving warnings to be issued. In North America, severe, fast-moving weather poses an unrelenting problem. The continent's extensive coastlines breed volatile conditions, and vast interior plains lack east-west ranging mountains that would help keep hot air masses from the south from colliding violently with masses of cold air from the north.

The United States is plagued by more destructive storms than any other country, causing it to endure an annual average of 10,000 severe thunderstorms, 1,000 tornadoes, 5,000 floods, and 2 hurricanes. Sporadically occurring phenomena, like the three-to-seven-year El Niño cycle in the Pacific Ocean, only exacerbate these statistics. An abnormal warming of the eastern Pacific, El Niño brings extreme temperatures, heavy rainfall, and drought to the Americas.

While the satellite eyes in the sky cannot tame the rampages of nature, they can bring some order into the climatic chaos. Increasingly, scientists rely on them to help monitor soil saturation that might cause flooding, the weather effects of ash fallout from volcanic activity, and, of course, hurricanes, tornadoes, and El Niño.

MISSISSIPPI, 1988

Curling into each other just north of St. Louis, Missouri, the courses of the Mississippi (upper) and Missouri (lower) Rivers merge, thus forming a thin, well-defined line on the landscape. Landsat made this image July 4, 1988, when drought lowered river flow; the average gauge reading for the day—an indication of river depth— measured 1.8 feet.

MISSISSIPPI, 1993

During the Great Flood of 1993, inky lakes of inundation spread far beyond the normal paths of the Mississippi and Missouri, driving gauge readings to 46.5 feet on July 18. Heavy spring and summer rains brought the flood, and by July river waters had invaded urban areas (pink) as well as less developed areas (green) in much of the Midwest.

HURRICANE FRAN

White whirl of death swirling in the western Atlantic, infamous Fran bears down on the Florida peninsula in early September 1996. Like many previous hurricanes, Fran changed her course and headed north along the Eastern Seaboard, slamming the Carolinas with 115-mile-an-hour winds. NOAA's

GOES-8, a Geostationary Operational Environmental Satellite, captured Fran's ominous image, giving meteorologists at the National Hurricane Center in Florida a good view of the approaching storm. Using the satellite as their eye in the sky, they could watch Fran's movement toward the coast and send out timely warnings to people living in her path.

The continent's west coast is its most geologically active region. Part of the Pacific Ring of Fire, sections of it straddle or rest near the edges of oceanic and continental plates whose movements cause frequent earthquakes and occasional eruptions. The cloud-piercing volcanoes that grace the Pacific Northwest are young by geologic standards—and dangerously active, as Mount St. Helens proved in 1980.

The coastal region to the south is less volcanic, but it is no more stable: Alternating rains and droughts bedevil its farmers and homeowners. During dry spells, hot Santa Ana winds can ignite brushlands into uncontrolled blazes that destroy communities and the area's considerable, if precarious, natural beauty.

MOUNT ST. HELENS

As seen in these oblique views by WorldSat, Mount St. Helens rose in 1972 (upper) like a beauty mark on the landscape of southwest Washington. Then, on March 20, 1980, the young volcano in the Cascade Range shook itself awake, as it does every 100 to 200 years, setting off an earth tremor and spewing a cloud of ash and steam from its snowcapped summit. Two months later, on May 18, the volcano exploded in a violent eruption that collapsed the summit and left a sagging wasteland, as shown in this 1985 view (middle). The powerful blast from the eruption destroyed thousands of trees and killed a large number of wildlife; heavy mudflows and ash fallout claimed 60 lives and some 200 homes. By 1996, although the catastrophe was far from forgotten, plant life had returned to St. Helens, greening its slopes once again (right).

OAKLAND HILLS, CALIFORNIA

In October 1991, a TM simulation made this aerial view of burned wildlands (orange) and blazing buildings (yellow) in the Oakland hills (opposite). The costliest urban fire in U.S. history raged across 1,500 acres and 26 miles of city streets, killing 25 people and destroying 3,000 homes.

The national borders originally drawn to carve out political claims are now, in some places, clear lines across the landscape when seen from high in the sky. Urban development patterns, farming and ranching techniques, government land-use policies, population pressures, and natural features have all contributed to these demarcations.

In North America, the boundaries between the United States and its neighbors, Canada and Mexico, are particularly obvious. Canada's population is only one-ninth that of the U.S., and many of its people dwell in the eastern third of the country, residing in large metropolitan areas that are farther south than the northernmost section of the lower 48 states. Most of the western half of the contiguous U.S. reaches as far north as the 49th parallel, a line of latitude that has served as part of the border since the signing of an agreement in 1818. Over the decades, this arbitrary political boundary has been etched into the continent itself (below). Large-scale farming and development in the midwestern U.S. extends all the way to the border and stops abruptly; less populated rangelands lie north of the border.

Far to the south, the border between the U.S. and Mexico (opposite, top) appears as a long thin line when seen from space. This boundary is one of the few places in the world where a developing country directly adjoins a modern, highly developed one. Fences rise along parts of the border in an effort to control population movements that result from the economic disparity between the two nations. Farther east, the Rio Grande forms a natural boundary for about half the border's length.

CANADA/UNITED STATES

Montana's patchwork of wheat fields ends abruptly at the 49th parallel, where the open rangeland of Canada begins. Though both areas share similar soil, their approaches to land use clearly differ. Ignoring the boundary, the Milk River slices across this Landsat image from northwest to southeast.

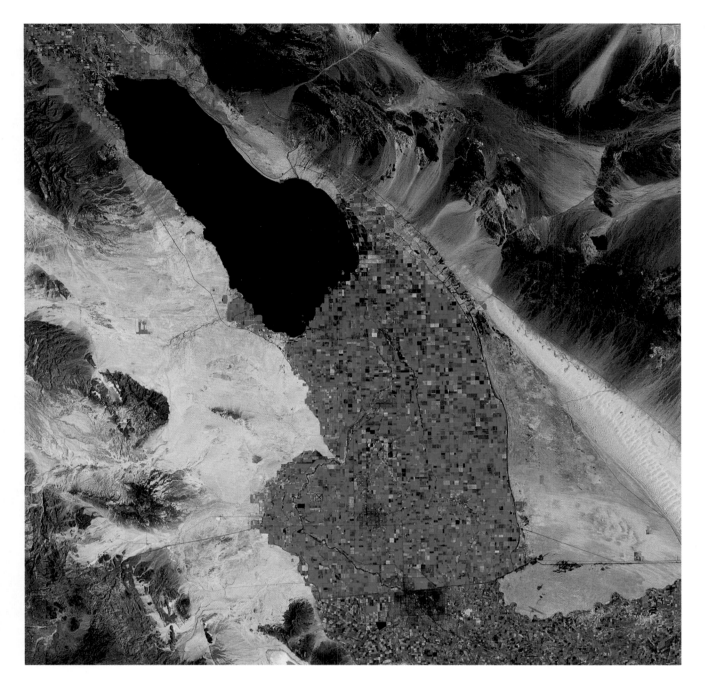

South of the large black blot made by the Salton Sea, 232 feet below sea level, the green fields of southern California's Imperial Valley stretch toward Mexico (left). At the border, visible in the lower part of this Landsat image as a thin west-to-east line, the green quickly gives way to Mexicali's less verdant farmlands.

Hoping to feed many mouths, farmers in southeastern Mexico strip trees from the land and plow them under, denuding much of the rain forest—shown here as the much lighter area (right). Less populated Guatemala preserves its forest, which appears as the dark green area to the south and east, exactly marking the border with Mexico.

Human tracks drawn across the landscape—highways, causeways, canals, railroads, and even oil pipelines—show clearly from above, as do the effects they have on the environment around them. Two centuries ago, before canals and railroads were built, no such imprints of progress marked the surface of North America. But just in the past half century, superhighways have radically altered the speed and style of ground-based transportation. Now these highways and other systems used for transporting people and their goods form an enormous network across a large part of the continent, piercing national boundaries, burrowing through mountains, bridging expansive bodies of water, and making the planet a smaller, if not always better, place.

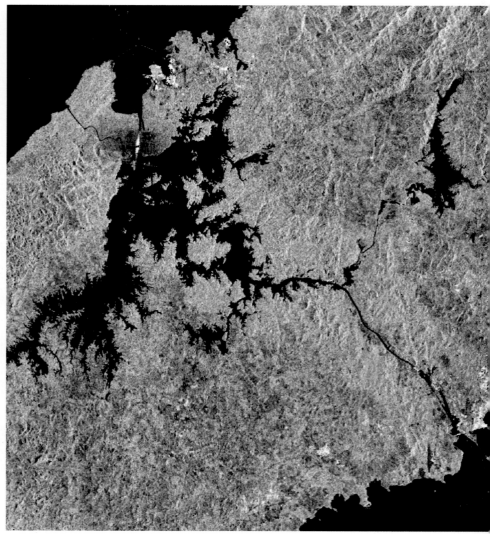

GREAT SALT LAKE, UTAH

Railroading the Great Salt Lake into higher salinity levels, a Southern Pacific causeway separates the northwest part of the lake from the natural freshwater tributaries that once fed it. The lighter blue in this Thematic Mapper scene comes from salinity levels three times higher than the rest of the lake water.

PANAMA CANAL

Linking the Atlantic and Pacific, the 40.3-mile-long Panama Canal begins in the north at Bahía Limón, reaches inland to Gatún Lake, then narrows into a system of locks leading to Panama Bay—all visible in this radar mosaic. Radar penetrates clouds, revealing ships waiting at both ends of the canal.

TRANS-ALASKA PIPELINE

Paralleling the Koyukuk River, the Alaska Pipeline and a gravel maintenance road snake through the foothills of the Brooks Range, as shown in this view from a NASA high-altitude airborne camera (opposite). The pipeline pumps oil from Prudhoe Bay to the port of Valdez about 800 miles to the south.

VANCOUVER, BRITISH COLUMBIA

Watery wonderland, peninsular Vancouver (right, at lower right) faces the Strait of Georgia, its northern coastline scooped by Burrard Inlet and its southern side cut by the Fraser River Delta. Beyond the inlet, Howe Sound and a series of finger lakes chisel into the spectacular Coast Mountains. The Gulf Islands, partly filling the lower left corner of the image, lie across the strait, just off the much larger Vancouver Island. The country's biggest port and third largest city, Vancouver receives kudos for creating a lively metropolis in a superb natural setting.

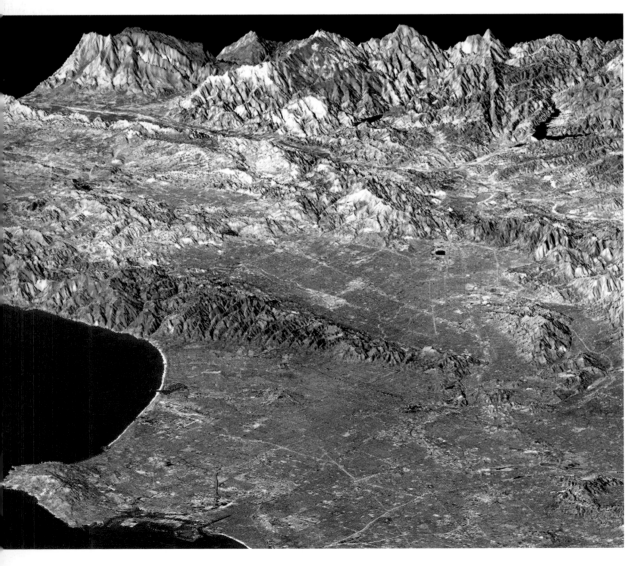

LOS ANGELES, CALIFORNIA

As seen in this 3-D view, a coastal plain edged by Pacific beaches and bounded by mountains holds southern California's City of Angels (left). "An untidy jumble of human diversity and perversity," writer George Will called the metropolis that encompasses the lavish homes of Beverly Hills, the inner-city hopelessness of South Central L.A., and the perpetual hopefulness of Hollywood. Sprung from an 18th-century Spanish pueblo, Greater L.A. now ranks as one of the largest metropolitan areas on the continent.

SAN FRANCISCO BAY AREA, CALIFORNIA

Hilly San Francisco (opposite) occupies a peninsula jutting between the Pacific Ocean and San Francisco Bay. Its East Bay sisters, Oakland and Berkeley, lie just over the double-deck Bay Bridge, which anchors itself in mid-sweep to Yerba Buena Island. To the city's north, the Golden Gate Bridge leads to Marin County and rugged headlands. For all its beauty, the Bay Area must contend with active faults, including the unpredictable San Andreas. In 1906 and 1989, earthquakes dealt the area major seismic blows.

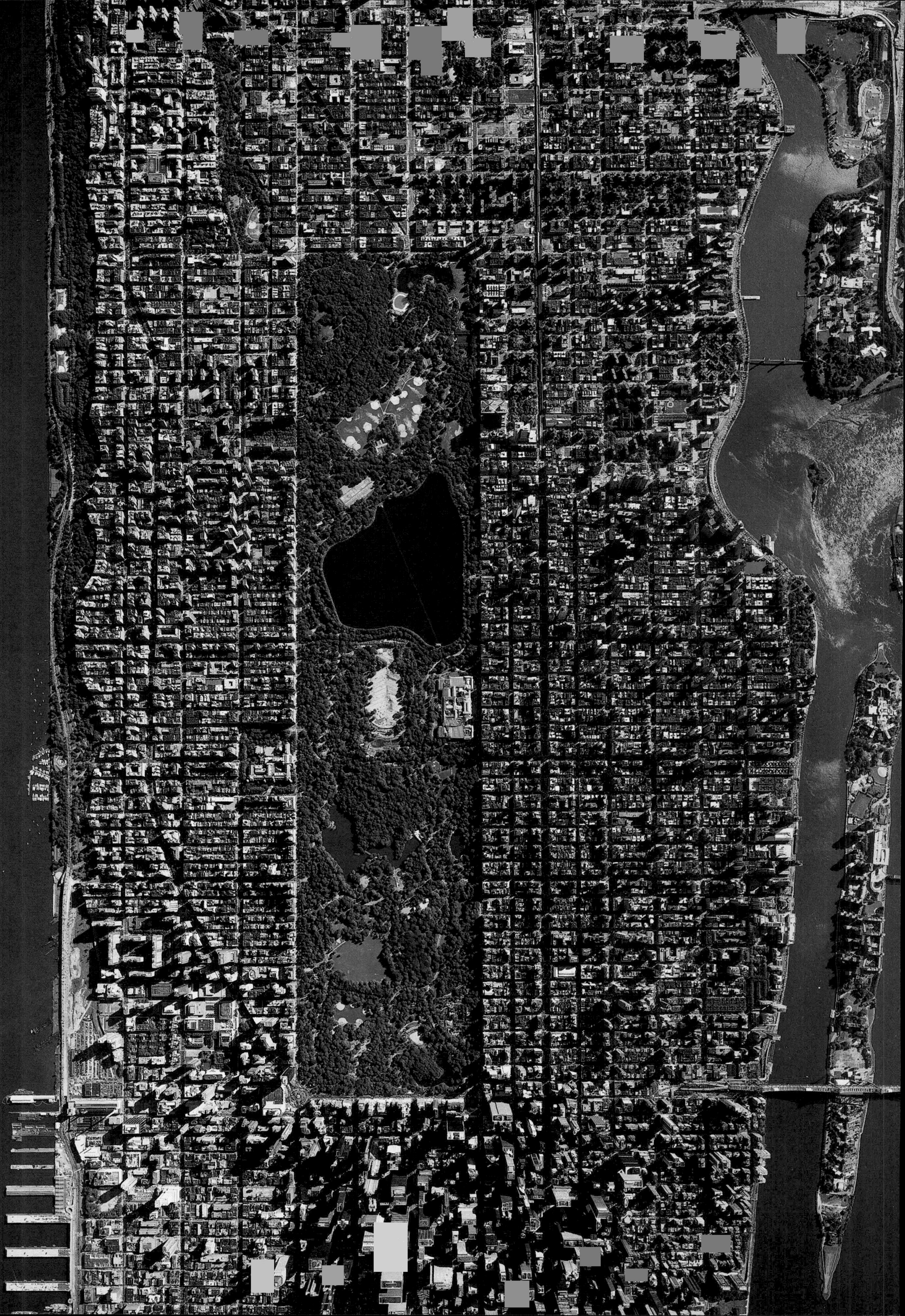

QUÉBEC, QUÉBEC

Birthplace of French-Canadian culture, the city of Québec (right) has occupied its strategic site on Cape Diamant promontory (bluish area) since 1608, when Samuel de Champlain established a trading post here. Overlooking the St. Lawrence River and almond-shaped Île d'Orléans, Québec still includes the long lots typical of early French settlement—a striking feature in this image. Now the capital of French-speaking Quebec Province, the city has led the movement for Québécois independence from Anglo-oriented Canada.

CHICAGO, ILLINOIS

Chicago (right) leans against the shoreline of Lake Michigan, a muscular cityscape of high-rises laced with ethnic neighborhoods. Settled in the 1770s by a fur trader of French, Canadian, and African descent, the site became a major port and railroad town by the mid-19th century. Railroads still radiate from downtown, carrying passengers and freight in nearly every direction. While no longer strictly a gritty transportation and industrial center, Chicago remains—in the words of poet Carl Sandburg—the "City With Broad Shoulders."

NEW YORK, NEW YORK

Heart of America's most populous city, Manhattan Island (opposite) stands at the forefront of world culture and finance. The densely packed island crowds a population of some 1.5 million souls into 22 square miles. As seen in this aerial view, Central Park separates the upper east and west sides. The 843-acre haven of gardens, waterscapes, and woodland paths owes its personality to Frederick Law Olmsted and Calvert Vaux, who in 1857 began transforming a bog into a "place where city dwellers could go and forget all about the city."

NEW ORLEANS, LOUISIANA

Looped by the levee-protected course of the Mississippi River, the Big Easy curls itself along the edge of Lake Pontchartrain in this SPOT image (below). Louisiana's largest city lies about 110 miles upriver from the Gulf of Mexico and has long served as the Mississippi's major deepwater port, shipping out local resources such as cotton, rice, and oil, as well as products from areas farther up the river. Since the city's founding nearly 300 years ago, Spanish, French, and American flags have flown over it. Long, narrow lots still stretch from the river's shores, visible reminders of early French settlement. With its compelling mix of cultures, cuisines, and moods, New Orleans attracts large numbers of writers, artists, musicians, and tourists. Each year, in February or early March, the city plays host to the pre-Lenten carnival it calls Mardi Gras.

WASHINGTON, D.C.

The merging of panchromatic imagery from an Indian satellite with a TM image (for color) produced this detailed view of Washington, D.C. In 1790, George Washington, first President of the United States, chose this marshy spot at the confluence of the Potomac (west) and Anacostia (east) Rivers as the site for the new nation's capital city. Conceived in grand, Baroque style by French-born architect Pierre Charles L'Enfant, the city took nearly two centuries to become a reality of marble monuments, broad avenues, and fountained greenswards. The cornerstone for the city's oldest government building, the White House, dates from 1792. British troops set fire to the building and much of Washington in the War of 1812. Arlington National Cemetery, honored resting place for the country's military dead, occupies a knoll overlooking the river.

MEXICO CITY

Some 17 million people call Mexico City home (below), making it one of the world's most populous urban centers. The Aztec people founded the city almost 700 years ago, when their gods directed them to a marshy bowl in the central highlands of Mexico. Now sprawling across more than a thousand square miles, the metropolitan behemoth must deal with severe air pollution, a lack of clean water, and an ever present threat from Popocatépetl, an active volcano within striking distance of the city's megamillion people. Beautiful but potentially deadly, snowcapped "Popo" (to the right of center) looms on the horizon in this three-dimensional image viewed from the northwest.

SOUTH AMERICA

Wispy dendrites from space, tributaries of the Amazon River converge to create the world's second longest river, after the Nile. Stretching from the Andes in the west to the Atlantic in the east, the Amazon Basin occupies nearly half of South America and defines the planet's largest, most biologically diverse rain forest. The Amazon floodplain covers more area than Florida and is twice the size of England.

South America also boasts what may be the world's driest desert, the Atacama of northern Chile, and other natural features that exemplify the great variety of the fourth largest continent. In the north, several Andean landmarks climb from tropical forest floors to glacier-covered summits more than 20,000 feet high; such ecological extremes may have given rise to half of Earth's plant and animal species. Spine of the continent, the Andes travel virtually its entire length,

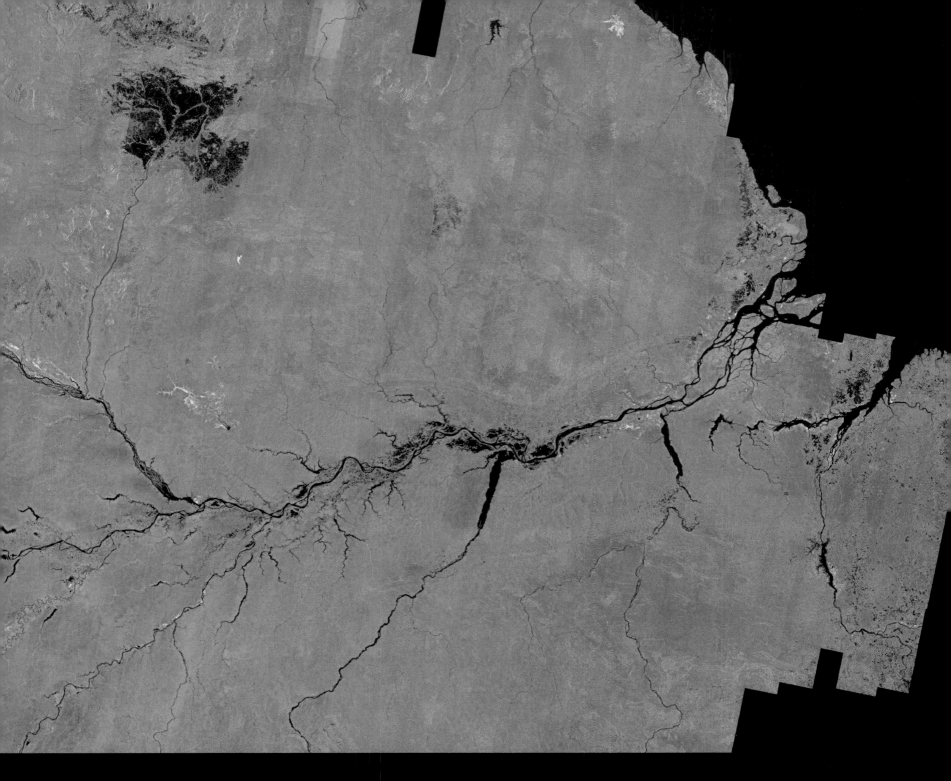

some 4,500 miles along the Pacific coast. The lower and broader highlands of Guyana and Brazil, and Argentina's Patagonia, rise away from the Atlantic coast.

In addition to the vast basin of the Amazon, two other lowland regions are drained by mighty rivers. The Orinoco in the north flows through alluvial plains and mesas of its basin, called the llanos. In the south, the Paraguay-Paraná system scores the flat expanses of the Pampas and the Gran Chaco.

THE AMAZON BASIN

Preliminary mosaic of JERS-1 radar images hints at the Amazon Basin's trove of interconnected ecosystems. Sweeps of color code vast areas of the mosaic: Purple represents open water; pink highlights the low vegetation that often fringes rivers and other bodies of water; green shows the forest. Yellow areas indicate flooded sections of the rain forest. About 800 images compose this coast-to-coast view of northern South America,

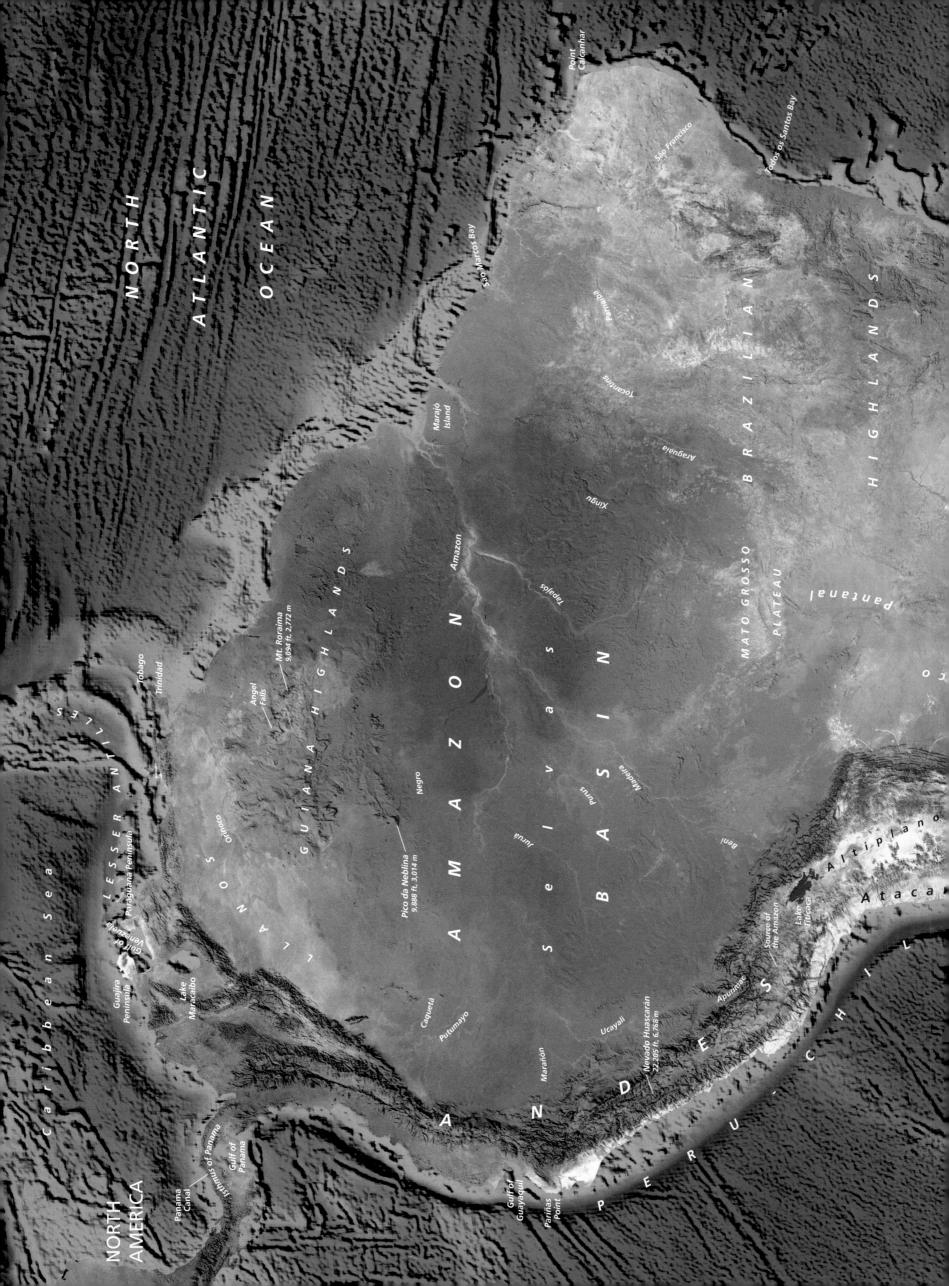

NORTH ATLANTIC OCEAN

NORTH AMERICA

Caribbean Sea

Panama Canal

Isthmus of Panama

Gulf of Panama

LESSER ANTILLES

Tobago
Trinidad

Gulf of Venezuela

Guajira Peninsula

Paraguaná Peninsula

Lake Maracaibo

Point Calcanhar

São Francisco

São Marcos Bay

Marajó Island

Amazon

Todos os Santos Bay

Parnaíba

Tocantins

Araguaia

Xingu

BRAZILIAN HIGHLANDS

HIGHLANDS

GUIANA HIGHLANDS

Mt. Roraima
9,094 ft. 2,772 m

Angel Falls

Soledad

Tapajós

Pantanal

MATO GROSSO PLATEAU

Pico da Neblina
9,888 ft. 3,014 m

Negro

Orinoco

L L A N O S

A M A Z O N

S e l v a s

B A S I N

Madeira

Purus

Beni

Altiplano

Atacama

Lake Titicaca

Source of the Amazon

Caquetá

Putumayo

Juruá

Marañón

Ucayali

Apurímac

Nevado Huascarán
22,205 ft. 6,768 m

A N D E S

Gulf of Guayaquil

Pariñas Point

P E R U - C H I L E

C H I L E

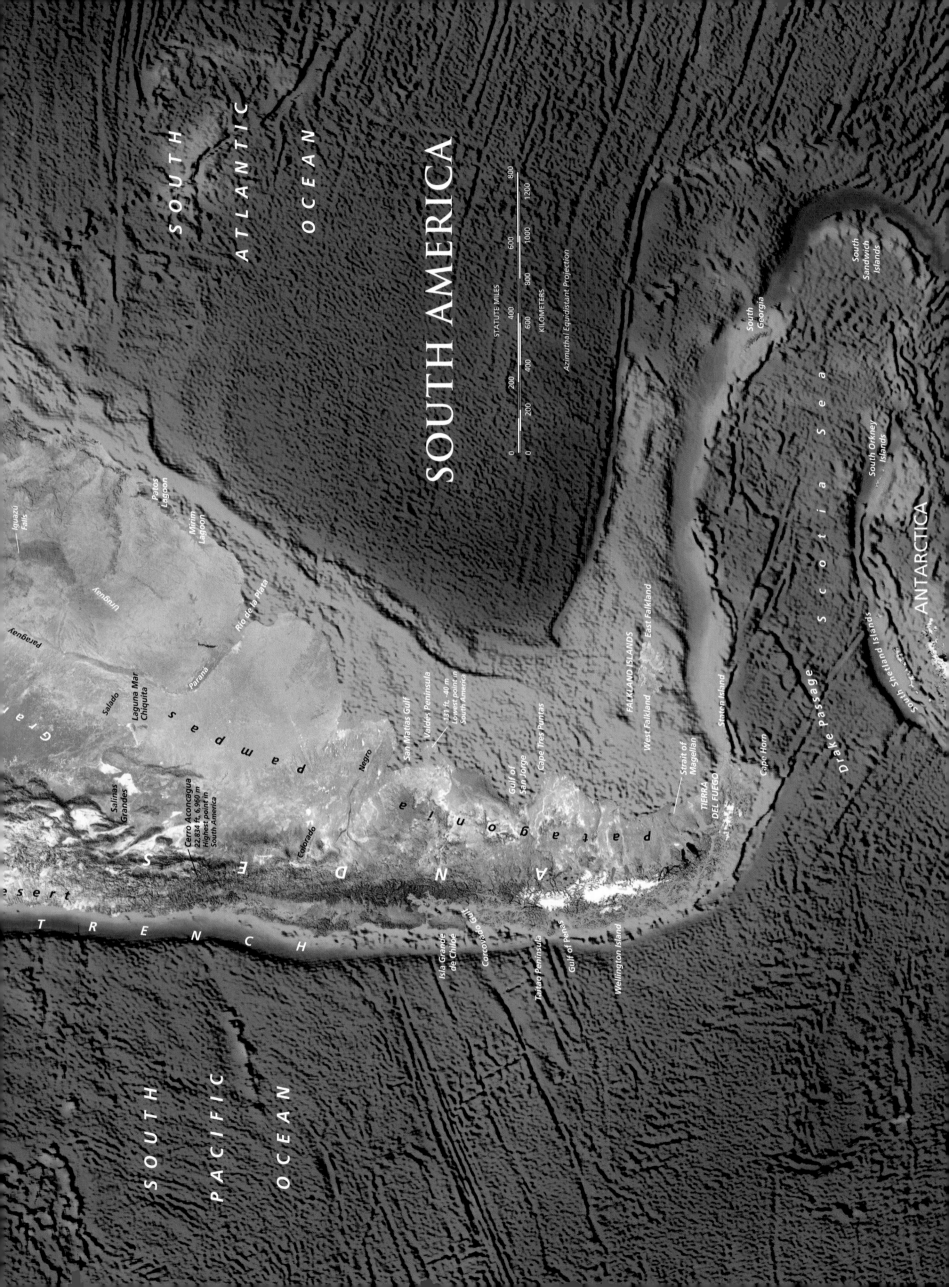

SOUTH
ATLANTIC
OCEAN

SOUTH AMERICA

STATUTE MILES
200   400   600   800

KILOMETERS
200   400   600   800   1000   1200

Azimuthal Equidistant Projection

South
Georgia

South
Sandwich
Islands

S c o t i a   S e a

South Orkney
Islands

ANTARCTICA

Drake Passage

South Shetland Islands

Iguazú
Falls

Patos
Lagoon

Mirim
Lagoon

Uruguay

Paraguay

Río de la Plata

Paraná

Gran

Salado

Laguna Mar
Chiquita

P a m p a s

Negro

San Matías Gulf

Valdés Peninsula
131 ft. -40 m
Lowest point in
South America

Gulf of
San Jorge

Cape Tres Puntas

FALKLAND ISLANDS

East Falkland

West Falkland

Strait of
Magellan

Staten Island

Salinas
Grandes

Cerro Aconcagua
22,834 ft. 6,960 m
Highest point in
South America

Colorado

P a t a g o n i a

TIERRA
DEL FUEGO

Cape Horn

Desert

A N D E S

Isla Grande
de Chiloé

Corcovado Gulf

Taitao Peninsula

Gulf of Penas

Wellington Island

SOUTH
PACIFIC
OCEAN

T R E N C H

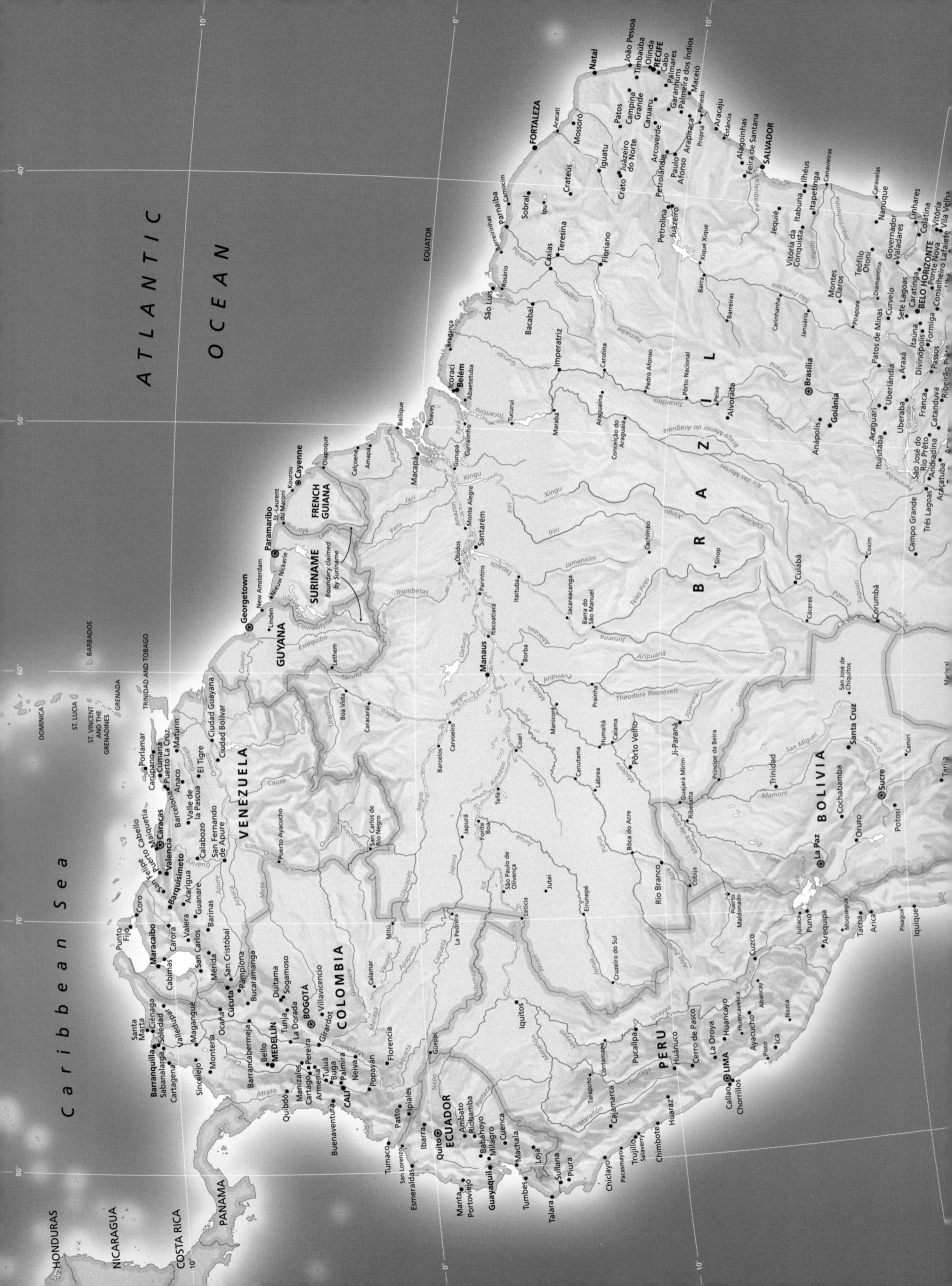

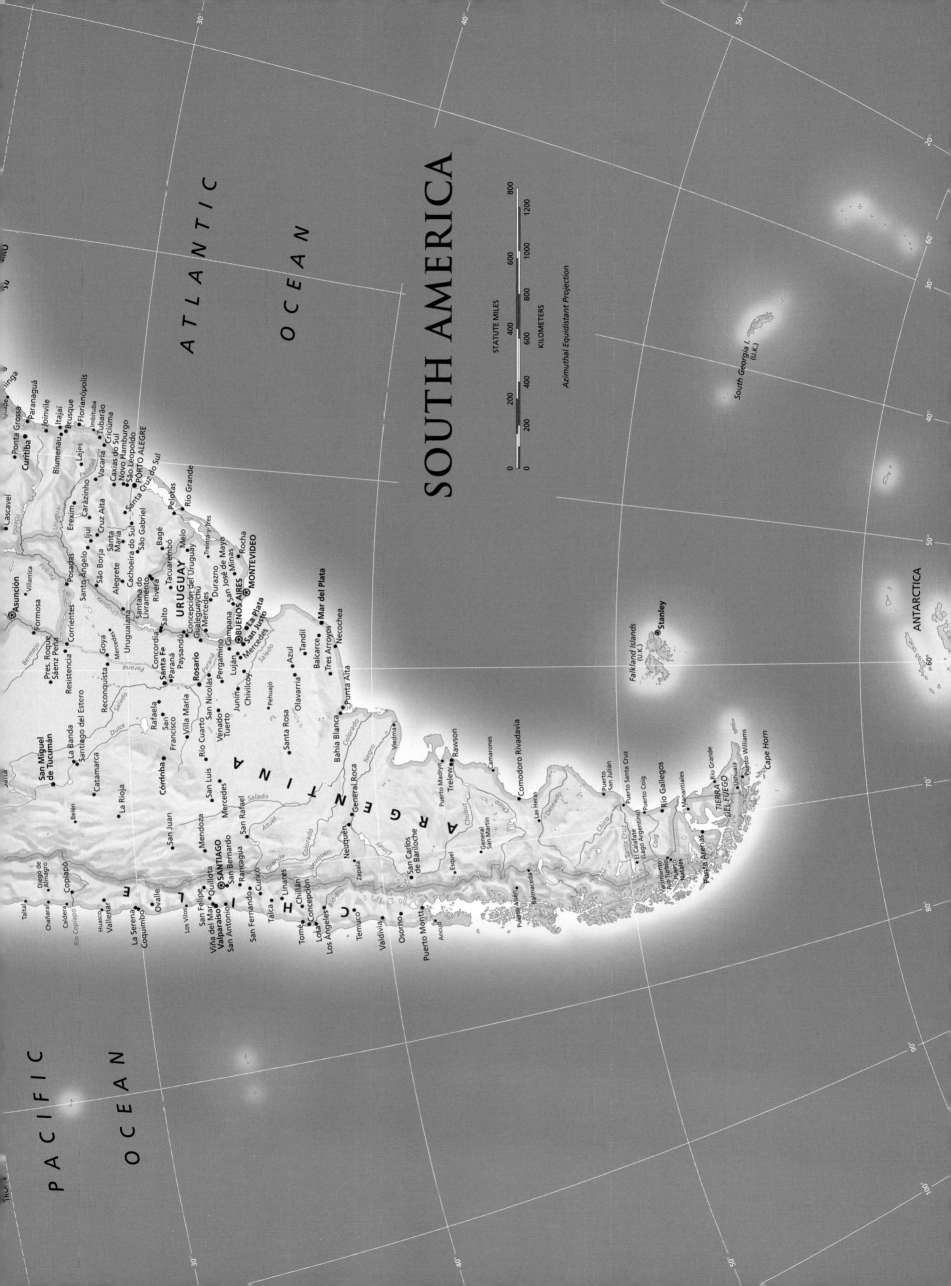

SOUTH AMERICA

PACIFIC

OCEAN

ATLANTIC

OCEAN

STATUTE MILES

200   400   600   800

0   200   400   600   800   1000   1200

KILOMETERS

Azimuthal Equidistant Projection

ANTARCTICA

South Georgia I.
(U.K.)

Falkland Islands
(U.K.)
⊕ Stanley

Asunción
Villarrica
Lascavel
Iguaçu
Ponta Grossa
Paranaguá
Curitiba
Joinvile
Blumenau Itajaí
Brusque
Florianópolis
Imbituba
Tubarão
Criciúma
Vacaria
Caxias do Sul
São Leopoldo
Novo Hamburgo
PORTO ALEGRE
Santa Cruz do Sul
Pelotas
Rio Grande
Lajes
Erexim
Carázinho
Cruz Alta
Jiju
Santa Maria
São Borja
Alegrete
Santo Angelo
Posadas
Cachoeira do Sul
São Gabriel
Bagé
Formosa
Corrientes
Goyá
Resistencia
Pres. Roque
Sáenz Peña
Reconquista
Santana do
Livramento
Rivera
Tacuarembó
Melo
Durazno
San José de
Minas
Rocha
Treinta y Tres
MONTEVIDEO
URUGUAY
Salto
Paysandú
Concepción del Uruguay
Gualeguaychú
Mercedes
BUENOS AIRES
La Plata
San Justo
Mercedes
Campana
Luján
Pergamino
Mar del Plata
San Nicolás
Rosario
Santa Fe
Paraná
Concordia
Uruguaiana
Rafaela
San Francisco
Villa Maria
Río Cuarto
Venado
Tuerto
Junín
Chivilcoy
Pehuajó
Santa Rosa
Azul
Tandil
Olavarría
Necochea
Tres Arroyos
Balcarce
Punta Alta
Bahía Blanca
Viedma
Carmen de
Patagones
San Miguel
de Tucumán
La Banda
Santiago del Estero
Catamarca
Belén
La Rioja
Córdoba
San Luis
Mercedes
San Juan
Mendoza
San Rafael
Aconcagua
SANTIAGO
San Bernardo
Rancagua
San Felipe
Quillota
Viña del Mar
Valparaíso
San Antonio
San Fernando
Curicó
Talca
Linares
Chillán
Tomé
Concepción
Lota
Los Angeles
Temuco
Valdivia
Osorno
Puerto Montt
Ancud
Diego de
Almagro
Copiapó
Caldera
Chañaral
Taltal
Huasco
Vallenar
La Serena
Coquimbo
Los Vilos
Ovalle
General Roca
Neuquén
Zapala
Esquel
San Carlos
de Bariloche
Puerto Aisén
Balmaceda
Coihaique
Puerto Madryn
Trelew
Rawson
Camarones
Comodoro Rivadavia
Las Heras
General
San Martín
Puerto
San Julián
Puerto Santa Cruz
Puerto Coig
Río Gallegos
El Calafate
(Lago Argentino)
Río Turbio
Puerto Natales
Manantiales
Punta Arenas
Río Grande
TIERRA
DEL FUEGO
Puerto Williams
Ushuaia
Cape Horn

ARGENTINA

CHILE

URUGUAY

Paraguai
Uruguay
Paraná
Bermejo
Salado
Dulce
Salado
Río Copiapó
Atuel
Grande
Colorado
Colorado
Neuquén
Bío-Bío
Limay
Negro
Colorado
Chubut
Chico
Deseado
Santa Cruz
Coig
Chico

Stretching north of the Equator and south to the subantarctic zone, South America takes in a greater range of latitudes than every other continent except Asia. The presence of the world's second highest mountain range, the Andes, amplifies the natural variety of landforms into a series of extremes, as does the range's proximity to the Pacific Ocean.

In the south, where the continent tapers toward Cape Horn, the Andes cast a rain shadow that combines with the cold Humboldt Current to make the Atacama Desert an almost lifeless environment of extraordinary aridity. In western Argentina rises Aconcagua, the highest mountain among dozens of South American peaks in the 20,000-foot range. But the single largest feature of the Andes is the Altiplano of Peru and Bolivia, a vast massif studded with hills and wide plains, grooved with steep valleys, and watered by rivers, marshes, and lakes, including the huge, freshwater Titicaca. More than two miles up, Titicaca is one of the world's highest lakes.

Lake Titicaca
Atacama Desert
Mount Aconcagua

LAKE TITICACA

Loftiest of the world's large navigable lakes, with an elevation of 12,500 feet, Titicaca straddles the border of Bolivia, to the east, and Peru (left). Nearly as large as Jamaica, the 3,200-square-mile lake nestles in a great north-south depression between the Cordillera Oriental, visible to the east of the lake in this Landsat image, and the Pacific coast's Cordillera Occidental. Like every other lake and marsh within the 500-mile-long complex of high Andean plateaus known as the Altiplano, Titicaca lacks an outlet to the sea.

ATACAMA DESERT

Starburst-like, in SPOT imagery, snowcapped volcanoes rise above northern Chile's Atacama Desert (left). To their west, the Atacama Fault slices north to south. This desert ranks as the driest place on Earth; in some areas rain has not fallen for as long as people have kept weather records. Dry lake beds at upper right reflect the Atacama's abundance of saline minerals, which originate in Andean volcanoes. Particularly prevalent, nitrate began yielding material for explosives and fertilizer in the 19th century.

MOUNT ACONCAGUA

Summit of the Western Hemisphere, Argentina's Mount Aconcagua, at upper right in this Landsat image (opposite), rises to 22,834 feet less than 100 miles from Chile's Pacific shore. Extremes crowd this sliver of land at the continent's western edge. Atop Aconcagua, for instance, windchill factors plunge to minus 100°F. Yet just 40 miles to the west, the farmlands around San Felipe remain free of snow year-round. Less than 70 miles from the volcano, capital city Santiago boasts a mild Mediterranean climate.

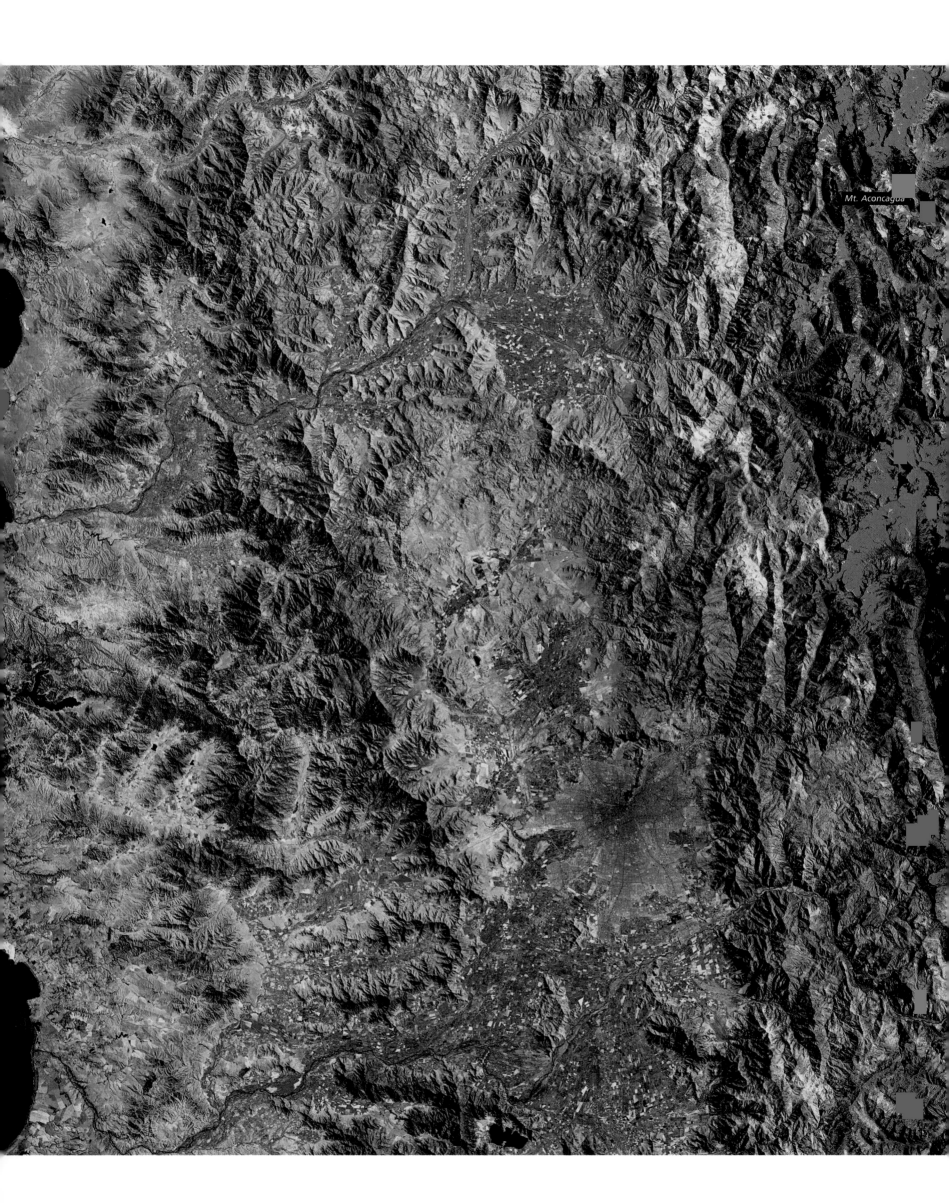

Mt. Aconcagua

The world's largest river by volume, the Amazon discharges more than three trillion gallons of fresh water each day into the Atlantic Ocean, an amount equivalent to ten times the Mississippi's flow. A tributary, the Rio Negro, carries a volume exceeded only by the Amazon itself. Yet most of the region's rainfall evaporates, cycling through a formidable weather machine whose effects reverberate far beyond the South American landmass.

Prodigious rainfall and tropical temperatures also give rise to the world's richest biodiversity. Science has yet to identify many of the Amazon Basin's ecosystems, much less the unique plant and animal species that depend on them; the task becomes ever more urgent as deforestation

AMAZON AND RIO NEGRO CONFLUENCE

The inky Rio Negro and the muddy-brown Solimões (upper Amazon), shown as scarlet in the color-enhanced TM image at left, converge beyond the city of Manaus, Brazil—seen here as the lighter area at top right. To the east, the sediment-laden Solimões continues to underrun the Rio Negro's lighter flow.

Mouth of
the Amazon

Amazon and Rio
Negro Confluence

MOUTH OF THE AMAZON

Branching into Canal do Norte, the "northern channel," and Canal do Sul, the "southern channel," the Amazon River (below) carves its Atlantic delta into an archipelago that holds a vast tidal habitat. The northern hump of Marajó, the largest island in the estuary, fills much of the lower half of this Landsat TM mosaic. Stretching nearly 200 miles inland to the mouth of the Xingu River, the estuary defines a zone of tidal forests that receive twice-daily inundations of fresh water.

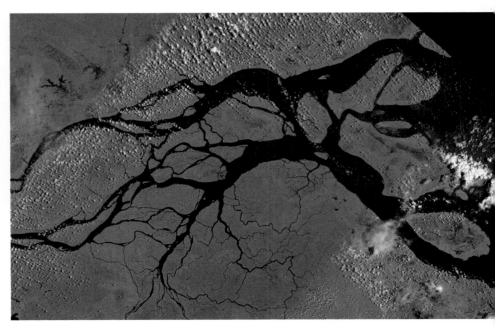

81

Inspiration for Arthur Conan Doyle's 1912 novel *The Lost World*, Venezuela's tepuis remain, in part, true to their mysterious reputation. More than a hundred of the sheer-sided tepuis—meaning "mountains" in the Pemón Indian language—soar from the forests and savannas of Venezuela and Guyana, culminating in mesas thousands of feet high. But scientists and explorers, hampered by the region's extreme ruggedness and isolation, have closely explored fewer than half of them.

More is known of the tepuis' geological history. At least 1.8 billion years ago, some of the world's oldest sandstone deposits settled over the Guayana shield, giving rise to vast plateaus. Later, tectonic forces helped shape the

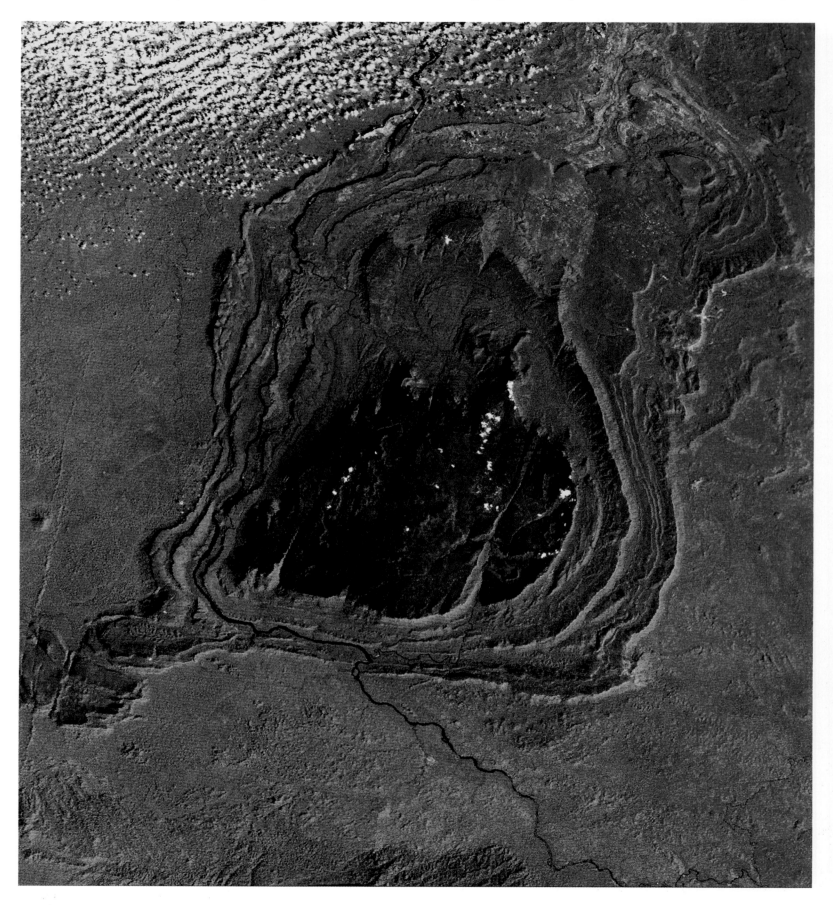

MOUNT GUAIQUINIMA

Dusky green and mottled red, the summit of Mount Guaiquinima stands at almost 7,000 feet in an area west of Canaima National Park. Parallel fault lines score the mesa in this Landsat MSS image. Appearing to swirl around the summit, Guaiquinima's escarpments fall sharply away in tiers interrupted by talus slopes. Color distinguishes the progress of erosion along the tepui's walls: Green indicates less resistant areas of rock, already worn away, while shades of red denote more solid areas, little altered so far. Evergreen forests of the surrounding upland region appear in tones of green. Small white clouds float above the tepui and fill the image's upper left corner.

tepuis, fissuring and fracturing here, uplifting individual blocks there. But erosion has played the main sculpturing role over the past 20 million years. Today's tepuis are a small remnant of the original sandstone plateau; most deposits were washed to sea long ago. As the whittling proceeded, summits became arks holding species uniquely adapted to their harsh environments.

ANGEL FALLS

Copious cloudbursts spilling over the 3,212-foot-high edge of Auyán Tepui create the world's tallest waterfall, Angel Falls (above, center). Thundering into the Cañón del Diablo—"devil's canyon"—the flow eventually joins the Caroní River, the sinuous feature flowing north in this Landsat MSS image. Largest, but not highest, of the mesas, Auyán Tepui means "mountain of the god of evil" in the Pemón language. Nevertheless, some areas of the generally soil-poor summit grow Edenic gardens bearing hundreds of orchids, bromeliads, and other plant species. Part of Mount Guaiquinima, on the opposite page, appears in the image above, at far left.

To one 19th-century immigrant, the continent's southern extremity was "the uttermost part of the earth." A largely unpopulated region, it holds some of the world's most dramatic landscapes. Huge ice fields, glaciers, rivers, lakes, peaks, and fjords confound the region, which includes the southern reaches of Patagonia, the island of Tierra del Fuego and its archipelago, and the Falkland Islands, 300 miles east of the mainland in the Atlantic. No other landmass in the Southern Hemisphere dips beyond the 50th parallel, or as close to Antarctica, lying south of the 60th parallel.

Fierce westerlies that sweep unhindered around the globe's southern latitudes blast Tierra del Fuego and bring heavy rains to the area's western

landfall. To seamen, the passage around Cape Horn before the Panama Canal opened in 1914 was notorious for storms, icebergs, and towering waves. Nevertheless, the region enjoys milder winters than Labrador and other northern locales at comparable latitudes. Arid grasslands, remnants of the Patagonian steppe to the north, hold enormous ranches that give the region its traditional products, wool and mutton; on the smaller holdings of the Falkland Islands, sheep outnumber humans.

The discovery of oil in recent decades has fueled new interest and development, along with geopolitical tensions that have contributed to strife between the United Kingdom and Argentina.

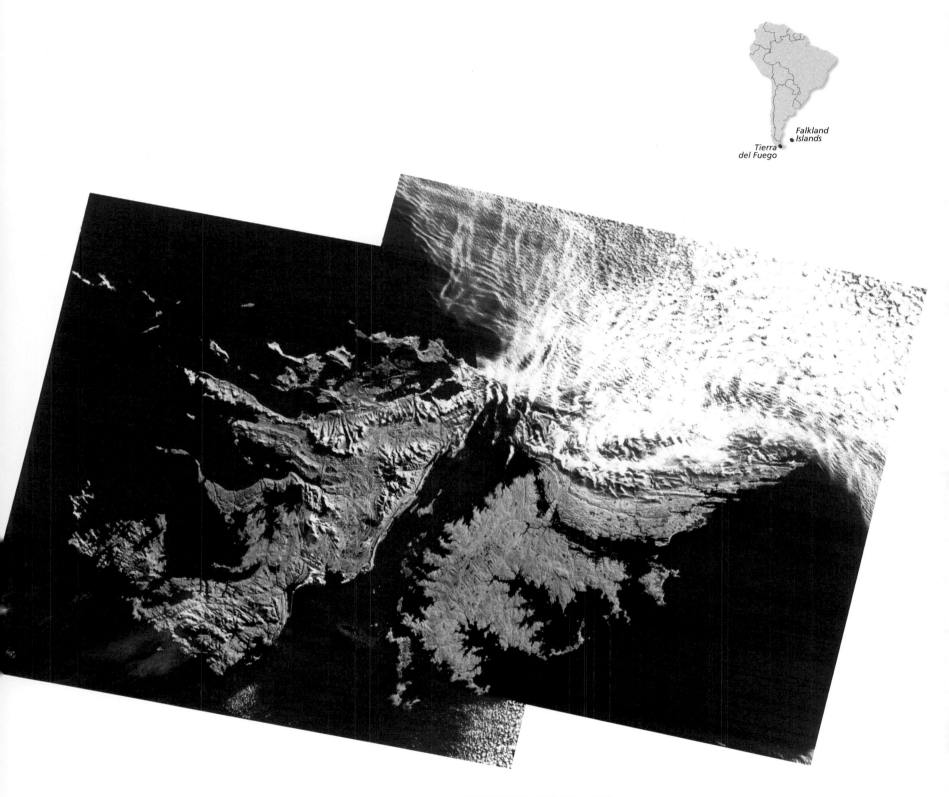

TIERRA DEL FUEGO

Three combined ERS-1 radar images from the 1992-93 austral summer reveal 62-mile-long Lake Fagnano, surrounded by parkland on the Argentine half of Tierra del Fuego's main island (opposite). Fuegian settlements in both Chile and Argentina vie for fame based on latitude. On the Beagle Channel's north shore, Argentina's Ushuaia, Tierra del Fuego's oldest settlement, claims to be Earth's southernmost city. Across the channel, on Navarino Island, Chile's Puerto Williams calls itself the southernmost settlement.

THE FALKLAND ISLANDS

Clouds part long enough to uncover West Falkland Island, but much of East Falkland remains shrouded in a Landsat TM image from another day (above). Numerous inlets and bays indent the coastline of this archipelago, which includes hundreds of smaller islands. Obscurity prevailed until 1982, when 12,000 Argentine troops began arriving to claim the islands they called the Malvinas. British warships steamed in to defend the Crown's dependency, wresting surrender in a bloody but undeclared war.

Ramparts of the Andes rise almost continuously along South America's Pacific coast, breaking the continent into lopsided parts of essentially different character. Forming the southeastern wall of the volcanic Ring of Fire that encircles the Pacific, the Andes began to rise some 20 million years ago. In a tectonic process known as subduction, the dense, heavy, basaltic crust of the ocean floor slowly dived beneath the relatively lighter continental crust, thrusting it four miles upward in places.

Today the Andes bristle with superlatives. One area, for example, holds more stratovolcanoes topping 16,000 feet than any other region on the planet. At an elevation of 22,834 feet, Aconcagua is the world's highest volcano; 22,310-foot Tupungato, also on the border between Chile and Argentina, is the tallest active volcano. Ruggedness, earthquakes, volcanic eruptions, and avalanches have deterred human occupation of the heights, but not completely: The highest archaeological site and one of the loftiest working mines in the world both ride Andean crests.

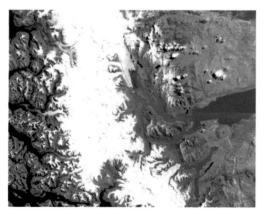

ANDEAN GLACIERS

Glaciers cap the line of Andean peaks rising to the west of southern Patagonia's Lake Argentina (above). Fingerlike fjords penetrate the Pacific coastline, at left in this MSS image.

ANDEAN PERSPECTIVE

Following continental contours, the Andes bend around the Arica Elbow, a geological deflection zone. This 3-D elevation model adds mass to might, showing parallel ranges, or cordilleras.

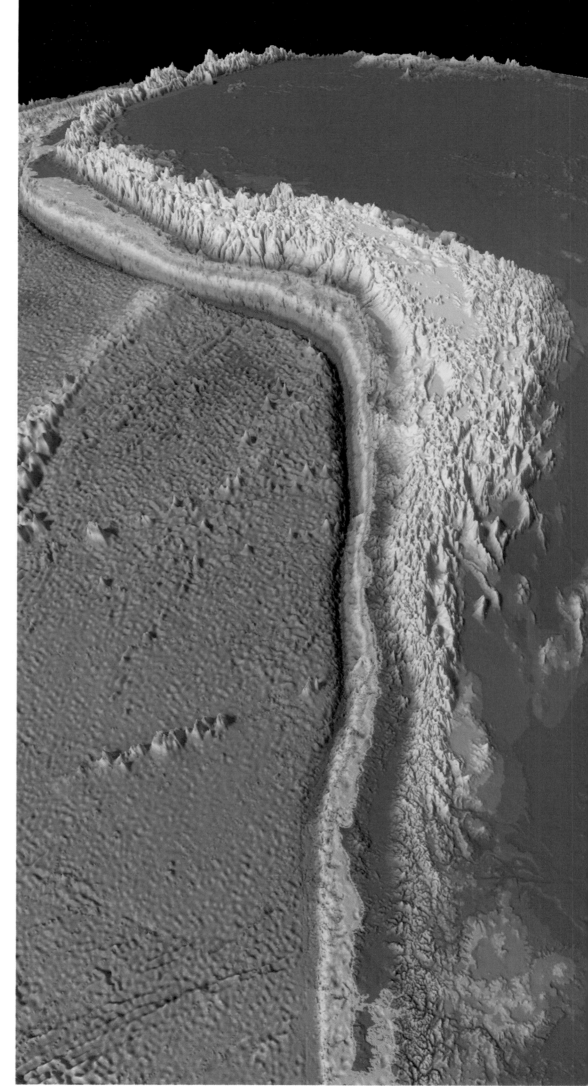

VOLCANIC SOILS

In this Landsat Thematic Mapper scene, a patchwork of farm plots climbs toward a volcanic mountain looming east of the Argentine town of San Luis. The richness of the volcanic soils in the central Andes encourages the spread of agriculture in the region. But the wind often blows away much of the soil that erodes from the steep volcanic slopes, and the meager amounts of annual rainfall remain a constant challenge to farmers struggling to grow their crops.

Landsat images provide stark evidence of the accelerating pace of deforestation in South America. Brazil's government, for instance, relies primarily on satellite imagery to measure destruction of the Amazon rain forest. The government's estimates, based on year-to-year comparisons, indicate that at least 20,000 square miles of forest disappeared in 1997, triple the rate of loss in 1994. Environmental organizations generally interpret the data to reflect even more widespread deforestation from selective logging, conferring upon Brazil the dubious distinction of a number one world ranking in rain forest destruction. Traditional slash-and-burn practices, used by countless generations of farmers in developing

BEFORE DEFORESTATION

Wilderness at the heart of a continent, the Gran Chaco extends southward from the eastern Bolivian farming community shown in this 1975 Landsat image. For countless centuries the vast alluvial lowland, which reaches into Paraguay and Argentina, held only indigenous peoples.

Bolivian
Deforestation

countries, continue to be a major problem. But increasingly, selective logging that thins forest stands subjects them to wildfires.

When trees are felled, openings appear in the rain forest canopy and high humidity levels eventually drop, especially at the forest edges. Just one spark from a brush fire or a stroke of lightning can more easily start a fire, which then races through a forest. Scientists have discovered that when large sections of a rain forest have been removed, local weather patterns eventually become affected. The deforested areas release less moisture into the atmosphere. As a result, fewer clouds form, and neighboring areas of the forest get less rainfall. They, too, become drier and more vulnerable to fire.

AFTER DEFORESTATION

The footprint of human endeavor transforms the same area of Bolivia two decades later, in a 1996 Landsat image. Croplands cleared by Japanese and Mennonite settlers replace humid forest and chaparral near a bend in the Rio Grande; the grid at upper left shows government-run "national farms."

Changing land-use patterns reflect conflicting imperatives in South America as the 20th century comes to a close. A booming population in most of the continent's nations means that increasing numbers of people, in a desperate search for land and livelihood, are drawn into lightly inhabited, ecologically fragile regions such as the Amazon Basin and the Brazilian Pantanal (below, at right).

Elsewhere in South America, traditional lifeways reach intersections where they collide with the demands of the outside world: Cultivation of the coca plant, in particular, has expanded into a major force in the global economy, keeping pace with the growing international demand for processed cocaine. But at the same time, environmental awareness has been steadily increasing, not just among members of the international community but also at local levels. As a result, more and more countries in South America have begun setting aside potential farmland for national parks.

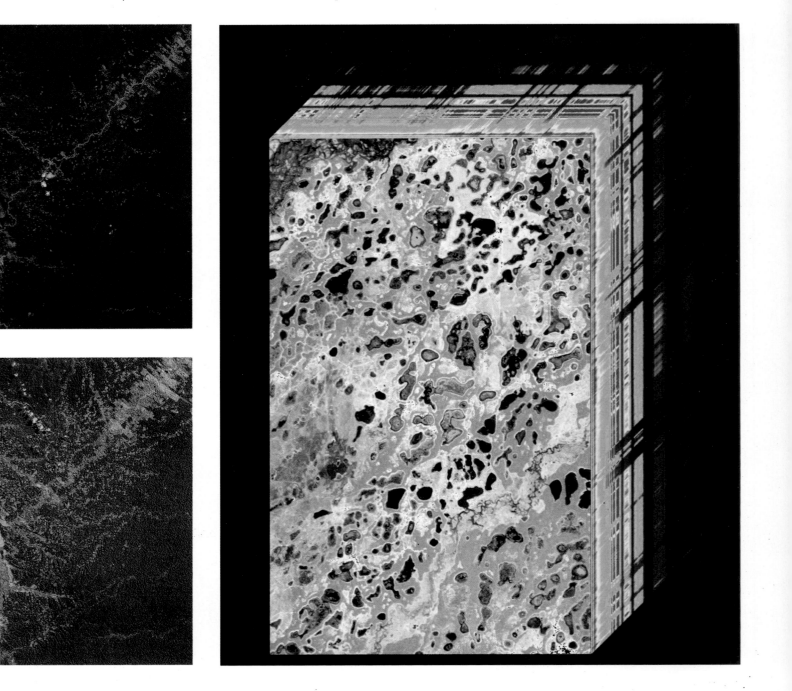

DRUG FIELDS

Tentacles of the international drug trade reach through the Andean backcountry, where indigenous peoples of South America have grown and chewed energy-giving coca leaves for 4,000 years. Thematic Mapper images taken just two years apart (above left) attest to the change in an area flanking the Huallaga River Valley in Peru. In the earlier of the two (upper), imaged on September 7, 1985, a light dusting of turquoise dots represents the extent of coca cultivation amid the red tones of other vegetation. In the later image, from August 28, 1987, the area under cultivation has become a thicker, broader coating of turquoise. Because the lucrative profits of the cocaine trade have trickled down toward subsistence farmers, the slowing of coca farming looms as a formidable task.

PANTANAL

The entire solar-reflected portion of the electromagnetic spectrum—224 bands, compared with Thematic Mapper's 7 bands—imparts breathtaking detail to Brazil's Pantanal (above) in an image made by the Airborne Visible/Infrared Imaging Spectrometer (AVIRIS). A vast alluvial plain located on the Mato Grosso Plateau, this wildlife-rich region undergoes dramatic seasonal changes. In the August 1995 image, made at the beginning of the dry season, floodwaters recede and leave behind small ponds. Black areas indicate clear water; light blue areas denote floating vegetation, and dark blue areas show high salinity. Changes wrought since the introduction of cattle show up as large areas of brown and red, where grazing on ranches has degraded the vegetation. The sides of the cube show the AVIRIS spectral response.

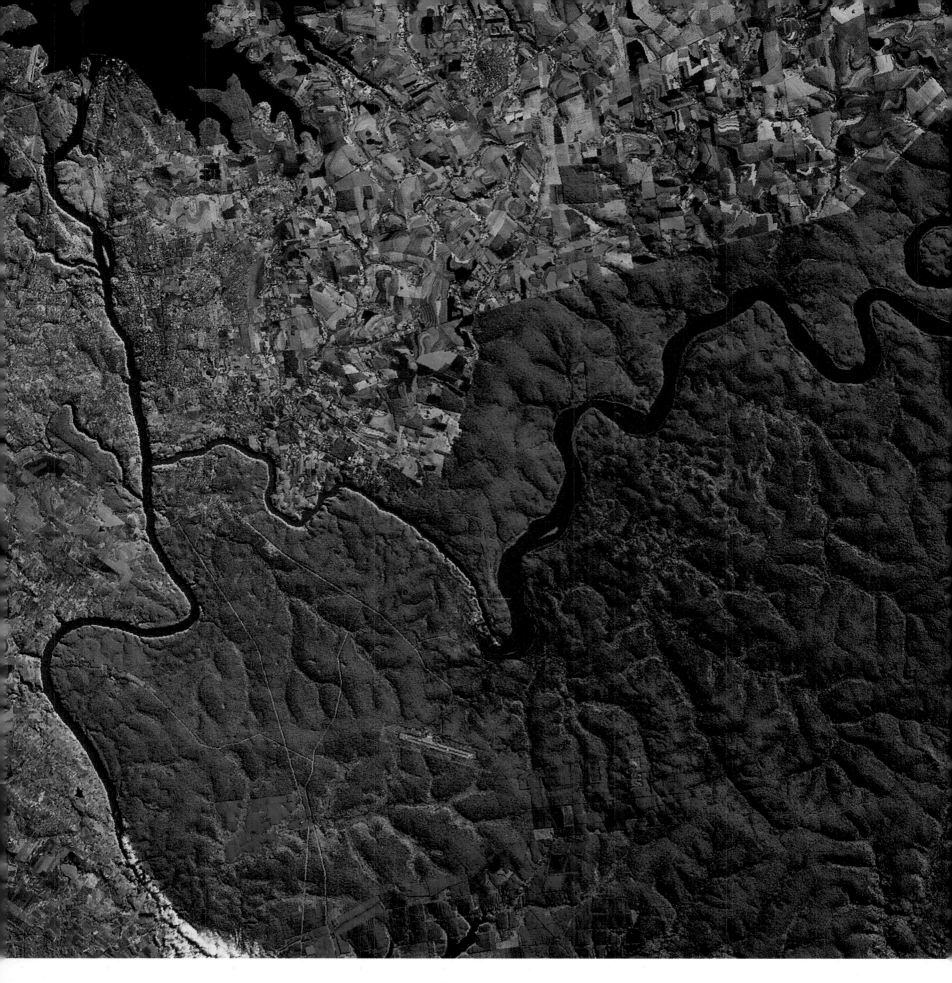

IGUAÇU FALLS AREA

Flowing from north to south, the 2,485-mile-long Paraná River serves first as the border between Paraguay, to the west, and Brazil. South of its confluence with the east-west flowing Iguaçu River, it separates Paraguay from Argentina. The Iguaçu, in turn, separates parts of Brazil and Argentina. But development and relative prosperity unite these areas into one of South America's wealthiest regions. Here lie temperate farmlands. And the Itaipú Dam on the Paraná River—its reservoir appears at the top of the image—generates enormous hydroelectric power. The Iguaçu River boasts a natural dazzler: Iguaçu Falls, located below the center of this TM image, where the river narrows. Iguaçu National Park preserves the lush setting around the falls, serving as a verdant buffer between them and deforested cropland to the north.

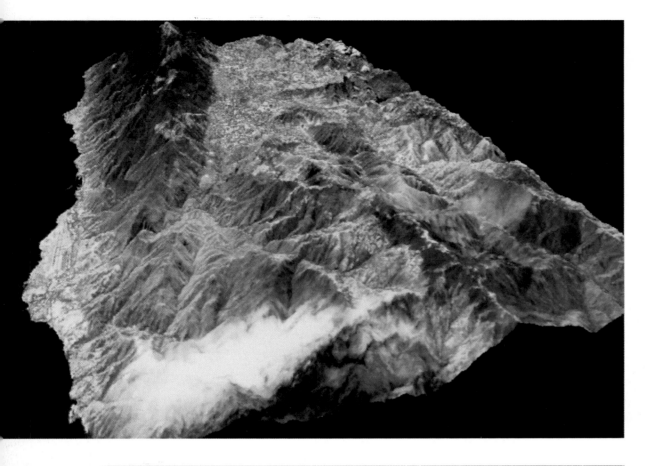

CARACAS, VENEZUELA

Three-dimensional Landsat modeling reveals the dramatic setting of Venezuela's capital (left), birthplace of Simón Bolívar, South America's George Washington. Some three million people live here, inhabiting a 3,000-foot-high rift valley enclosed by Andean hills; in 1812, a powerful earthquake rumbled through the valley and nearly destroyed the "city of eternal spring." The 8,600-foot-high coastal mountains, at left, form a wall to the north, separating Caracas from the Caribbean coast, just seven miles way.

BOGOTÁ, COLOMBIA

Bordered by national parkland to its east, Colombia's capital, Bogotá, spreads across a plateau that rises nearly 8,700 feet above sea level (left). This SPOT scene, imaged on June 24, 1994, uses shades of blue to highlight the city. Vegetation, depicted as red in the image, climbs the slopes of two-mile-high peaks that ring this city of some six million people. High tablelands characterize much of Colombia's densely populated Cordillera Oriental, one of three Andean ranges that score the country.

LIMA, PERU

Known locally as El Pulpo—"the Octopus"— metropolitan Lima (opposite) reaches far beyond the town founded by Francisco Pizarro in 1535. About a third of Peru's 25 million people crowd into the metropolitan area shown in this false-color image. In Spanish Pizarro called it City of Kings, but Lima, the name that stuck, came from the Quechua Rímac, which means "talker," the name of the river that flows through the city to its port of Callao, on the Pacific, and waters the barren coastal desert.

BRASÍLIA, BRAZIL

A bold vision realized, Brasília rises in the midst of Brazil's vast, lightly populated central plateau. The "capital that will unite the whole nation"— according to then President Juscelino Kubitschek— materialized in the 1950s as an attempt to draw people and economic activity inland from Brazil's densely populated coast. In this TM image, the undisturbed vegetation of Brasília National Park lies to the northwest; Lake Paranoá extends an embrace from the east. Unplanned satellite cities, often shantytowns, spread outward.

SÃO PAULO, BRAZIL

*Largest city in the Southern Hemisphere,
São Paulo (left) holds 17 million inhabitants
in a 3,000-square-mile metropolitan area of
southeastern Brazil. Hundreds of thousands of
newcomers each year, most from impoverished
areas of northeastern Brazil, fuel the growth that
often overwhelms São Paulo with 60-mile-long
traffic jams. Paulistas find respite in the forested
reserves of the northerly Cantareira Range, and
on the beaches near the port of Santos—visible
to the southeast in this image.*

RIO DE JANEIRO, BRAZIL

*Ranked among the world's natural wonders,
Guanabara Bay—"arm of the sea" in the native
Tamoio language—stretches 20 miles inland
beyond its narrow opening to the Atlantic Ocean
(below). Early Portuguese explorers mistook the
bay for a river. Their name, Rio de Janeiro—
"river of January"—today applies to a metropolis
of more than ten million people on the western
side of the bay. The hills and isolated peaks that
interrupt the sea of buildings appear as dark
forms in this natural-color TM image.*

LA PAZ, BOLIVIA

Loftiest capital city in the world, La Paz actually lies in a valley some 12,000 feet above sea level (right). Just beyond, peaks of Bolivia's Cordillera de La Paz, laden with snow in this SPOT image, tower above the city. The population of La Paz—more than a million—and that of the rest of the densely populated Altiplano in Bolivia remains largely indigenous. In 1548, Spanish conquistadores founded La Paz as a way station for llama trains bearing silver to the Pacific.

SANTIAGO, CHILE

Rugged peaks that rise steeply to the city's east confine Chile's booming capital (left) to a narrow basin lying between the coastal range and the high Andes. In this SPOT image, Santiago and its population of about five million spread to the south, encroaching on agricultural lands that appear red. Central Chile's mild climate and good soils have long attracted farmers, but the corridor that includes Santiago and its Pacific port, Valparaíso, also accounts for two-thirds of Chile's industrial employment.

BUENOS AIRES, ARGENTINA

Growing almost five times faster than Argentina as a whole, Buenos Aires sprawls toward the fertile Pampas in the west. The capital city of 12 million people counts proximity to productive farmland as only one of its several geographical assets. Buenos Aires also prospers as the continent's largest port, although sediment confines large oceangoing vessels to a channel in the River Plate estuary. In this Thematic Mapper image, vivid red at the head of the estuary identifies the relatively unaltered marshlands of the Paraná River Delta. The Uruguay River, top center, also empties into the head of the Plate. North of the Plate lies the grain-growing province of Colonia, in Uruguay.

EUROPE

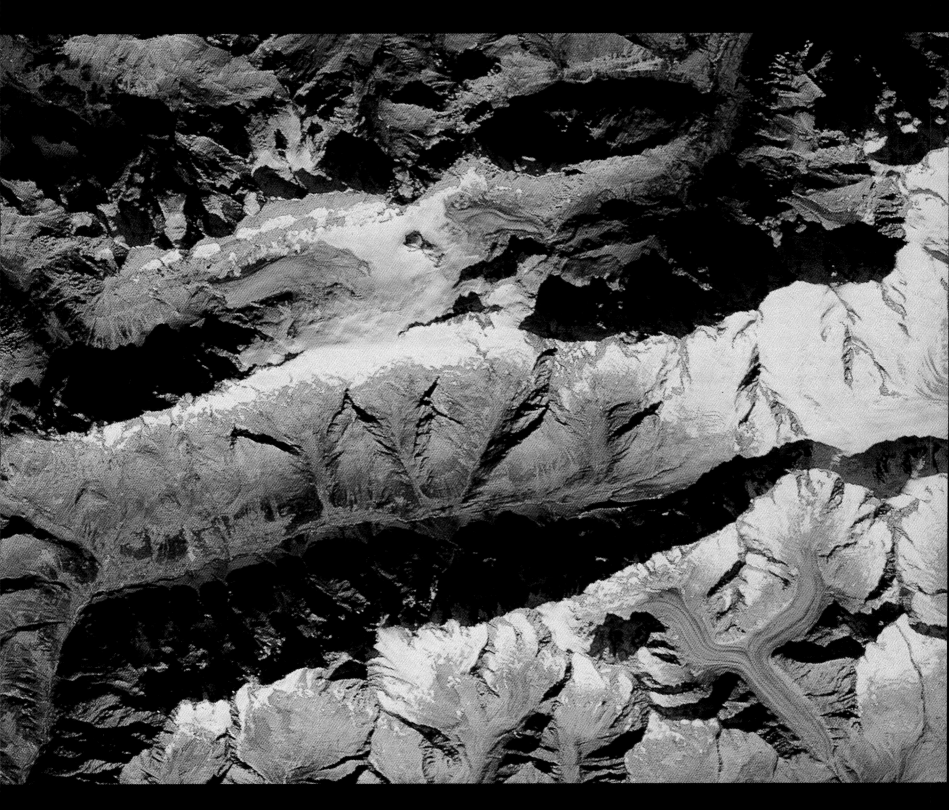

E urope covers barely 7 percent of Earth's land surface. Smaller than every other continent except Australia, it appears from space as a cluster of peninsulas making up less than a fourth of the great Eurasian landmass. Even so, Europe has more than 40 countries, only 13 of which are landlocked. The long coastline, shaped by four major seas and two oceans, has many gulfs, bays, inlets, and fjords. With such easy access to the sea,

Europeans have historically been great mariners, traders, and explorers, leaving few regions in the world untouched by their languages, customs, or forms of government.

Within the continent, the landscape has been shaped by colliding tectonic plates and retreating Ice Age glaciers. The Caledonian Ridge, slanting across the north from Scandinavia to southern Wales, rose 400 million years ago. Later, glaciers softened its contours and carved fjords seen

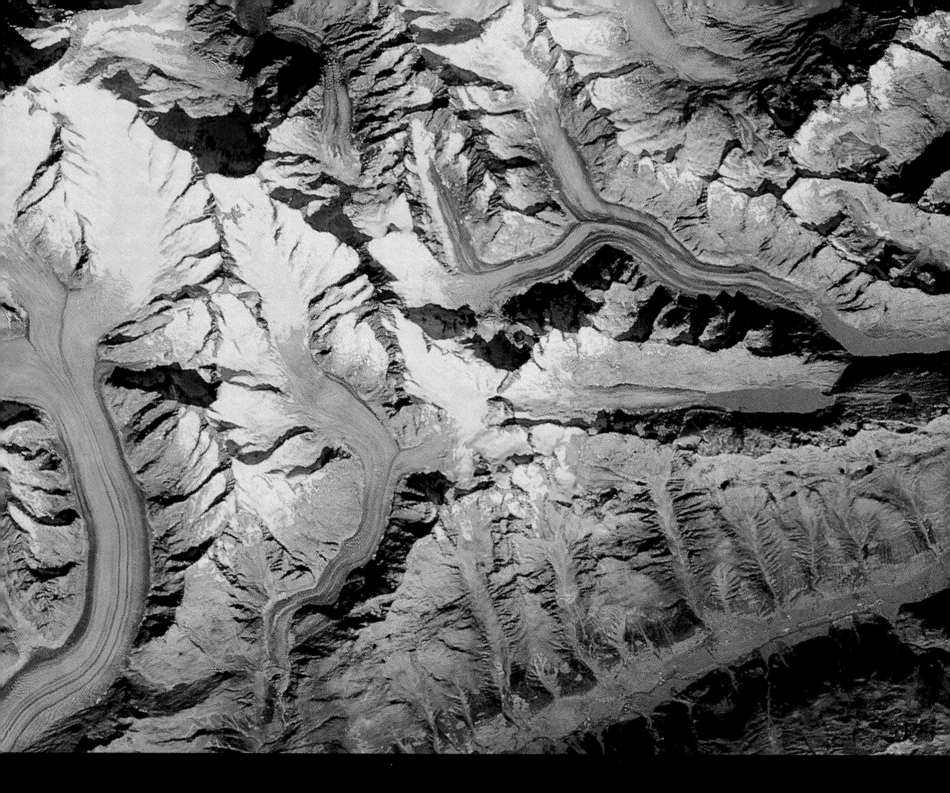

at sea level. More dramatically rugged are the Alpine ranges that appeared across southern Europe 65 million years ago. They were forced upward when the African plate slammed into the Eurasian plate, causing earthquakes and volcanic eruptions that continue today. Although the Ice Age ended about 10,000 years ago, its glaciers have not yet disappeared from the Alps and associated ranges. They feed several principal rivers, including the Danube, Rhine, Rhône, and Po,

ALETSCH GLACIER

Switzerland's Aletsch Glacier, at the center of this Thematic Mapper image, lies between the 13,642-foot Jungfrau and the 13,763-foot Aletschhorn. Though constantly retreating, this 66-square-mile body of ice in the south-central part of the country ranks as the most formidable glacier in the Alps. Tons of rock and earth scraped from valley walls form dark lines of moraine at the sides and centers of its icy tongues.

Aletsch
Glacier

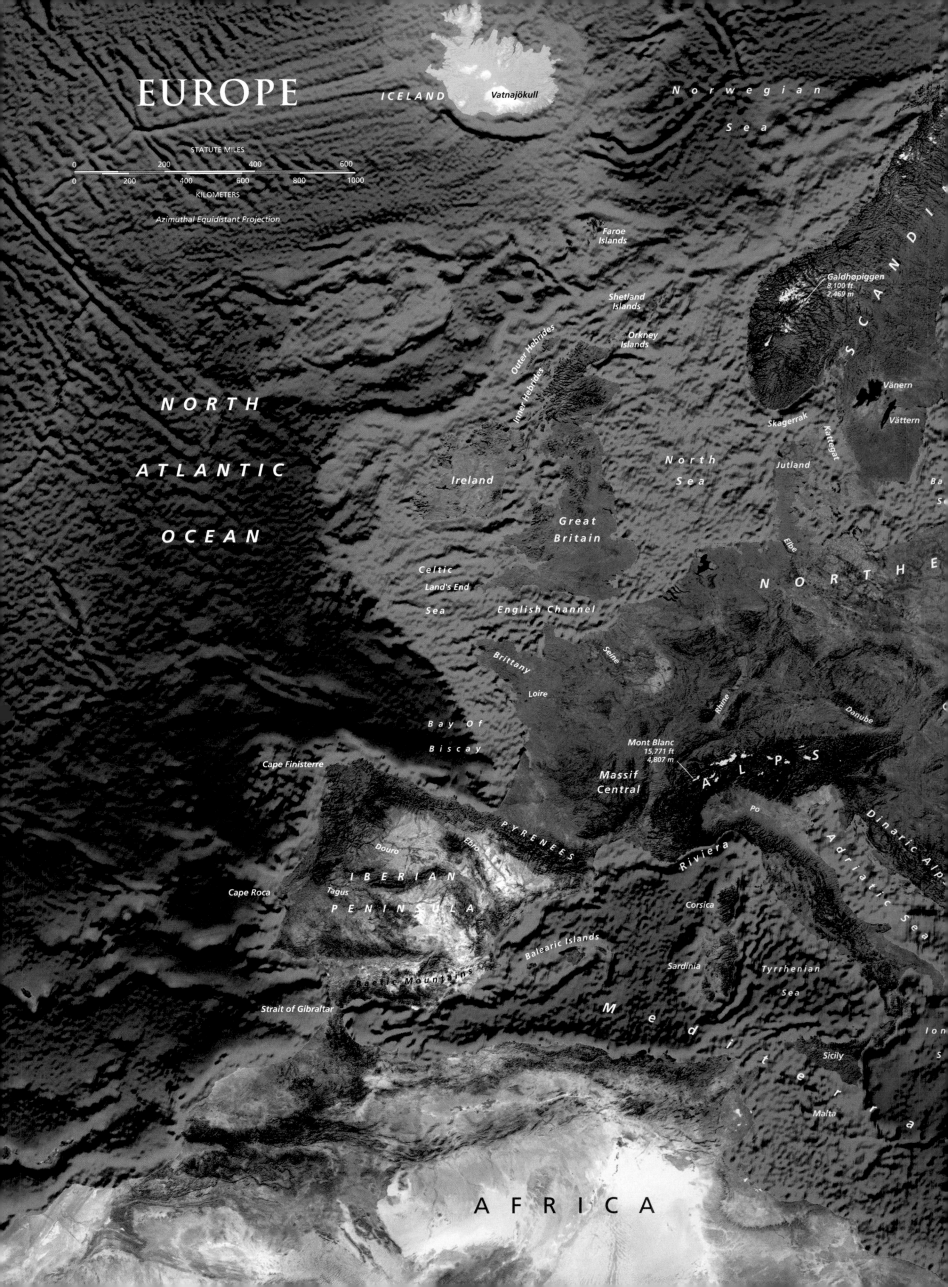

EUROPE

ICELAND   Vatnajökull

N o r w e g i a n

S e a

STATUTE MILES
0   200   400   600

0   200   400   600   800   1000

KILOMETERS

Azimuthal Equidistant Projection

Faroe
Islands

Shetland
Islands

S C A N D I

Galdhøpiggen
8,100 ft
2,469 m

Vänern

NORTH

Orkney
Islands

Outer Hebrides

Inner Hebrides

Skagerrak

Vättern

Kattegat

ATLANTIC

Ireland

North
Sea

Jutland

N O R T H E

Ba

Elbe

Great
Britain

OCEAN

Celtic

Land's End

Sea

English Channel

Brittany

Seine

Rhine

Danube

Loire

B a y   O f

Mont Blanc
15,771 ft
4,807 m

Po

Dinaric Alps

B i s c a y

Massif
Central

A L P S

Cape Finisterre

Riviera

Adriatic Sea

P Y R E N E E S

Douro

Ebro

Cape Roca

Tagus

I B E R I A N

Corsica

P E N I N S U L A

Balearic Islands

Sardinia

Tyrrhenian

Sea

Baetic Mountains

M

Sicily

Strait of Gibraltar

e

d

i

t

e

r

r

Malta

a

Io

A F R I C A

Barents Sea

Kola
Peninsula

White Sea

Timan Ridge

URAL MOUNTAINS

ASIA

Northern Dvina

Lake
Onega

Lake Region

Lake
Ladoga

Rybinsk
Reservoir

Kama

EUROPEAN PLAIN

Gulf of Finland

Lake
Peipus

Volga

Gulf
of
Riga

Ural

CENTRAL

RUSSIAN

UPLAND

Pinsk Marshes

Volga

Caspian Depression

-92 ft, -28 m
Lowest point
in Europe

Dnieper

Don

Dniester

ian Mountains

Sea Of
Azov

CRIMEA

El'brus
18,510 ft, 5,642 m
Highest point
in Europe

Caspian Sea

Transylvanian Alps

CAUCASUS MOUNTAINS

Black Sea

Balkan Mountains

BALKAN

Bosporus

PENINSULA

Aegean
Sea

ASIA

Crete

an   Sea

Barents Sea

White Sea

FINLAND

RUSSIA

EUROPE ASIA

RUSSIA

KAZAKHSTAN

ESTONIA

LATVIA

LITHUANIA

BELARUS

Black Sea

Sea of Azov

CRIMEA

Caspian Sea

UZBEKISTAN

TURKMENISTAN

ROMANIA

MOLDOVA

UKRAINE

BULGARIA

GREECE

MACEDONIA

TURKEY

GEORGIA

ARMENIA

AZERBAIJAN

Aegean Sea

Sea of Crete

CYPRUS

LEBANON

SYRIA

IRAQ

IRAN

ISRAEL

JORDAN

SAUDI ARABIA

EGYPT

LIBYA

KUWAIT

BAHRAIN

QATAR

Gulf of Finland

Lake Ladoga

Lake Onega

Lake Peipus

MURMANSK

ST. PETERSBURG

MOSKVA (MOSCOW)

RIGA

VILNIUS

MINSK

KYYIV (KIEV)

KHARKIV

DONETS'K

DNIPROPETROVS'K

ROSTOV NA DONU

VOLGOGRAD

SAMARA

KAZAN'

PERM'

NIZHNIY NOVGOROD

SARATOV

ASTRAHAN'

ODESA

BUCURESTI (BUCHAREST)

SOFIYA (Sofia)

ISTANBUL (CONSTANTINOPLE)

ATHINAI (Athens)

THESSALONIKI

BAKI (BAKU)

Danube

Don

Volga

Ural

Dnieper

Northern Dvina

The gateways to Europe have traditionally opened from the sea. To reach the continent's Mediterranean shores, ships can enter by the Strait of Gibraltar, in the west; the Bosporus, Sea of Marmara, and Dardanelles, in the east; and the Suez Canal in the south. Europe's northern and western edges front the Arctic and Atlantic Oceans and their associated bodies of water.

The eastern boundary with Asia, however, is much harder to define. The Ural Mountains and the Ural River are generally accepted as the line of demarcation across Russia and Kazakhstan, reaching from the Arctic to the Caspian Sea. But the dividing line that runs from the Caspian to the Black Sea causes much controversy. Many mapmakers like to use physical features, and for them the Caucasus Mountains seem a natural choice. But the mountains cut through countries, and for practical reasons other cartographers prefer to use national borders to demarcate Europe, thereby including all of Georgia, Armenia, and Azerbaijan.

Strait of Gibraltar

Bosporus

STRAIT OF GIBRALTAR

Named for the tiny British enclave on Spain's southern coast, the Strait of Gibraltar (above) separates the rugged European and African coasts. This narrow channel between Spain and northern Morocco measures only eight miles across and connects the Atlantic to the Mediterranean Sea. Until the age of air travel, it served as a strategic gateway to southern Europe and northern Africa. In this radar image, a large wave pattern enters the Mediterranean, triggered by a sea ridge just west of the strait's narrowest part.

BOSPORUS

Nineteen miles long, the Bosporus (opposite) separates Asian Turkey from its European peninsula. The waterway also divides Turkey's largest city, Istanbul. In 1973 engineers linked the eastern and western halves of the city by completing a 3,540-foot-long suspension bridge at the channel's narrowest point. One of the world's most important bodies of water, the Bosporus provides the only exit for Black Sea ships, which must pass through it and the Sea of Marmara to reach the Mediterranean.

A great system of rugged highlands extends across southern Europe into Asia. It reaches from Spain's Baetic Mountains to the Pyrenees, at the French border. From there, the Alps stretch across France, Switzerland, northern Italy, and Austria. The Carpathian Mountains curve through a large part of eastern Europe, and the Balkan range extends south and east across Turkey. The Caucasus Mountains, between the Black and the Caspian Seas, hold Europe's highest peak, 18,510-foot El'brus. Mountains of the older Caledonian system rise in northern Europe. These ranges often mark country boundaries, artificially dividing important biogeographic areas, but a number of transfrontier national parks now protect endangered species such as ibexes, golden eagles, and many high-elevation plants.

PYRENEES

Looking southwest, a 3-D image shows the lofty Pyrenees reaching from the Mediterranean Sea, on the left, to the Bay of Biscay, an arm of the Atlantic 270 miles away, at upper right. Like a barrier across the neck of the Iberian Peninsula, the Pyrenees separate Spain and Portugal from France and the rest of the European continent. Today the folded ranges, flat-topped massifs, and permanently snowcapped peaks attract sports lovers and vacationers from both sides of the mountains. Tax-free shopping and a six-month skiing season, as well as the scenery, draw millions of visitors annually to Andorra, a tiny principality occupying six glacial valleys atop the Pyrenees.

ALPS

Spreading across southern Europe, the Alps reveal their valleys, glaciers, ridges, and summits in this 26-image Thematic Mapper mosaic (below). The scene comes from a larger mosaic comprising more than 250 images of Western Europe. The governments of Italy, Austria, Switzerland, and France regard the Alps as important national assets: Mountain streams produce cheap hydroelectricity for industry, and the area's many attractions draw more than 100 million tourists a year from around the world. But new ski areas, housing complexes, and roads threaten the fragile Alpine environment. A dramatic 3-D image (bottom) shows the Swiss, French, and Italian Alps arcing south toward the Mediterranean, enclosing Italy's fertile Po Valley in their sweep. The massif of Mont Blanc, in upper center, dominates the range.

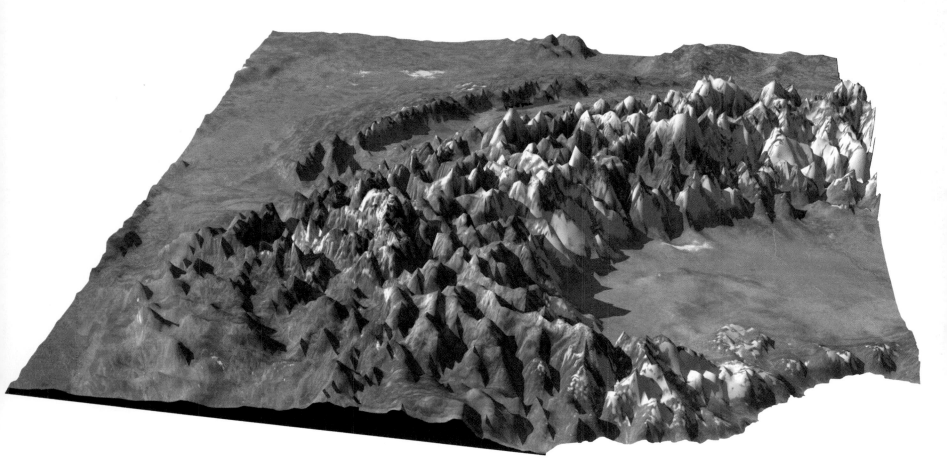

A singular landform found only at high latitudes is the fjord—a Norwegian word for a long, narrow inlet reaching inland from the sea through mountainous terrain. Frequently flanked by cliffs hundreds of feet high, fjords are actually flooded coastal valleys that were formed by the action of glaciers.

When the Ice Age came to an end some 10,000 years ago, retreating glacial ice exposed valley floors at depths far below sea level; the valleys then became submerged as the great volume of water released by the melting ice caused the world sea level to rise. The greatest depth of a fjord, often measuring thousands of feet, is likely to be found along the middle of the valley floor and in the farthest inland reaches, where the heavy glacier had exerted its greatest force.

Fjords can be seen in several countries in the high latitudes, notably in Norway, Iceland, Greenland, and western Canada in the Northern Hemisphere, and in Chile and New Zealand in the Southern Hemisphere.

ICELAND

Fjords indent Iceland's coast, and glaciers cap vast areas farther inland, as shown in a thermal satellite image (left). The broad Vatnajökull glacier, below center, covers an area of 3,150 square miles, making it the largest glacier in Europe. Its coldest areas appear blue and green in the image. The subarctic country straddles the Mid-Atlantic Ridge, where giant tectonic plates diverge and occasionally cause earthquakes and eruptions. Iceland includes about 200 volcanoes, and geologists consider many of them still active.

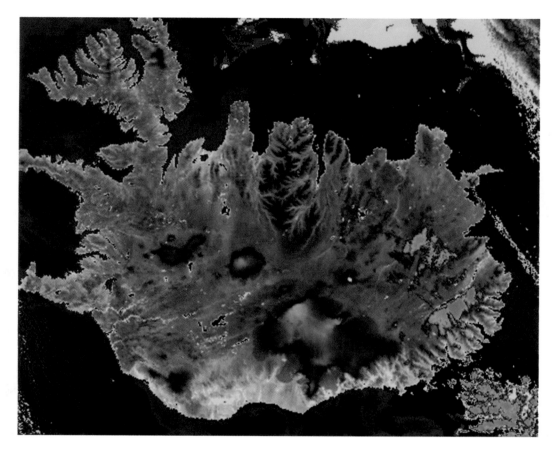

NORWEGIAN FJORDS

In this Landsat view (right), Norway's southwest coast shows fjords extending far inland. Because the land's geological structure runs perpendicular to the coast, some fjords reach 100 miles into the mountains. Norway's jagged coastline measures 1,645 miles, but if the figure included shorelines of all the fjords and bays in the country, it would total more than 13,000 miles. Surprisingly, the fjords rarely freeze. Gulf Stream waters warm the winter air over the ocean to temperatures far higher than the average for the latitude.

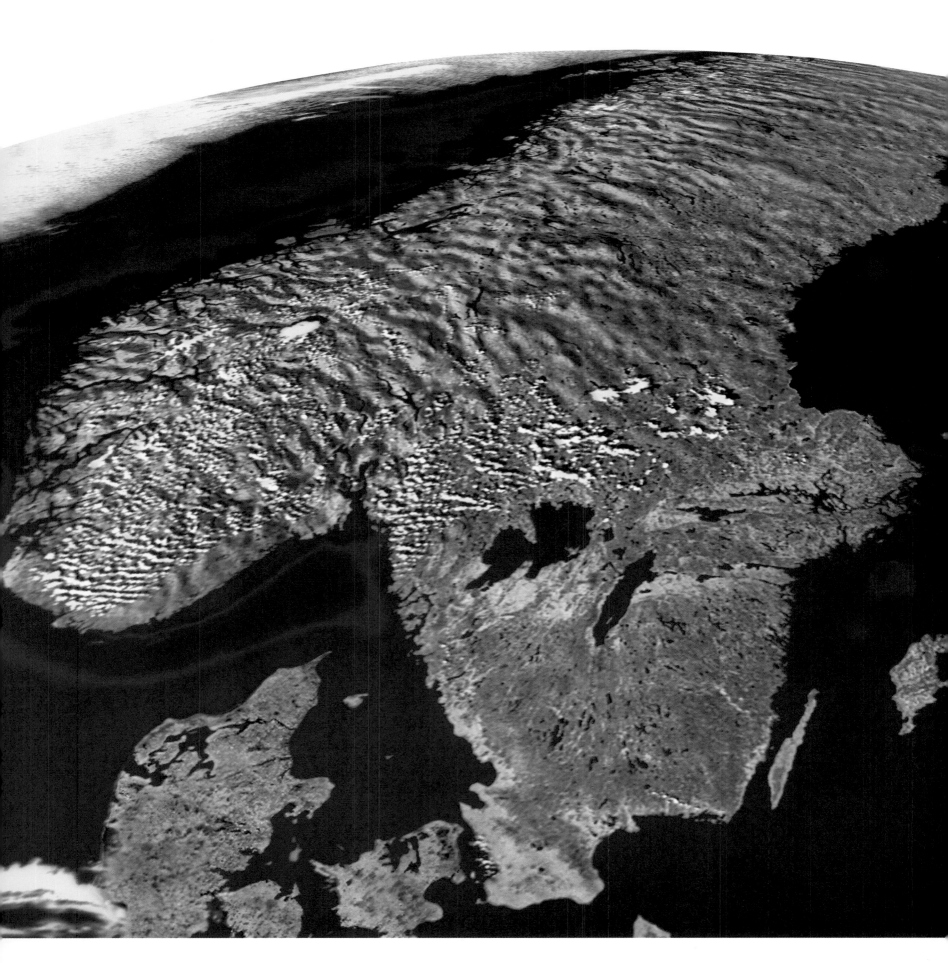

SCANDINAVIA

Norway and Sweden, on the huge Scandinavian Peninsula, fill most of this composite (above), along with Denmark, at lower left. The peninsula lies between the Norwegian and North Seas on the west and the Gulf of Bothnia and Baltic Sea on the east. The merging of two sets of data at different resolutions—from NOAA's AVHRR (for the background) and Resurs's MSU-SK (for the foreground)—eliminated the out-of-focus effect that sometimes occurs when creating a perspective.

In Europe, the powerful forces of nature play hardest in the south, where mountains continue to rise even as glaciers grind them down, earthquakes occur, and volcanoes pose a constant threat. This diverse region is, in fact, bound together by a belt of mountain ranges, anchored by the Alps, that stretches across the continent from eastern Spain to Turkey.

The geologically dynamic zone came into being millions of years ago when converging tectonic plates crumpled the southern European bedrock into mountains. This event was not a simple head-on collision of the enormous African and Eurasian plates, however. Microplates beneath the Mediterranean Sea exerted lateral pressures as well, causing several mountain chains to be pushed into S-shaped arcs.

The mountain-building process goes on, producing earthquakes most often on the Balkan Peninsula and in the Aegean Sea, and periodic eruptions in southern Italy, on the island of Sicily, and in the island arc of the southern Aegean.

Italy
• Mount Vesuvius
Mount Etna •

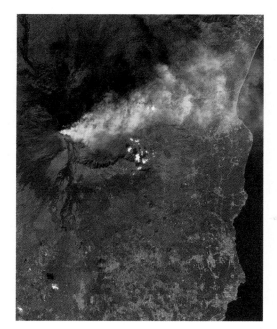

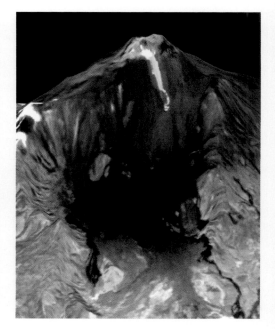

MOUNT ETNA

Europe's highest and largest active volcano, Mount Etna rises over 10,000 feet and covers 600 square miles of Sicily's east coast (above). The volcano first rumbled to life more than 2.5 million years ago, and it now averages about 15 eruptions every century or so. Over the past hundred years, at least five such outbursts damaged nearby villages and farmland. The SPOT image at left shows an ash plume drifting eastward and dispersing over the coast. In the center TM image, dark areas indicate recent lava flows. The 3-D thermal image on the right shows lava erupting from the summit of Mount Etna in 1984 and flowing into a deep depression on the volcano's eastern flank.

MOUNT VESUVIUS

Mount Vesuvius (left) climbs 4,203 feet above Italy's Gulf of Naples, but its elevation changes with each major eruption. Lush, lava-enriched vegetation appears in the SPOT image as red on the volcano's lower slopes and nearby hills, while the blue-gray of urban development covers the coastal plain. Vesuvius, less than 200,000 years old, performs erratically. It lay dormant for centuries before erupting in A.D. 79 and burying the cities of Pompeii and Herculaneum. The most recent eruption occurred in 1944.

BOOT OF ITALY

Italy possesses one of the most recognizable outlines in the world: It resembles a high-heeled boot, as seen in this AVHRR image enhanced with elevation data (opposite). The Adriatic Sea, a 500-mile-long arm of the Mediterranean, separates the east coast from the continental mass of Europe, creating a peninsula. In northern Italy, the lofty Alps join the Apennines, which extend along the peninsula and curve west into Sicily. Cupped between the two ranges in the north, lies the broad and fertile valley of the Po River.

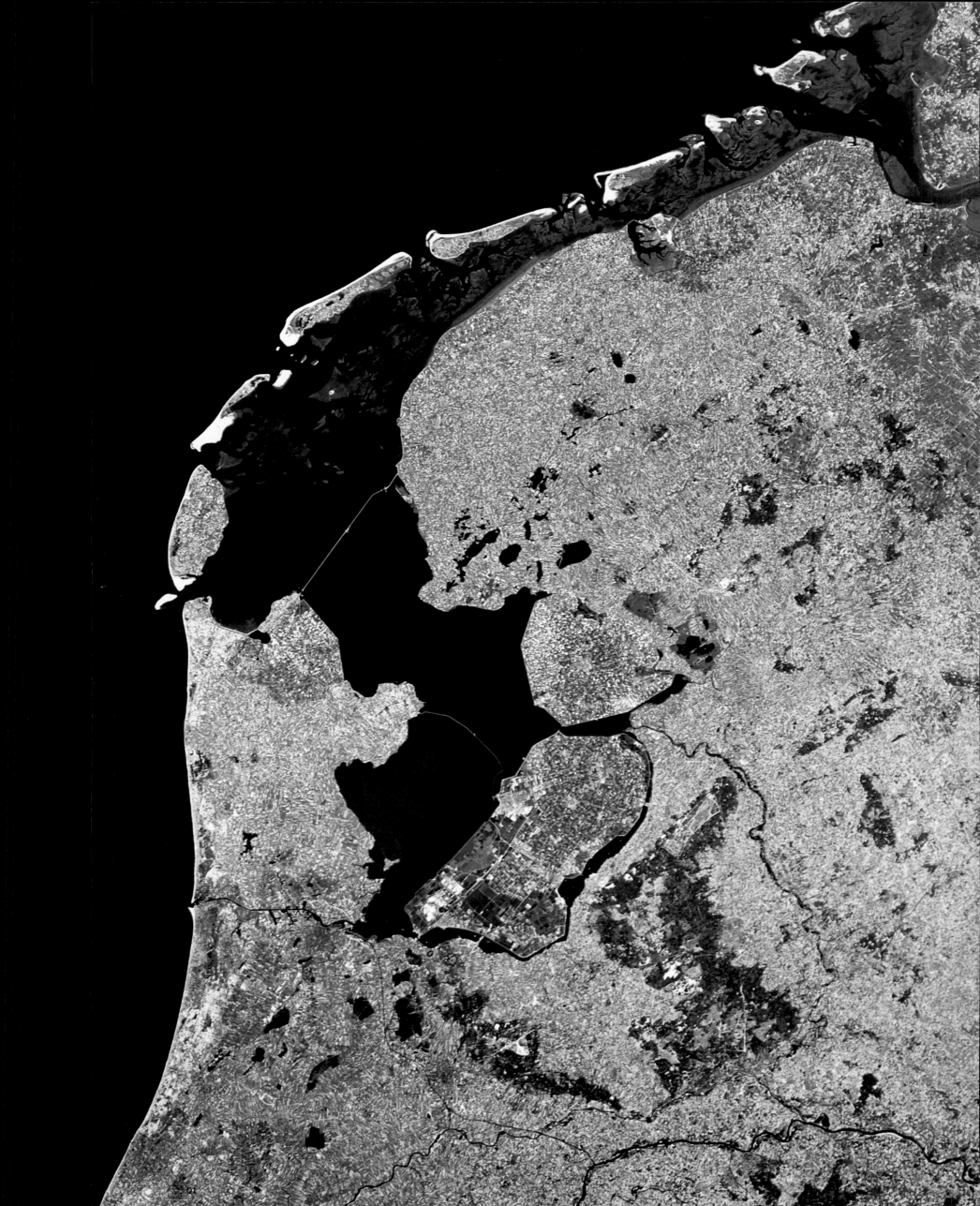

Of all the continents, perhaps Europe has experienced the greatest changes to its environment. Beginning 2,000 years ago with the Roman Empire, good roads spanned the continent, aqueducts brought water to growing urban centers, and towns were built where none had existed before. From the early Middle Ages, the primeval forest that had covered much of Europe since the Ice Age was systematically cut down to make way for cultivation and to supply wood for towns and ships.

By the 20th century, people had left scarcely any part of the continent untouched. Only areas that were too inaccessible, or too hard to farm, remained unaltered. Most of these sites, and pockets of wilderness kept as royal hunting preserves, have been gathered into national parks, but they must constantly withstand pressure from industry, agriculture, and commercial interests. Nearly every river has been reshaped by dams, dikes, canals, or embankments. And Holland's polders created a new shoreline. As a consequence, while human society becomes better integrated and enjoys a high standard of living, the food chains and migratory patterns of other species become disrupted. The most insidious threat comes from air and water pollution caused by highly concentrated industries.

Concern for the environment finally has caught the attention of Western European governments, and the establishment of the European Union holds out hope for unified environmental policies and the possibility of enforcing them. Only by concerted effort and political will can people hope to maintain their habitat in a livable condition.

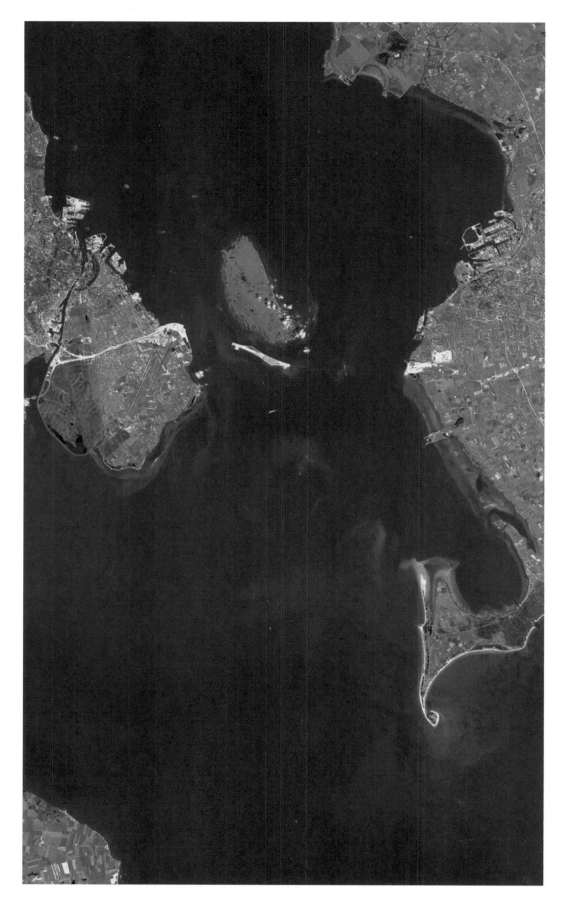

NETHERLANDS

Reclaiming land from the sea, a technique used by the Netherlands (opposite), ranks as one of Europe's greatest engineering feats. In the 13th century, the North Sea breached protective sandbars, flooding inhabited lands and creating the Zuider Zee. In 1932, the country completed a long dike across the Zuider Zee, dividing it into an outer coastal sea, called the Wadden Zee, and an enclosed lake named the IJsselmeer. By 1968, four large polders, or reclaimed lands, had reduced the IJsselmeer by almost half.

SCANDINAVIA'S "ØRESUND LINK"

By the year 2000, a road-and-rail link may connect Copenhagen, Denmark (above, at left), and Malmö, Sweden, which face each other across a stretch of water known as the Øresund. South of Saltholm, an uninhabited island lying between them, an artificial island whimsically called Pepparholm will act as the junction for a tunnel to Copenhagen and a bridge to Malmö. Three million people will use the link each day, cutting the time shore-to-shore from a 45-minute ferry ride to a 10-minute car or train journey.

Pollution in the atmosphere has built up steadily since the Industrial Revolution began about two centuries ago. But only recently has it stirred worldwide alarm. With its dense population, high level of development, and concentration of industries, Europe was one of the worst polluters. Smog choked city streets, forests withered in the countryside, and great buildings and monuments began to crumble under the onslaught of acid precipitation. Western Europe has done much to clean up the air of its cities, but Eastern Europe must deal with antiquated industrial plants, a long legacy of carelessness, and a lack of funds.

The discovery of an ozone hole over Antarctica in the 1980s led to an international ban on chlorofluorocarbons, and cooperation becomes vital as problems multiply. Pollution carried by wind can do damage far from its source. Global transport systems produce abundant greenhouse gases, and industrial accidents rarely keep the consequences inside their own national borders.

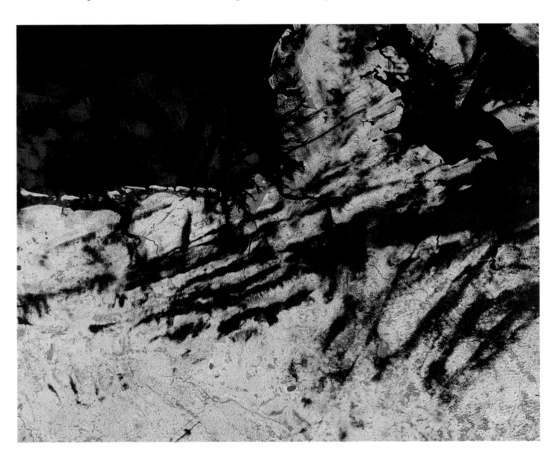

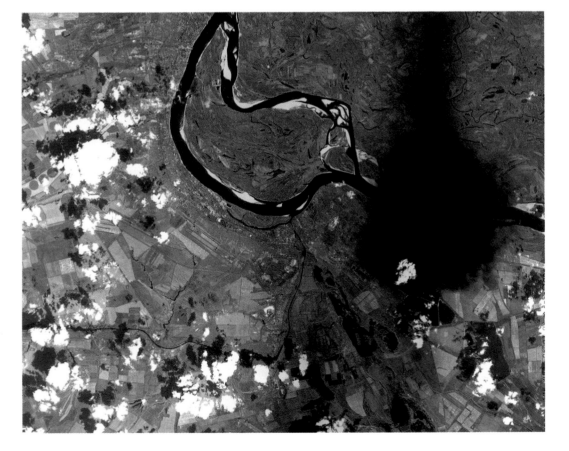

JET CONTRAILS

Red streaks represent contrails, or trails of condensed water vapor created by high-altitude jets, in a Nimbus satellite image (left) made over northern Germany. A larger image would show contrails above every important city in Europe. Aviation kerosene used by aircraft at about 30,000 feet produces exhaust made up mainly of water vapor and carbon dioxide, the principal greenhouse gas. The cloudlike vapor trails, which contribute to global warming, prevent the return of heat from Earth to the atmosphere.

VOLGOGRAD, RUSSIA

Made over southern European Russia in 1996, a SPOT image (left) catches an industrial disaster as it unfolds. A fire at a petrochemical complex south of Volgograd generates a black cloud about eight and a half miles across, visible at right in the image. The fire must have just started, because the dark smoke has not yet risen to the level of cumulus clouds in the area, one of which overlies it, nor has it lost its very regular shape. The large volume of smoke, reacting to sunlight, will soon blanket a wide area in brown haze.

CHORNOBYL', UKRAINE

On April 26, 1986, history's worst nuclear accident occurred at Chornobyl', in Ukraine (opposite). Because of technical and human errors, a nuclear power plant with four reactors suffered a sudden increase of thermal power in reactor 4. Two explosions followed, blowing the roof off the reactor, setting its graphite core on fire, and releasing nuclear material into the environment. A month later, a Thematic Mapper image shows the core of reactor 4 still burning as a bright red spot at lower left center.

Oceans cover more than 70 percent of Earth's surface, and for a long time they were believed to be immune to people's actions by virtue of their enormous size. In recent years, however, scientists have discovered the critical role that oceans and seas play in maintaining the world's environment and have warned of the damage that can be done to them. Nevertheless, people around the world continue to use them as dumping grounds for virtually every kind of waste.

Most solid waste eventually sinks to the bottom of the sea, but ocean currents and winds may propel floating waste such as garbage and oil for great distances, thereby endangering many forms of marine life. Industrial waste and dredge spoils dumped from barges are the primary pollutants of seawater. Highly toxic wastes are usually packed in drums before disposal. Alternative measures, such as recycling, are available, but because ocean dumping is usually much cheaper, it continues to be a problem.

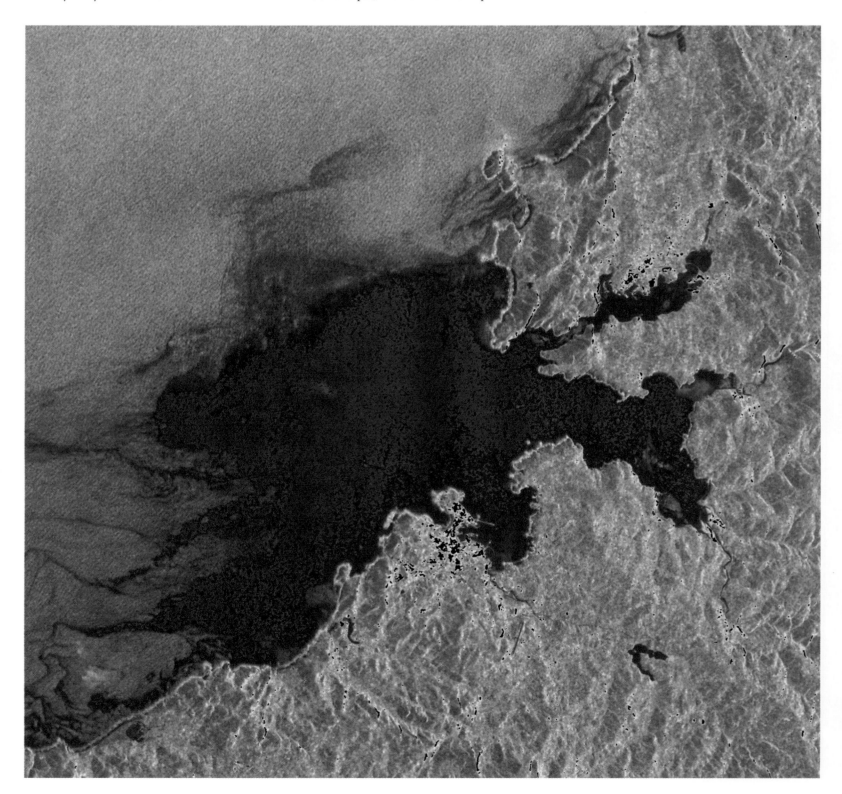

SPANISH COAST OIL SPILL

While in orbit high above Spain, the European Space Agency's ERS-1 made this radar image of a massive oil spill off the country's northwest coast. Taken ten days after a Greek tanker accident on December 3, 1992, the wide-view image reveals the extent of the disaster: Spilled oil, shown in red, reaches into the harbor of La Coruña and pollutes more than 125 miles of the Atlantic coastline. The dark gray areas in the water indicate volumes of oil that have started to disperse. Liability for damages and the huge expenses associated with cleaning up a major spill motivate the owners of tanker fleets to try to find ways of avoiding such accidents.

FROM AIR TO WATER POLLUTION

In this false-color satellite image, dead and dying forests downwind from two power plants in what is now the Czech Republic appear as a long, dark orange scar. Black stands indicate healthier trees. Smoke from the power plants shows up as blue plumes at lower right in the image, and the pink areas near the power plants denote agricultural fields. Wind carries pollutants across country borders, where they may fall as acid rain, a phenomenon that has damaged thousands of acres in Eastern Europe.

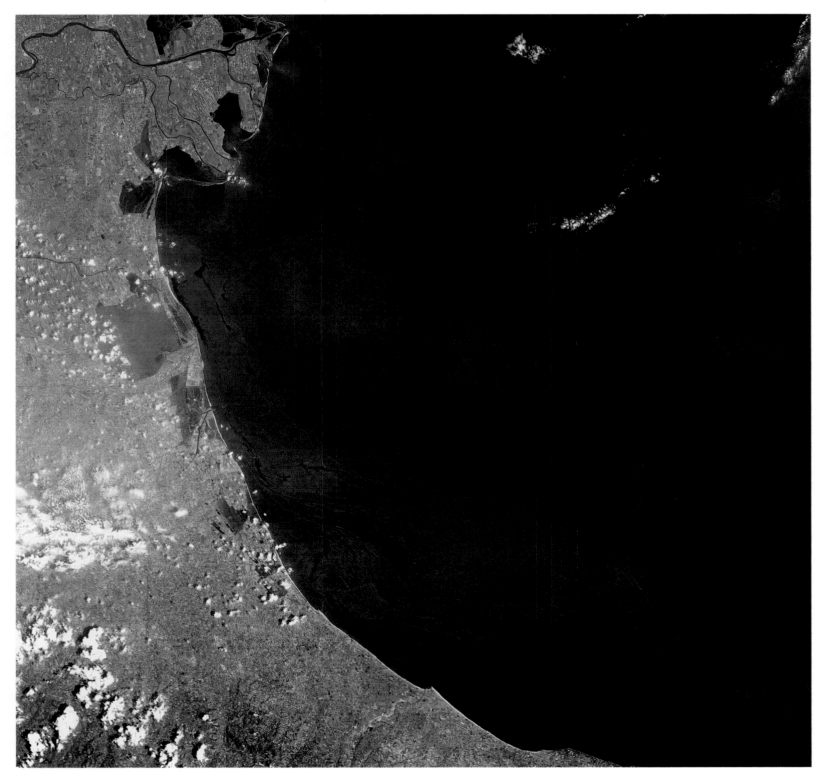

ADRIATIC SEA

South of the Mouths of the Po, near Ravenna, Italy, an algae bloom colors the Adriatic Sea red in this TM image. Algae may appear when large amounts of nutrients of human origin, such as sewage and agricultural runoff, enrich the water in a process called eutrophication. Scientists find increasing evidence of eutrophication along European shores, but the dense blooms of algae in the northern Adriatic seem to arise from some other cause. Theories suggest that water temperature may play a role, but the actual mechanisms for forming and sustaining large masses of algae remain a mystery. Italy's tourist industry voices deep concern, because algal slime on beaches drives away visitors.

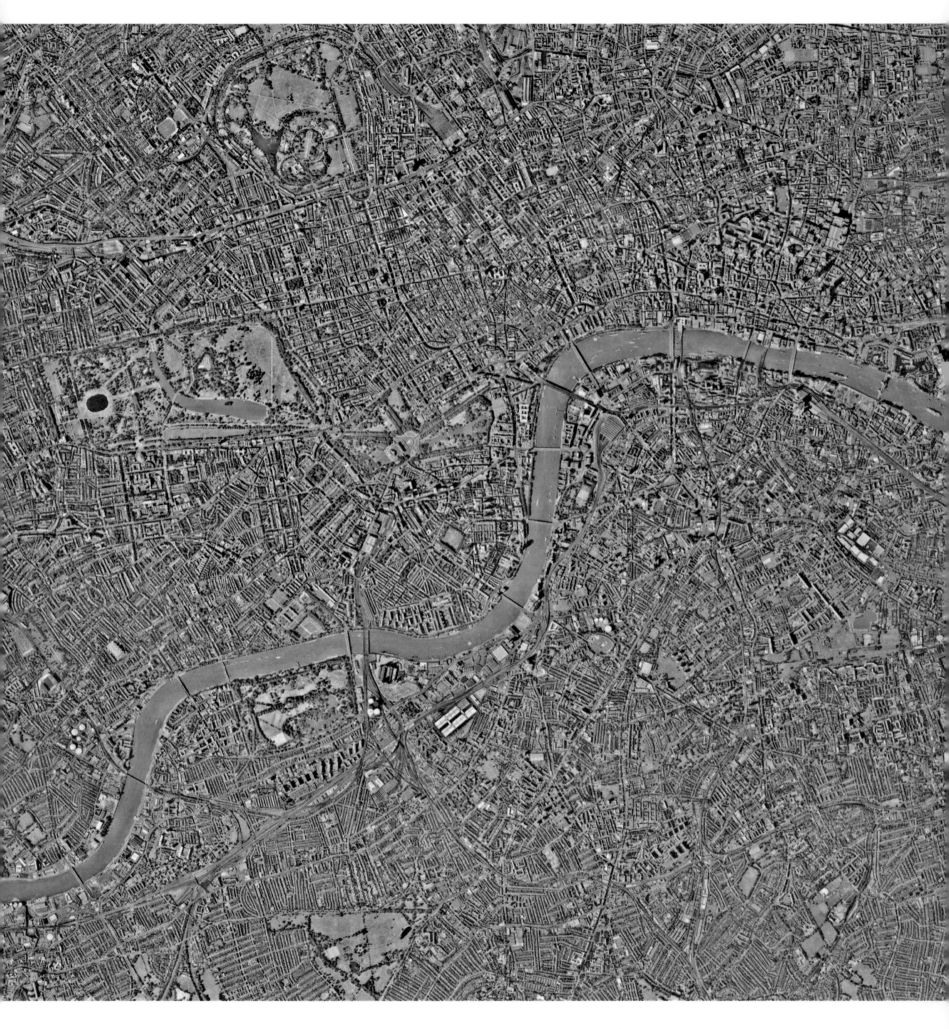

LONDON, ENGLAND

Made in the summer of 1994, this high-resolution aerial photograph of London shows remarkable detail. Hyde Park makes up the large rectangle at left center. To the right of the park rise Buckingham Palace and Westminster Abbey. Tower Bridge crosses the Thames River at right center.

PARIS, FRANCE

This 1995 SPOT image (right) shows Paris, the French capital, as a well-defined city of 41 square miles circled by a beltway and crossed by the Seine River. The darkest areas reveal wooded parks. The abrupt topography change outside the city represents a broad area of industrial suburbs; northern suburbs contain manufacturing industries, such as automakers and aeronautics firms. Flowing in from the east, the Marne joins the Seine near Paris.

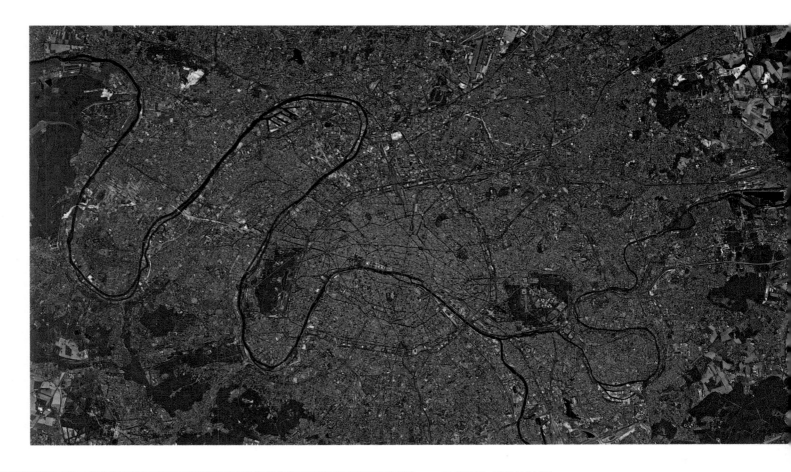

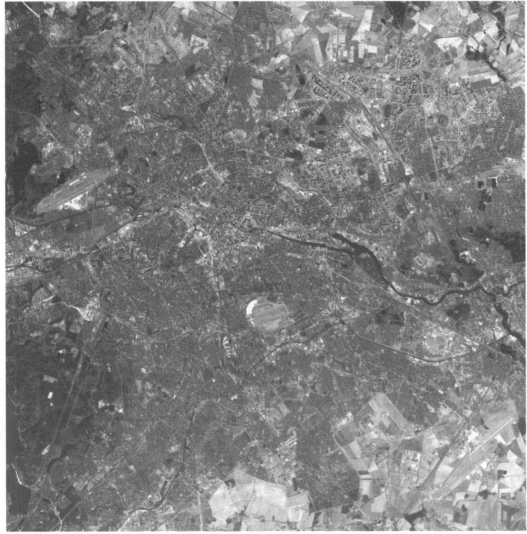

BERLIN, GERMANY

Berlin (left) covers an area eight times greater than Paris. This 1997 image shows the German city in natural color with its suburbs extending into agricultural areas. In the years following World War II, Berlin rebuilt itself into a modern city, but from 1961 to 1990 the infamous Berlin Wall divided the city almost in half, its two sectors remaining hostile throughout the Cold War years. Tempelhof Airport, a light patch in the center of the image, welcomed hundreds of supply planes a day during the 1948-49 Berlin Airlift. In 1991, the newly reunified Germany declared Berlin its capital.

STOCKHOLM, SWEDEN

As seen in this SPOT natural-color image of May 12, 1993, Sweden's largest city, Stockholm, rises where a complex of lakes joins an arm of the Baltic Sea. Most residents live in apartment buildings—easier to heat than freestanding homes—and enjoy efficient public transport by bus, train, and subway.

ST. PETERSBURG, RUSSIA

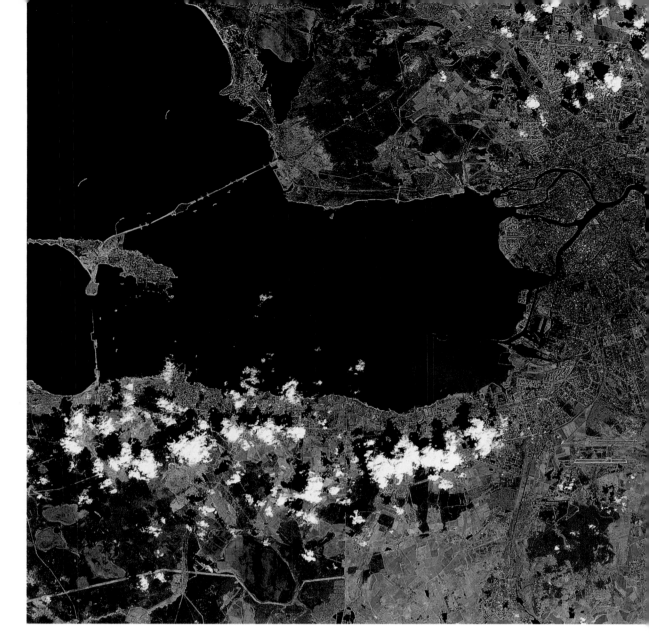

The second largest city in Russia covers several islands in the Neva River Delta (right). Ever since Peter the Great founded the city in 1703, waves have damaged it every few decades. To deal with the threat, in 1980 the country began to construct a 115-foot concrete barrier (at left in this Landsat image) that crosses the Gulf of Finland at Kotlin Island. But urban and industrial wastes, now unable to escape, seriously pollute the waters around the city.

MOSCOW, RUSSIA

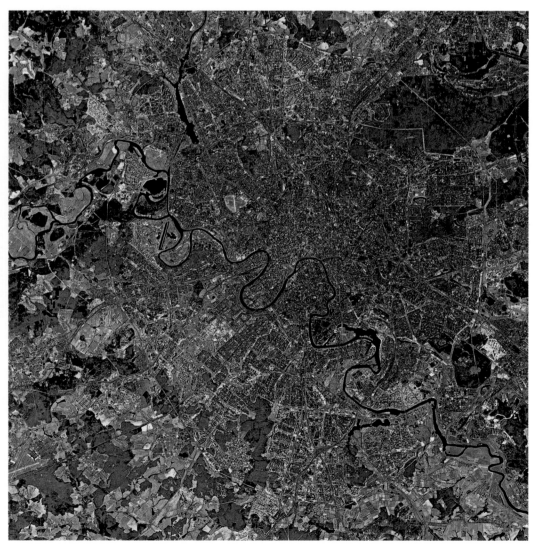

At left, a SPOT image reveals the radial-ring pattern of Moscow, Russia's capital. The Moskva River shows as a dark, sinuous line across the city of nine million people. The inner ring holds the Kremlin, a 15th-century fortified enclosure; the middle ring dates from the industrialized 18th and 19th centuries; and the outer zone contains 20th-century factories and new suburbs. Recent reductions in smog make the parts of a motor beltway visible across parklands.

LISBON, PORTUGAL

Lisbon, the westernmost capital in continental Europe, lies on the north shore of a bay formed by Portugal's Tagus River (above). Named "Sea of Straw" for its golden hue, the bay has served as an important harbor since ancient times. In 1755, an earthquake destroyed Lisbon, but the city revived and grew into a spacious, modern capital. Agricultural land northwest of the city, visible at the top of this SPOT image, produces mainly grain crops. The bay's south shore, opposite Lisbon, holds a large industrial center.

VATICAN CITY

This Russian satellite image of Vatican City shows the world's smallest independent country in detail (opposite). Built behind a high wall on a hill in Rome, Vatican City looks to the Pope as its leader. The Castel Sant'Angelo, a papal refuge surrounded by a star-shaped park, rises beside the Tiber River at right. From there, an avenue leads to the colonnaded ellipse of Saint Peter's Square, with its Obelisk. Saint Peter's Basilica, the world's biggest church, extends to the left, with its famous dome visible at the crossing.

ROME, ITALY

Scientists combined TM information with elevation data to produce a 3-D "drape" of Rome, as seen from the Italian coast. The Tiber River, a dark line winding through the city, empties into the Tyrrhenian Sea at the bottom of the image. On the left, the image shows Leonardo da Vinci International Airport and the town of Fiumicino. Rome lies 15 miles inland. The central part of the city, built on seven hills, sat at the heart of the Roman Empire 2,000 years ago.

BUDAPEST, HUNGARY

This SPOT image shows Budapest's two sides (left), separated by the south-flowing Danube River. To the west, medieval Buda climbs from the river into the Buda Hills. Stretching to the east and south, a plain holds the larger area of Pest, which began to develop into a center of commerce and industry in the 18th century. The cities merged and joined names in 1873. World War II greatly damaged Budapest, and reconstruction dominated the years following the war.

VENICE, ITALY

Two and a half miles square, Venice's historic center (right) occupies a fish-shaped area in the center of the image. The Grand Canal forms a reversed letter S across it, and a causeway links it to mainland Italy at Mestre and Marghera, industrial boroughs lying south of an agricultural region. A tidal lagoon created by peninsulas and islands separates Venice from the Adriatic Sea. Flooding about 40 times a year, the city continues to sink below sea level, partly due to overuse of groundwater.

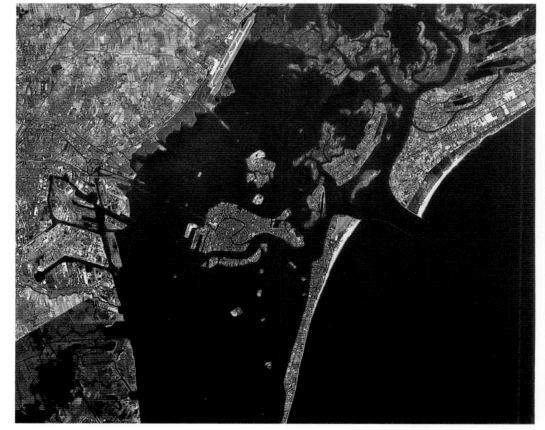

ATHENS, GREECE

Seen by the SPOT satellite, Athens appears as the dark core of a light gray area of urban development. Reddish brown areas define the surrounding mountains on an arid peninsula in southeastern Greece. Piraeus, a dark spot southwest of Athens on the Saronic Gulf, serves as the region's main port.

ASIA

Largest and most diverse of all the continents, Asia comprises 30 percent of Earth's total landmass. High plateaus, mountains, and deserts spread across much of the middle latitudes. To the north, vast steppes merge with seemingly endless Siberian conifer forests that, in turn, meet Arctic tundra. Monsoon regions to the south, rich and wet, support rain forests and abundant green fields of rice and other grains.

Asia's wide range and diversity produce a string of spectacular features: Mount Everest, highest point on the planet, rises to 29,028 feet; the Dead Sea, at 1,337 feet below sea level, claims the lowest point; Lake Baikal fills the world's deepest continental trough, plunging to a depth of 5,371 feet. Many features arise from ongoing geologic activity: Volcanoes along the Pacific Rim and earthquakes in Japan, China, and western Asia bring periodic devastation.

In Central Asia, mighty mountain systems—the Himalaya, Karakoram, Hindu Kush, Pamirs, Tian Shan, and Kunlun, for example—give rise to such rivers as the Indus, Ganges, Salween, Mekong, Yellow, and Yangtze. Because most Asians live along rivers and coasts, very uneven population densities mark the continent. Eastern China, Southeast Asia, and the Indian sub-continent hold Earth's densest populations, but huge areas of Asia's northern and central sections have few people.

MOUNT FUJI AND TERRAIN

Japan's 12,388-foot-high Mount Fuji rises in snowcapped splendor above the heavily populated island of Honshu. Sagami Bay appears directly behind Fuji. At far right, below the arm of the Izu Peninsula, lies 8,000-foot-deep Suruga Bay, filled with wondrous sea life. The long, narrow strip of water to the left, separated from Sagami Bay by Miura Peninsula, forms Tokyo Bay, with the Tokyo-Yokohama metropolis on its western bank.

Mount Fuji
and Terrain

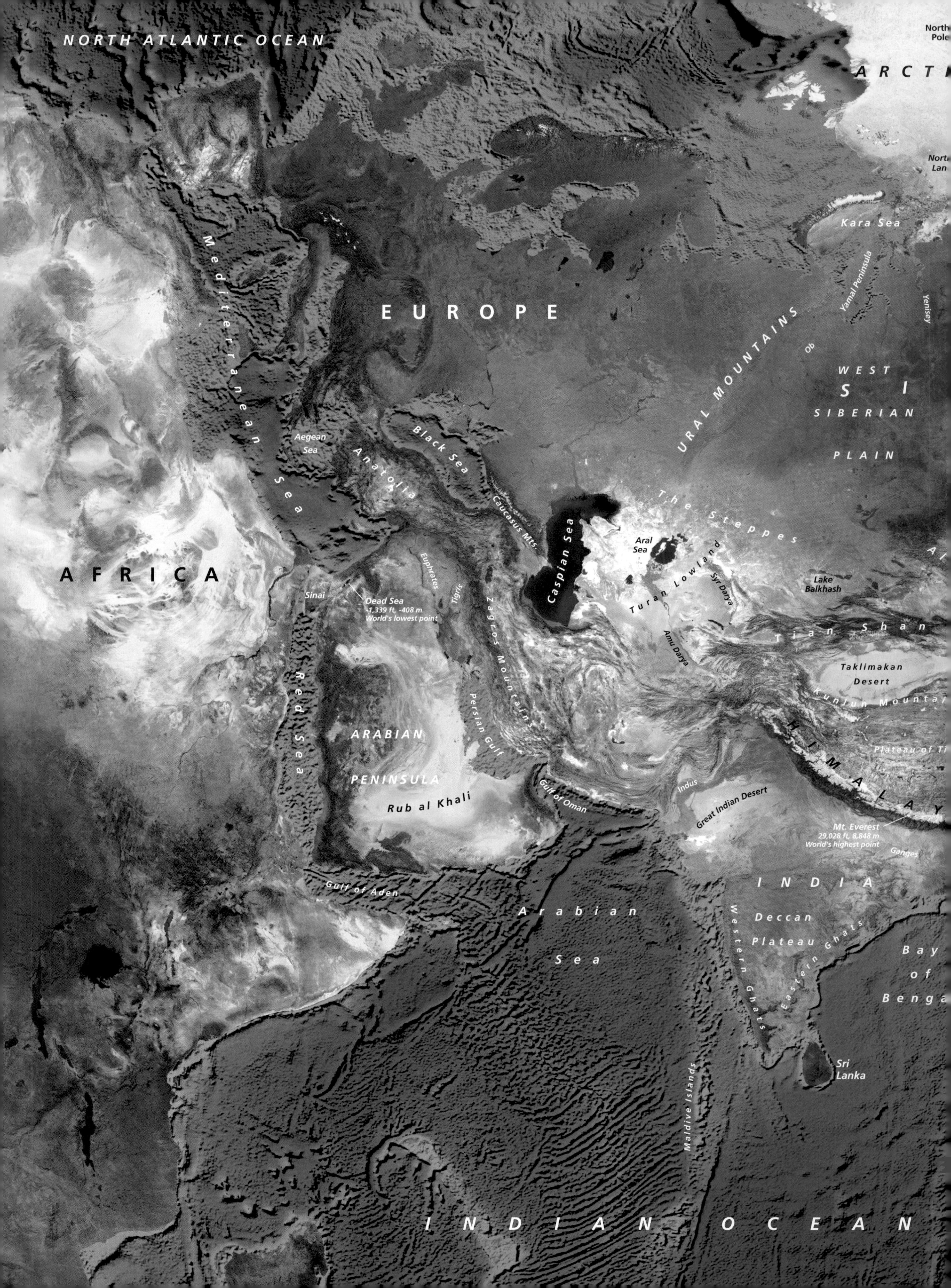

NORTH ATLANTIC OCEAN

ARCTI

North
Pole

North
Lan

Kara Sea

EUROPE

URAL MOUNTAINS

Yamal Peninsula

Yenisey

Ob

WEST
S I

SIBERIAN

PLAIN

Mediterranean Sea

Aegean
Sea

Black Sea

Anatolia

Caucasus Mts.

Caspian Sea

Aral
Sea

The Steppes

Ar

Lake
Balkhash

AFRICA

Sinai

Euphrates

Tigris

Dead Sea
-1,339 ft, -408 m
World's lowest point

Zagros Mountains

Turan Lowland

Syr Darya

Tian Shan

Amu Darya

Taklimakan
Desert

Kunlun Mountai

Red Sea

ARABIAN

Persian Gulf

HIMALAY

Plateau of Ti

PENINSULA

Gulf of Oman

Indus

Great Indian Desert

Mt. Everest
29,028 ft, 8,848 m
World's highest point

Rub al Khali

Ganges

Gulf of Aden

Arabian

I N D I A

Deccan

Plateau

Western Ghats

Eastern Ghats

Bay

of

Sea

Benga

Maldive Islands

Sri
Lanka

I N D I A N   O C E A N

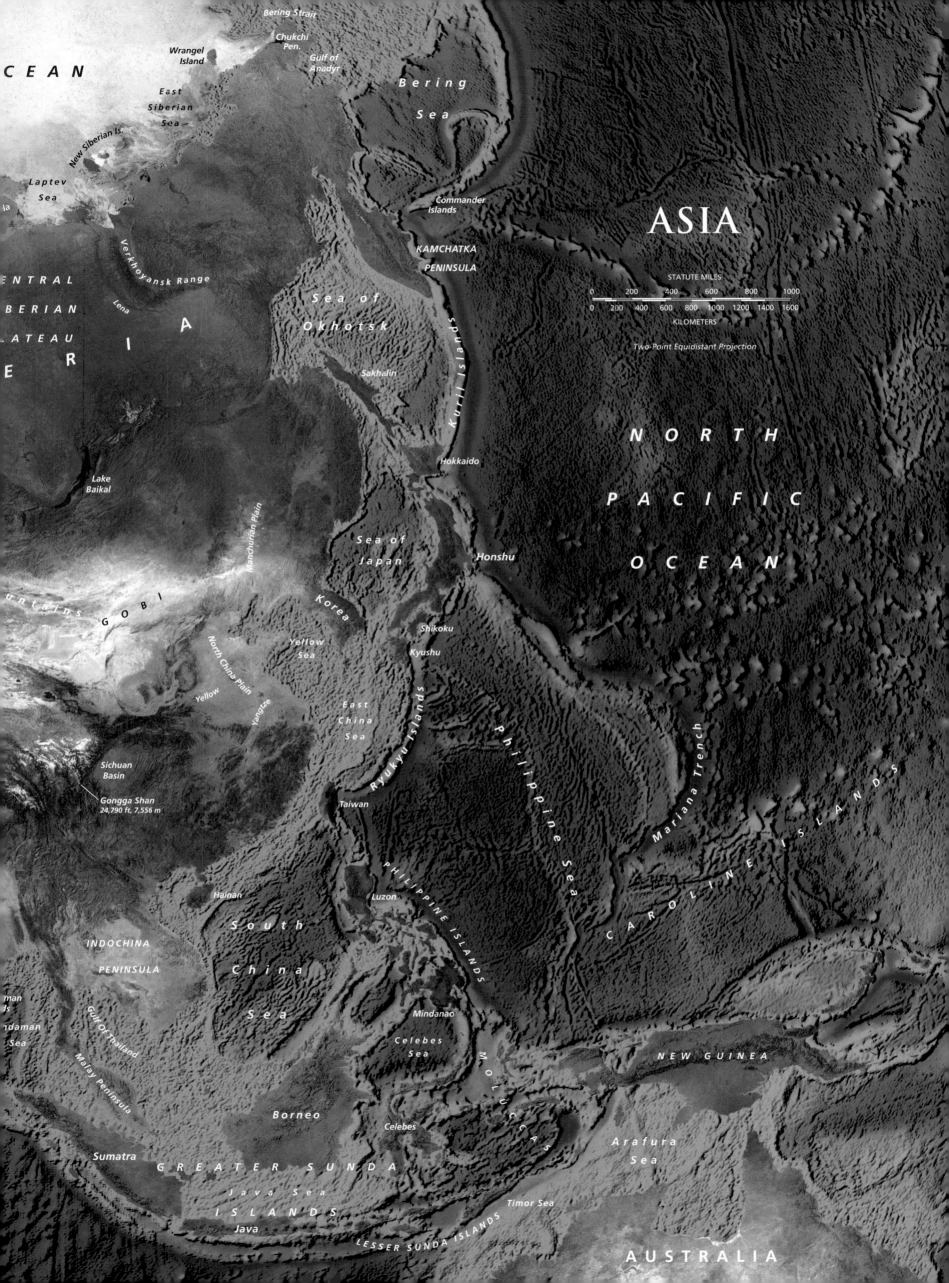

OCEAN

Wrangel
Island

Bering Strait

Chukchi
Pen.

Gulf of
Anadyr

East
Siberian
Sea

New Siberian Is.

Laptev
Sea

Bering
Sea

Commander
Islands

KAMCHATKA
PENINSULA

ASIA

CENTRAL

SIBERIAN

PLATEAU

ERIA

Verkhoyansk Range

Lena

Sea of
Okhotsk

STATUTE MILES

0   200   400   600   800   1000

0   200   400   600   800   1000   1200   1400   1600

KILOMETERS

Two-Point Equidistant Projection

Sakhalin

Lake
Baikal

Manchurian Plain

Hokkaido

A

Kuril Islands

NORTH

PACIFIC

OCEAN

Sea of
Japan

Honshu

untains

GOBI

Korea

Shikoku

Yellow
Sea

Kyushu

North China Plain

Yellow

Yangtze

East
China
Sea

Ryukyu Islands

Mariana Trench

Sichuan
Basin

Gongga Shan
24,790 ft, 7,556 m

Taiwan

Philippine Sea

CAROLINE ISLANDS

Hainan

Luzon

PHILIPPINE ISLANDS

South

INDOCHINA

China

PENINSULA

Sea

Mindanao

man
ls

Gulf Of Thailand

ndaman
Sea

Celebes
Sea

MOLUCCAS

NEW GUINEA

Malay Peninsula

Arafura
Sea

Borneo

Celebes

Sumatra

GREATER SUNDA

Java Sea

ISLANDS

Timor Sea

Java

LESSER SUNDA ISLANDS

AUSTRALIA

The world's early civilizations arose in Asia, establishing themselves between the Tigris and Euphrates Rivers in Mesopotamia, along the Indus River of present-day Pakistan, and in northern China near the Yellow River. Cultural innovations attributed to these civilizations include writing, complex societies, the wheel and chariot, irrigation, a decimal number system, and astronomy.

Trade and commerce, defense and warfare, and even religion and death have left behind physical remains as testaments to former empires. Monumental architecture, lost cities, roads, and irrigation works in many parts of the continent can be discerned by satellites orbiting high overhead. Ancient Greek ruins in Asian Turkey, gigantic key-shaped tumuli in Japan, and temple complexes of Southeast Asia, for example, are still awe inspiring several centuries after they were built. Most audacious of all, the Great Wall of China continues to wend its way over mountains and across deserts to proclaim its former splendor.

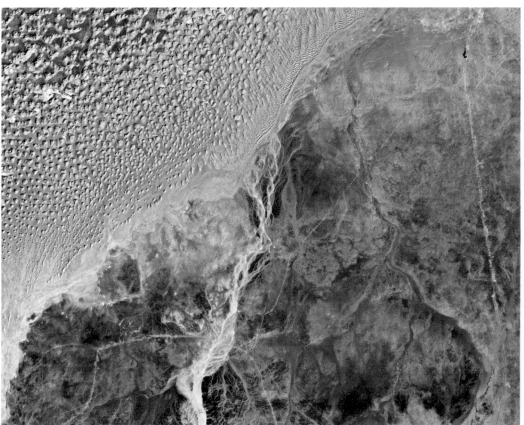

GREAT WALL

China's Great Wall appears in this radar image taken from the space shuttle Endeavor *in 1994 (top). A series of fortifications built over 2,500 years, the Great Wall functioned as a barrier against northern invaders. The Ming Dynasty (1364-1644) constructed the wall we see today, snaking some 3,000 miles from the Yellow Sea to northwestern China. In this image, the nearly 30-foot-high Ming structure cuts across northern Shaanxi province, paralleling a 1,500-year-old wall now reduced to rubble and hillocks.*

UBAR

An ancient city lost in the sands of southern Oman, Ubar reappeared after satellite imagery revealed camel tracks left in dunes centuries ago (above). The Arabian desert's barren floor takes up most of this TM image. A dry riverbed shows up at bottom center. Faint lines of modern gravel roads surround the village of Shisar, probable site of Ubar, where geologists and archaeologists have discovered the remains of watchtowers, city walls, pottery, and forgotten caravan encampments. Ubar might date from 2800 B.C.

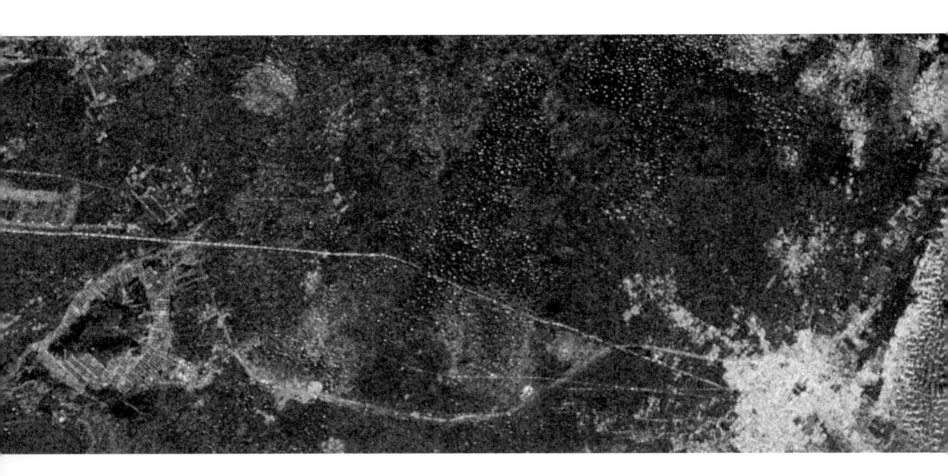

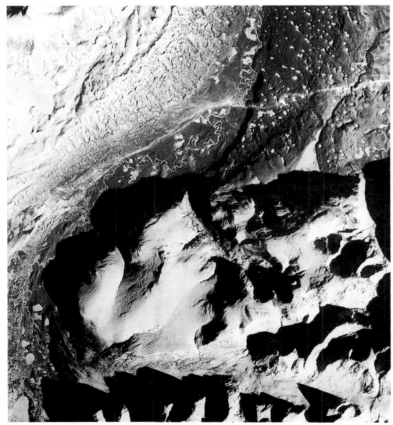

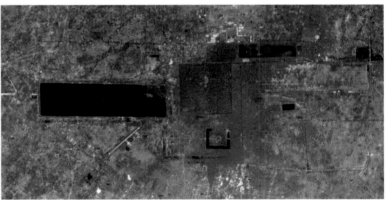

ANGKOR

Northwestern Cambodia's ancient Angkor (above), capital of the Khmer empire, grew to a million people between the 9th and 13th centuries. The Western Baray, a reservoir near the city's heart, appears as a large, dark blue rectangle in this December 1996 SPOT image. The famous Angkor Wat, a temple built in the 12th century of stone and brick and known for its exquisite bas-reliefs, appears as a square enclosed by a wide moat. Angkor Thom, a fortified city, lies within the larger square.

SILK ROAD

Viewing part of the border between southern Russia and northwestern China, a Russian image (above) reveals a possible northern branch of Asia's fabled Silk Road. The faint line arcing through the Altay Mountains from upper right to lower left might represent an ancient route followed by caravans carrying animals, traders, luxury goods such as silk, and new ideas between China, Central Asia, and the West. This Silk Road branch lies north of the main routes that sweep around China's Taklimakan Desert.

Asia's impulse to honor gods and lead humans along life's correct path has made it the homeland of the world's major religions. Over the centuries, Hinduism, Judaism, Buddhism, Jainism, Christianity, and Islam came to fruition in western and southern regions.

For millennia, the power of pilgrimage and the lure of sacred sites—holy rivers, mountains, trees, and lakes—have touched people here, connecting them to nature in intimate ways. India's Hindus gather at enormous festivals to wash themselves in the sacred Ganges River. Buddhists of China, Tibet, Japan, Korea, and Southeast Asia have built fabulous shrines, temples, and monasteries on propitious geographic sites, and they make pilgrimages to locations in India and Nepal associated with the Buddha.

Cities, too, attract through the power of religious association. Mecca's holy connection with ancient patriarchs and the prophet Muhammad beckons more than a billion Muslims to kneel and pray five times a day. From Turkey and Syria to Malaysia and Indonesia, the faithful bow in the direction of the city. Jerusalem speaks directly to Jews, Christians, and Muslims as a city of promise. It remains the sacred home of the Jewish Temple, destroyed by Romans in A.D. 70, and the site of Christ's teaching and crucifixion.

As Asia's traditional reverence for nature faces the 20th-century realities of industrialization and commerce, religious links to the land are threatened. And across the continent, religious discord continues to flare between groups that have their own faiths and holy places.

MECCA

Muslims around the world revere Mecca (above), birthplace of Muhammad, prophet of Islam and founder of the religion. The past two decades have seen this Saudi Arabian city spread north and southwest from the old area around the Sacred Mosque, visible in the image as a light spot left of center.

THE OLD CITY OF JERUSALEM

Settled since 1800 B.C., Jerusalem remains a site of holiness for Jews, Muslims, and Christians. As seen in this aerial view, walls built by the Ottoman Sultan Suleiman the Magnificent, in the mid-1500s, outline the Old City. The Dome of the Rock mosque occupies the large rectangle at right center.

GANGES

Giver of life to nearly 40 percent of India's 900 million people, the Ganges River arrives from the northwest to join with the Yamuna just east of the city of Allahabad. Rising in the central Himalaya, the Ganges drains nearly a quarter of India's land surface as it flows through the states of Uttar Pradesh, Bihar, and West Bengal before entering Bangladesh to help form that country's vast delta. Every dozen years or so, India's Hindu faithful immerse themselves in the holy waters at the Ganges-Yamuna point of confluence.

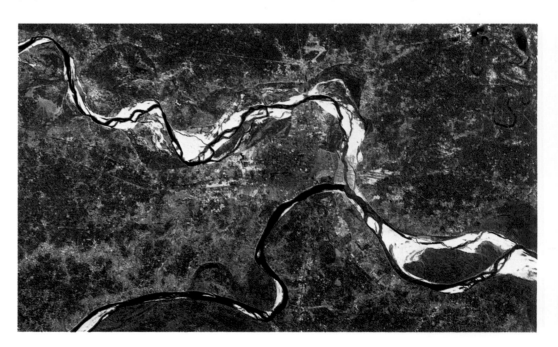

Jerusalem and
The Holy Land

Mecca

Ganges

THE HOLY LAND

*Enhanced by SPOT data for detail, this January
18, 1987, TM image reveals Israel's four main
geographic regions, as well as parts of Lebanon,
Syria, and Jordan. The cities of Tel Aviv-Yafo
and Haifa, in Israel, sit at the western edge of
the coastal plain, a historic bridge and route of
invasion from Asia to Egypt. On the coast at
the top of the scene lies Beirut, Lebanon.*

*East of Beirut rise the snowy Anti-Lebanon
mountains, crowned by 9,232-foot-high Mount
Hermon. The hilly regions in the north extend
southward to central Israel.*

*The north-to-south flowing Jordan River
divides the image, first crossing the Hula Basin,
then linking the freshwater Sea of Galilee and
the ultra-saline Dead Sea—Earth's lowest point
on land, at 1,337 feet below sea level. The Jordan
River's down-dropped valley forms part of the
greater rift system that runs through Israel, the
Gulf of Aqaba, and the Red Sea before cutting
deeply into East Africa.*

*Arid conditions mean extensive use of irrigation.
The Sea of Galilee provides water for nearly half
of Israel's agricultural land, and fields to the east
of the Jordan demand its water, too. This use,
combined with evaporation, causes the Dead Sea
to shrink. Bright blue mineral-evaporation pans
mark the Dead Sea's southern part.*

*The Negev desert stretches across most of
Israel's southern half; the desert's tawny northern
section appears at the bottom of the image.*

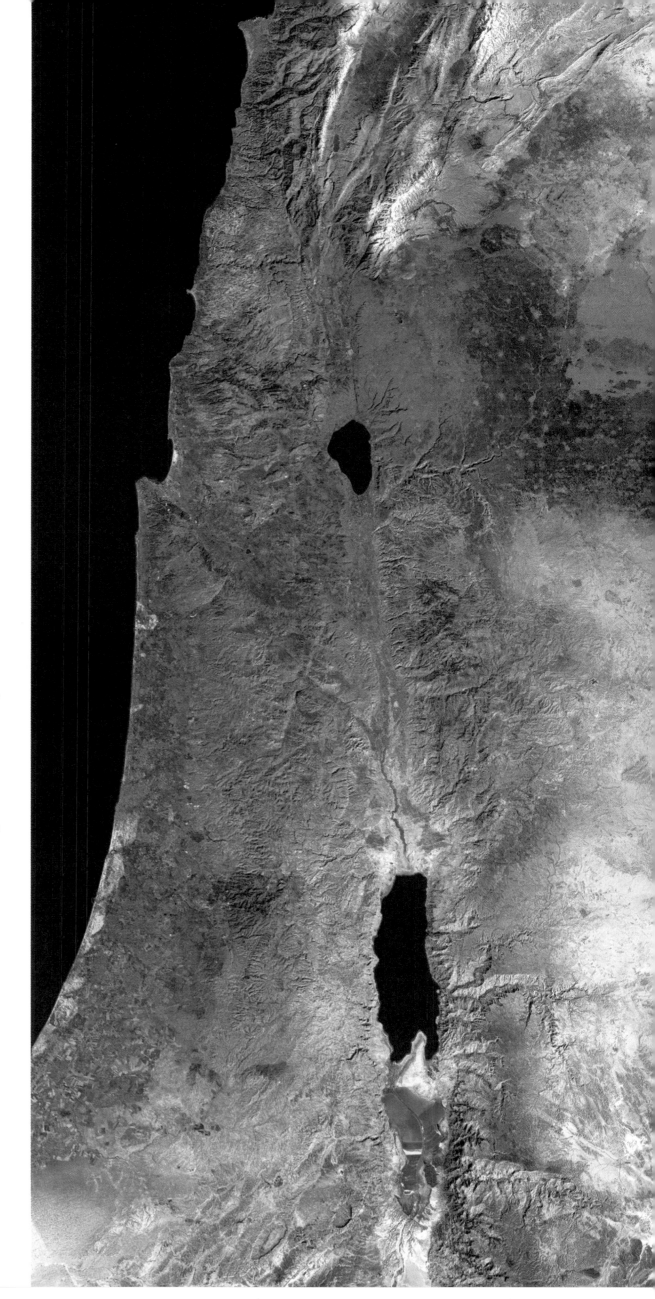

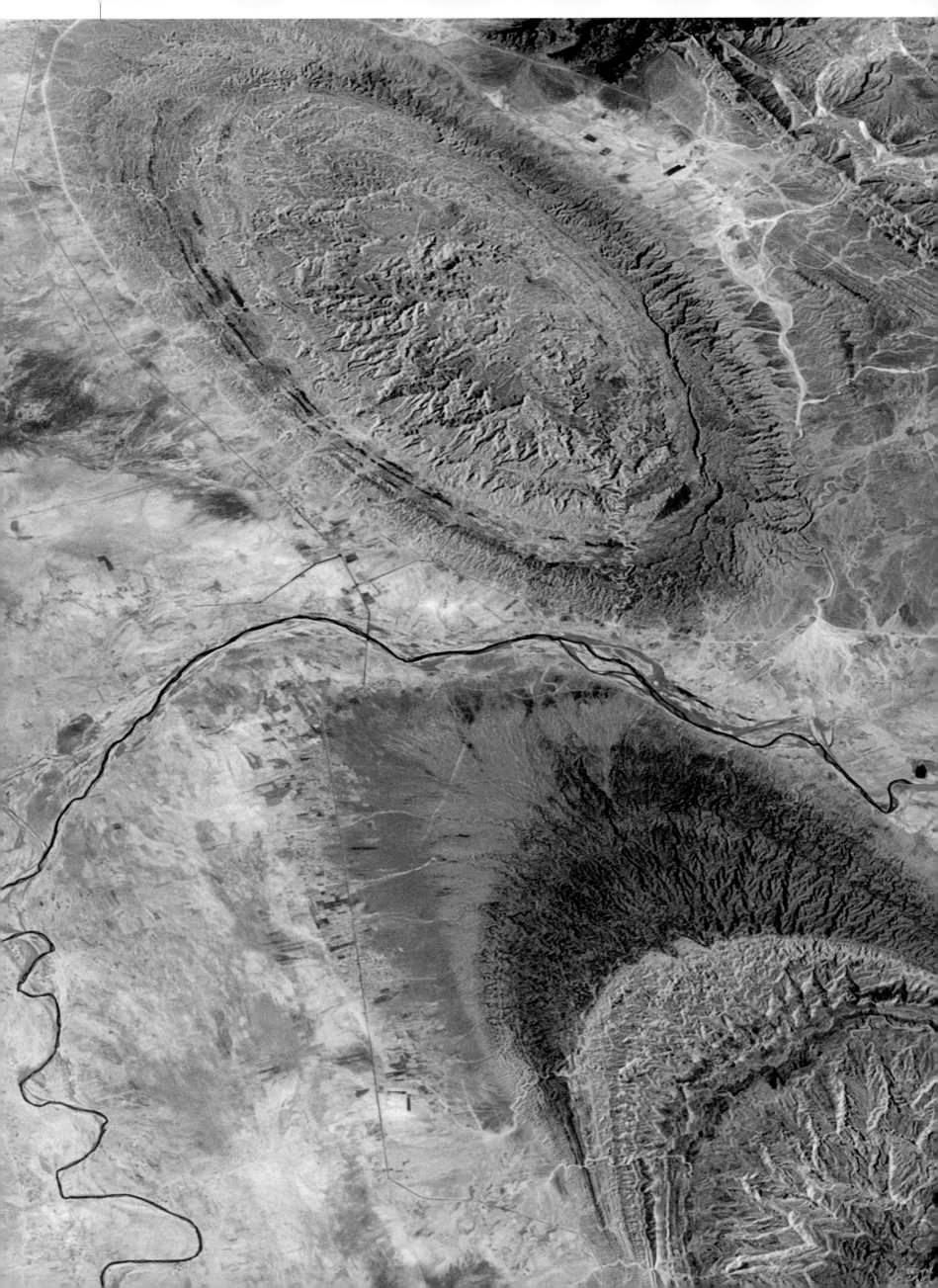

An arid band extends from the Red and Mediterranean Seas eastward through Central Asia and the northern part of the Indian subcontinent to Mongolia and northeastern China. Parts of this zone have sparse grass for grazing and enough precipitation to support limited agriculture and villages. But Arabia's Empty Quarter and China's Taklimakan Desert, parched and uninhabitable, represent dry lands at their harshest.

Northeast of the Himalaya, beyond Tibet, lies the awe-inspiring Gobi. Filling half a million square miles, the desert spans a thousand miles, including Mongolia's southern third and a large section of northern China's border region. Although most of the Gobi is made up of rocky expanses burned by sun and wind, it has semi-desert areas that allow for wild camels and asses, antelope, gazelles, small mammals, and isolated human populations. This land of extremes witnesses blazing summers and Siberian-like winters, with large fluctuations in a single day.

IRAN

Brilliant colors and high spatial and spectral resolutions mark this image of Iran just east of the Persian Gulf (opposite). The Mand River, with yellow-green riverside areas indicating sparse vegetation, flows between heavily eroded mountains at the southern edge of the Zagros Mountains.

GOBI

The Bogda Shan mountains of China's Xinjiang Uygur Autonomous Region help define the Gobi's southwestern limit. Above, green indicates vegetation, blue shows snow or water, and purple denotes alluvial fans sloping from the mountains. Sand dunes make up the reddish rippled area at bottom right.

ASIA · FORCES OF NATURE

The power of nature manifests itself in many ways. Ever so slowly continents collide and mountains rise, but nature also strikes with hellish swiftness, bringing earthquakes, eruptions, typhoons, forest fires, and tsunamis. Much of the blame for Asia's geologic troubles rests with the Pacific Ring of Fire, where shifting plates of the Earth's crust meet with astounding force, causing earthquakes and expelling molten rock from hundreds of volcanoes. Philippine volcanoes, such as Mount Pinatubo, erupt periodically. Japan's active volcanoes keep the people of that island nation always on alert. The volcanoes on Russia's Kamchatka Peninsula are among the world's most active, and their potential for destruction remains great.

NOVEMBER 25, 1989

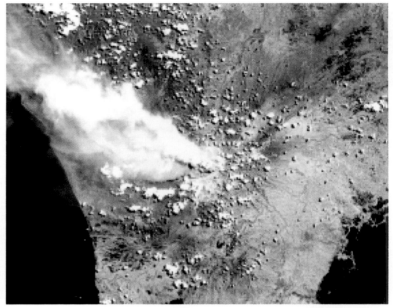

JULY 5, 1991

MOUNT PINATUBO

June 1991 saw multiple eruptions of Mount Pinatubo, just 55 miles north of the Philippine capital of Manila. The events killed 900 to 1,000 people and destroyed 42,000 houses. Before and after images (above left and right), taken 20 months apart by Japan's MOS-1, reveal the changed landscape. Where tropical forests and irrigated fields once lay, volcanic ash now mars the terrain. Pinatubo threw ash 98,000 feet high and released 20 million tons of sulfur dioxide.

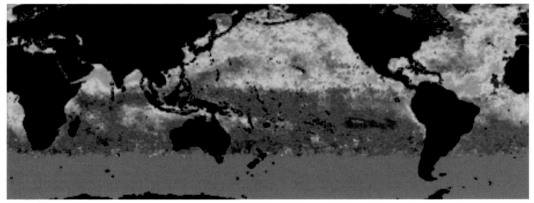

MAY 1991

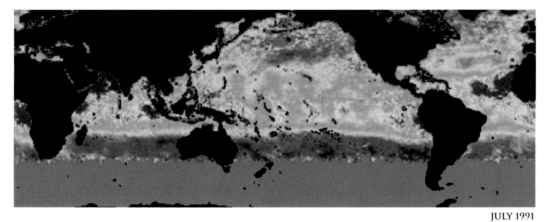

JULY 1991

PINATUBO'S GLOBAL ASH

At left, three images show how the 1991 eruption of Mount Pinatubo affected Earth's atmosphere. NOAA's AVHRR helped track the movement and spread of volcanic ash around the world, making the top image one month before the eruption, the middle image a month after, and the bottom image two months after the massive eruption. Following such a major volcanic eruption, the natural dispersal and removal of ash from the atmosphere can take from one to five years.

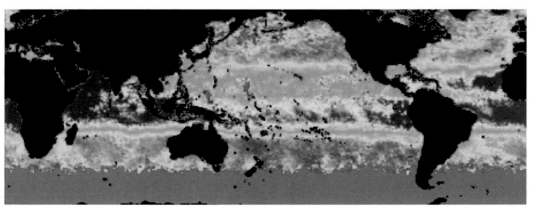

AUGUST 1991

RUSSIAN VOLCANOES

Volcanoes cluster together in a chain running 500 miles along the Kamchatka Peninsula in Russia's far east. This October 1994 SIR-C radar image penetrates 50,000-foot ash clouds ejected from the erupting Klyuchevskaya Sopka, which stands 15,584 feet tall and forms the dark triangle in the center.

LAKE TOBA

Sixty miles long and eighteen miles wide, Lake Toba (right) appeared in north-central Sumatra's Barisan Mountains after eruptions destroyed a much older volcano. Ash from those events fell as far west as Sri Lanka and India. In time, water filled Toba's crater, one of Earth's largest volcanic depressions. Waters 2,000 feet deep surround large, forested Samosir Island, then flow eastward into the Strait of Malacca. Prapat resort appears as a white spot on the Uluan Peninsula jutting into Toba's southeastern edge.

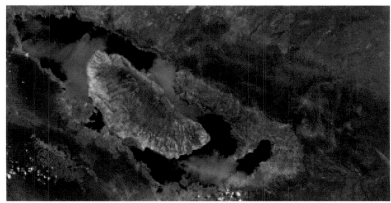

ASIA · HUMAN IMPACT

Since ancient times, people have altered Earth's environment through agricultural practices, the clearing and irrigation of land, and the building of towns. In China's Sichuan Basin, for example, scarcely any land has escaped 30 centuries of food production activities. In recent times, ingenuity has even led to the sprouting of cities and green fields in Asia's deserts. But human-caused disasters, with alarming ecological consequences, increasingly mar the record.

A slow-motion drama with dire consequences has been taking place in the Aral Sea basin. Water diverted from major rivers that flowed into the sea helped produce massive cotton harvests, but the sea shrank as the years passed. Once the world's fourth largest lake, it now claims sixth place.

TASHKENT

Uzbekistan's capital nestles between the reservoir at far left and the snowcovered mountains (blue) in this TM image (opposite). The Syr Darya river flows northwest to the Aral Sea, but most of its water never reaches the dying sea.

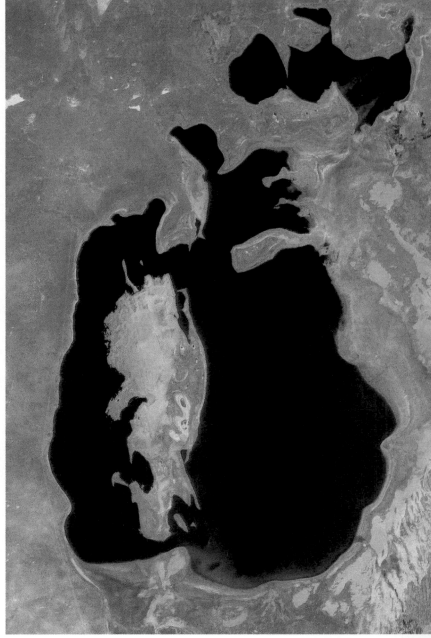

ARAL SEA, 1976

Satellite images of the shrinking Aral Sea confirm an environmental tragedy. In the early 20th century, the Soviet Union began irrigating vast areas of Central Asia for cotton production, taking increasing amounts of water from the Amu Darya and Syr Darya rivers. The Kara Kum irrigation canal opened in 1956 and diverted huge volumes of water from the Amu Darya, causing it to almost run dry by the time it reached the Aral Sea. Surface evaporation accelerated, and the sea began to shrink.

ARAL SEA, 1997

Between 1960 and 1990, the Aral Sea lost 40 percent of its surface area. Now the water line lies 50 miles or more from former shores. When blown into the air, millions of tons of salt, sand, and mineral particles from the former lake bed pose a severe health hazard, affecting millions of people. Problems include throat cancer, eye diseases, respiratory problems, and high infant mortality. Little can be done to save the Aral Sea. Although it may not disappear, it probably will shrink to a tenth of its former size.

Source of life and wealth, water increasingly plays a part in the interaction of nations and in the health and welfare of their people. Asia's arid regions especially demand water for agriculture, growing populations, and industry, but limited supplies and inefficiency compound the serious problem of shortages.

Thirsty Middle Eastern nations, all possessing very limited supplies of fresh water, apparently are not able to cooperate in sharing this essential resource. Separately, they try to achieve water security; future wars might be fought over it. In India, China, and elsewhere, large countries that dam their rivers deprive downstream nations of precious water.

Asia has one of the most degraded environments on Earth. In 1997 and 1998, unusually dry weather and slash-and-burn agricultural practices led to Indonesian fires that ruined huge forests and left neighboring nations choking in smoke and haze. And in 1991, war in the Persian Gulf fouled the air, land, and water of that region.

UNITED ARAB EMIRATES (U.A.E.), 1972

A confederation of seven tiny emirates founded in 1971 along the Persian Gulf, the U.A.E. evolved from a place of grinding poverty into a realm of great wealth. Abu Dhabi, the largest sheikhdom, grew with the oil boom of the 1960s. This 1972 MSS image shows early development in Al 'Ayn.

UNITED ARAB EMIRATES, 1990

This TM view of Al 'Ayn 18 years later shows dramatic expansion into the desert. Prosperity has built roads, sports centers, banks, shopping malls, conference complexes, airports, hotels, and hospitals. Foreign workers, up to 85 percent of the labor force, help construct and maintain the U.A.E.'s new cities.

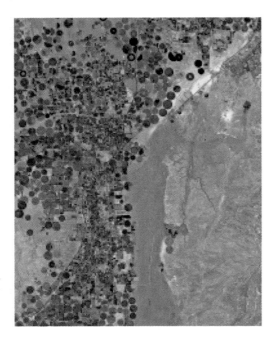

SAUDI ARABIAN OASIS

Mostly desert and dry steppe, Saudi Arabia suffers from extremes of heat and aridity. To reduce dependence on imported food and to improve rural life, the government encourages artificial irrigation. A 1992 SPOT image (left) shows As Sulaymaniyah oasis, southeast of Riyadh. The circles, as much as half a mile in diameter, indicate crops watered by overhead center-pivot irrigation systems. Colors reveal stages of growth: Black shows new cultivation; red, full crops just before harvesting; and tan, harvested fields.

KUWAITI FIRES

Made following the Gulf War, this 1991 image (opposite) shows numerous oil wells burning north and south of Kuwait City, at the head of the Persian Gulf. Retreating Iraqis set them on fire; wells to the south lie within the Burgan Oil Field, the second largest oil field in the world. Landsat imagery from 440 miles up reveals smoke streaming southeastward, where it blackens skies over the gulf. Clouds of oily soot rose to 22,000 feet while oil spread across the water, adding environmental devastation to the misery of war.

Despite burgeoning cities, most of Asia's countries remain over-whelmingly agricultural. Whether farming Himalayan slopes, planting rice in the Mekong River Delta, or practicing aquaculture in Thailand, rural Asians rely on land and water. Nowhere is this more evident than in densely populated Bangladesh; 85 percent of Bangladeshis live in the countryside as fishermen or farmers of rice, jute, tea, and other crops. This low-lying country, much of it only a few feet above sea level, defines itself through water. The great delta of the Ganges-Brahmaputra river system creates a delicate balance for life in a perpetually wet environment. Agriculture, transport, water, and survival itself go hand in hand here.

MEKONG RIVER · DELTA

This multicolor composite of the Mekong River Delta shows rice growing in Vietnam during May, June, and July 1996. Different colors designate the various stages of the rice. Vegetation along irrigation canals and in other built-up areas looks gray, indicating little change over weeks and months.

146

KATHMANDU VALLEY

In this February aerial, rice terraces climb the slopes of Kathmandu Valley near Bhaktapur, Nepal. The valley's population has grown rapidly over the past 30 years, yet agriculture has kept pace by exploiting the slopes. For centuries Nepalis have cultivated flat terraces, a type of farming that not only helps control water for wet rice fields but also retains soil and prevents erosion. After spring rice harvests, Nepali farmers plant the mountain slopes with wheat, potatoes, and vegetables. To make the furrows in the fields, farmers use shovel-hoes, not pulled plows.

BANGLADESH

Resource-poor Bangladesh has water and people in abundance. This riverine country, with a population of about 115 million living in an area the size of Illinois, relies on summer monsoon floods to enrich its land with silt. This TM image shows the Ganges-Brahmaputra confluence. These great Asian rivers merge and then join with the Meghna River south of Dhaka, Bangladesh's capital. Massive volumes of water carrying two billion tons of sediment a year flow into the Bay of Bengal to form the Mouths of the Ganges, an amphibious world of inlets, islands, shifting fingers of land, and mangroves.

PEARL RIVER DELTA

Cloud-free satellite imagery, a combination of four Landsat TM scenes, displays the Pearl River Delta and Hong Kong, on the South China Sea (above). The delta fills the left half of the image. Hong Kong's large, uneven peninsula and many islands take up the lower right. Britain's 156-year rule of Hong Kong, which ended in 1997 with a formal handover to China, saw the former colony grow from a few fishing villages into a trading, manufacturing, and banking power. Densely populated and dynamic, the Pearl River area has turned foreign investment and the spirit of commerce into an economic boom. Hong Kong acts as a major conduit of trade, boasting the world's largest container port. In a hurry to expand connections with the world, the area in the image has five major airports—at Guangzhou, Zhuhai, Macau, Shenzhen, and Hong Kong.

HONG KONG INTERNATIONAL AIRPORT

Hong Kong's new airport at Chek Lap Kok, off the north shore of Lantau Island, lies on a bed of reclaimed land. Opened in 1998, it replaces Kai Tak, an overtaxed airport jutting north of the island. At left, the upper image shows the future airport zone as a hilly island in 1988. The lower image shows it flattened and expanded to handle two giant runways in 1997. New rail, road, bridge, and tunnel links speed passengers to Hong Kong.

SINGAPORE

"Lion City" at the tip of the Malay Peninsula, Singapore (above) stands strategically where narrow sea routes join the Indian and Pacific Oceans. Founded as a British colony in 1819 and fully independent only since 1965, this vital city-state has proved a multiethnic success. Singapore's 3.5 million Chinese, Malay, and Indian inhabitants—highly educated and disciplined—have built one of Asia's richest nations. With its fine harbor at the entrance to the Strait of Malacca, Singapore has become an entrepôt for east-west exchange. Tiny Singapore Island, just 14 miles from north to south, relies on food imports and water by pipeline from neighboring Malaysia.

AIRPORT EXPANSION

Three images (from left to right) record expansion at Singapore's Changi Airport. The first image, taken in 1986, shows initial stages of a land-reclamation project. Image two, from 1991, reveals some progress. The third image, made in 1997, shows near completion. Runways, buildings, and support facilities on the new land will be in place by the early 21st century. The airport occupies the far eastern section of Singapore Island, as shown in the larger 1997 image above.

 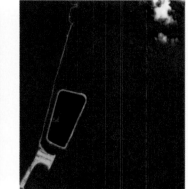 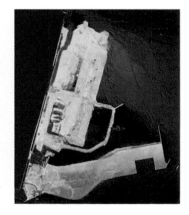

BAGHDAD, IRAQ

Baghdad, capital and major city of Iraq, stands at the heart of an ancient land. Some 5,000 years ago Sumerians used sun-dried mud to build the world's first cities along the courses of the Tigris and Euphrates Rivers. Water from these rivers, then as today, allowed for irrigation, agriculture, and the support of populations. Most Iraqis continue to live in towns and cities on the plains of these rivers. This Landsat TM image from March 16, 1991, shows the Tigris River winding through Baghdad's heart on its way to the Persian Gulf. Areas damaged by bombs that fell on the city during the 1991 Gulf War show up as dark blotches in the lower part of the image.

MUMBAI, INDIA

Mumbai, formerly called Bombay, now serves as the capital of India's Maharashtra state (right). Located on the Arabian Sea, at left in this 1994 SPOT image, Mumbai stands as India's main port and its principal financial and commercial center. One of the world's most densely populated cities, Mumbai extends northward past Thane, a new twin city visible at the top of the image. Sanjay Gandhi National Park, near top center, lies west of Thane, and Sahar International Airport appears south of that. Below Thane stretches the entire Mumbai peninsula, formerly seven islands but now linked together by landfill and causeways. The main port lies at western Bombay Harbour. Back Bay, forming Mumbai's southwest contour, culminates in Malabar Point. Colaba Point, the southernmost point on the peninsula, shows up at bottom left in the image.

BANGKOK, THAILAND

Sprawling Bangkok—Thailand's capital, cultural center, chief port, and center of industry—claims nearly seven million people, though the actual number may be much higher. Dramatic growth over the past 25 years made many people rich, but it also brought severe pollution and perhaps the world's worst traffic. Numerous canals, which once carried away 60 inches of rainfall annually, no longer thread the city. Nearly all of them have been filled in to build boulevards, and flooding now comes with every rainy season. Economic expansion caused Bangkok to spread east and south into agricultural land and marshy areas. The main features of this 1997 SPOT image include the Chao Phraya River, flowing south into the Gulf of Thailand, and the urban core above the large bend in the river. Bright blue coastal zones at lower left indicate mangroves.

BEIJING, CHINA

Near the center of a Landsat TM image (opposite), in shades of blue, lies Beijing's heavily populated and developed urban zone. Major avenues around the city show as well. This capital city holds some 13 million people within its borders, and an uncounted floating population of several million adds strain to the very polluted city. Rapid growth has led to development of a master plan that will eliminate almost all of the old city's one-story housing and eventually replace it with high-rises.

SEOUL, SOUTH KOREA

Flattened in the 1950-53 Korean War, South Korea's capital now stands as an Asian giant of some 11 million people (left). A mere 25 miles from the border with archenemy North Korea, Seoul powers the nation's economy of steel, cars, electronics, agriculture, and fishing. This Landsat TM image shows the Han River running through the middle of the city (blue). Inchon, Seoul's port on the Yellow Sea, lies at far left. Red denotes vegetation.

TOKYO, JAPAN

This striking 3-D land-use map of the greater Tokyo area (below) looks west and shows the Choshi peninsula, at bottom, jutting into the Pacific Ocean. Tokyo Bay lies beyond the long arm of the Boso Peninsula, with Tokyo, in red, at the bay's head. Japan's capital merges with Yokohama to the southwest,

creating a megacity of about 30 million people. Nearly every structure in the urban area dates from this century. Tokyo suffered the Great Kanto Earthquake of 1923, then endured heavy bombing during World War II. Mount Fuji rises near the center of the image. O Shima island, a favorite with vacationers, sits south of Sagami Bay at far left. Beyond lie the Izu Peninsula and Suruga Bay.

AFRICA

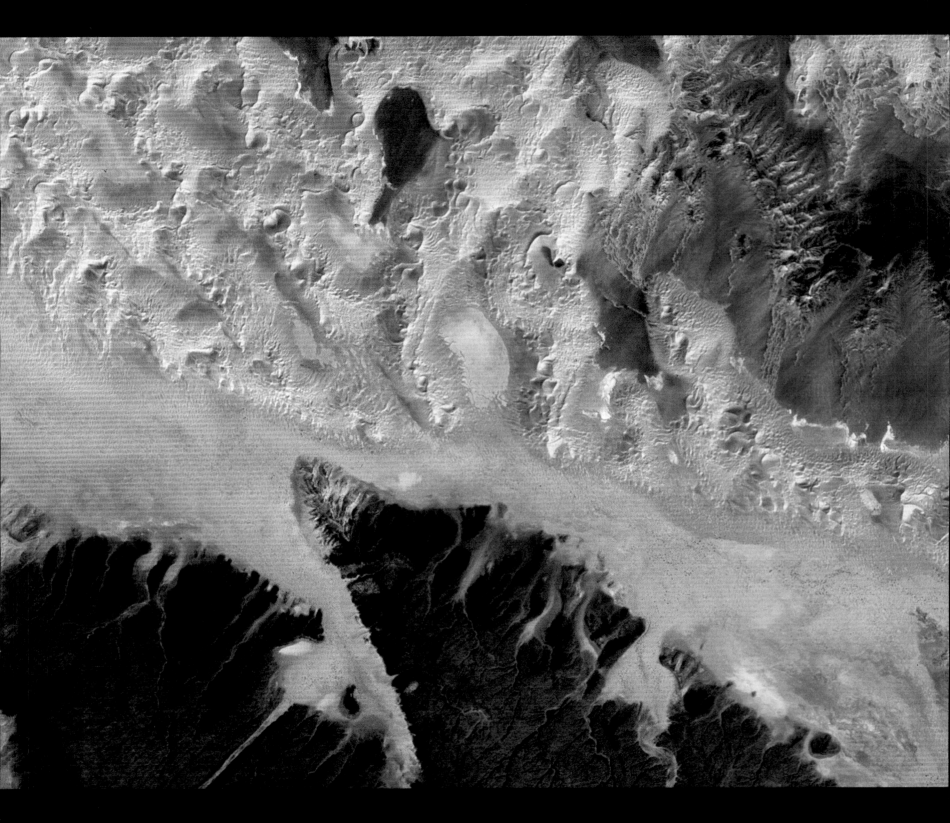

B irthplace of humanity and cradle of one of the Earth's greatest civilizations, Africa feels primal, a world somehow separate from the modern whirl of the late 20th century. Immense herds of antediluvian animals graze vast tropical savannas, while the desert sun bleaches ancient pyramids and temples. Huge lakes glimmer along the continent's eastern flank; balloon-sailed dhows catch breezes on the Nile River.

But this seemingly constant land is continually changing. The Sahara, sovereign of the northern third of the continent, pushes farther south, then recedes again; the Great Rift that threatens to pull apart Africa's eastern side contin- ues to widen; the now-dammed Nile, longest river in the world, grows more sluggish as it reaches its delta; and the tropical rain forests that green the center of the continent dwindle as more and more trees are cut down.

Today the place that European imperialists formerly called the "dark continent" steers by its own light. In these post-colonial decades, the people of Africa divide themselves among some 50 countries and converse in words from 1,000 different language groups. Most live as their ancestors did, subsisting as farmers on small plots of land. They pray for rain and hope that the seasons will cycle peacefully, trusting that the land will again sustain them.

THE SAHARA

Encompassing more than a third of the continent, the 3.5-million-square-mile Sahara holds North Africa in a tenacious desert grip. Though famous for its shifting sand seas, the chimerical Sahara consists mostly of gravel and stone, sometimes rising into formidable mountains, like Algeria's Tassili-n-Ajjer (above). At other points, the floor of this desert realm drops into depressions a hundred feet below sea level.

Tassili-n-Ajjer

ASIA

EUROPE

NORTH
ATLANTIC
OCEAN

Mediterranean Sea

Gulf of Sidra

Canary Islands

Cape
Verde

Senegal

Mauritania

S A H A R A

S A H E L

Great Western Erg

Great Eastern Erg

Ahaggar Mountains

Tibesti

Western
Desert

Libyan Desert

Eastern Desert

Nubian
Desert

Nile

Red Sea

Gulf of Aden

Somali Peninsula

-512 ft. -156 m
Lowest point
in Africa

Ethiopian
Highlands

Blue Nile

White Nile

Chari

Niger

Cameroon Mt.

Upper Guinea

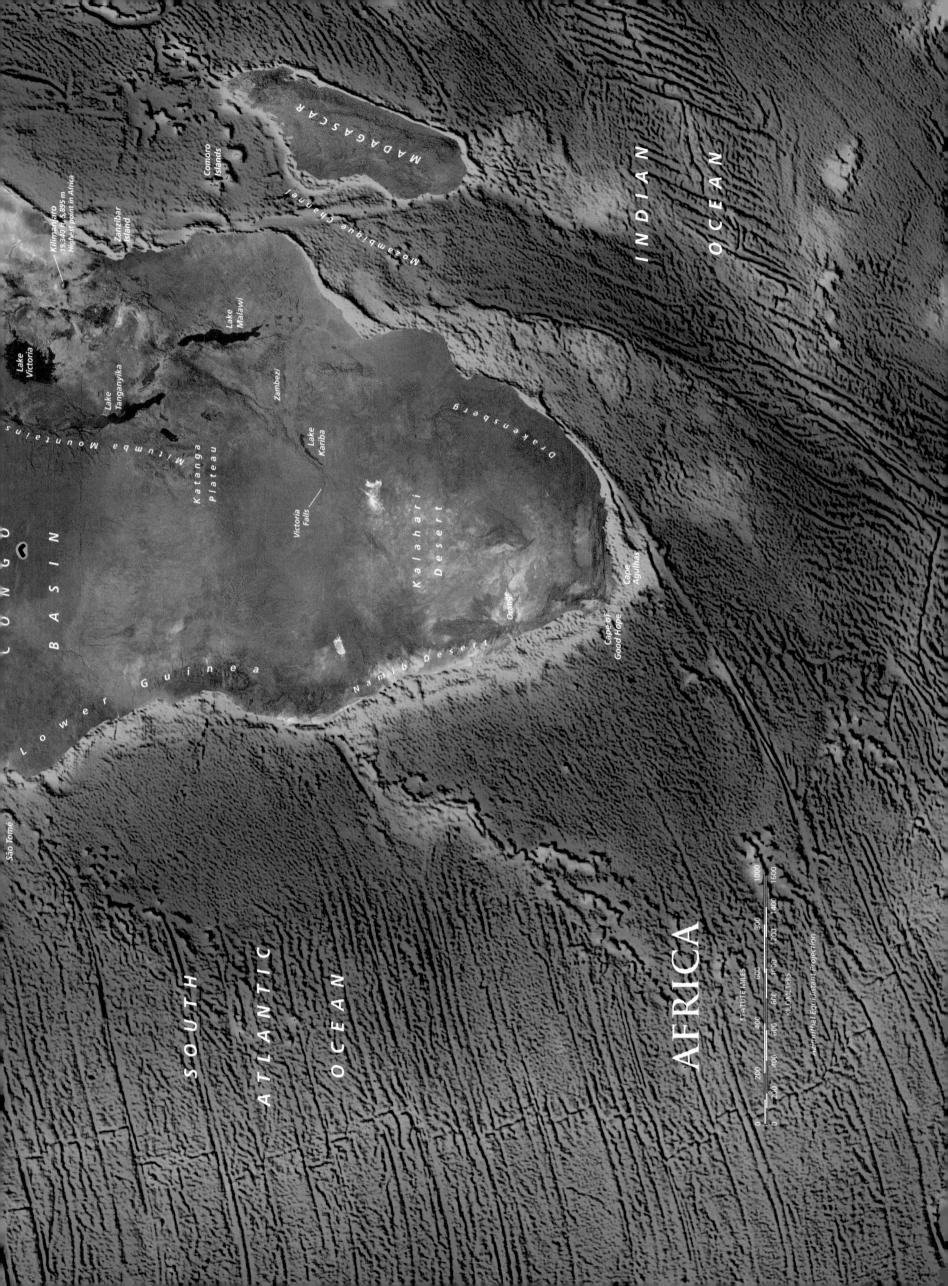

MADAGASCAR

Comoro
Islands

Mozambique Channel

Kilimanjaro
19,340 ft, 5,895 m.
Highest point in Africa

Zanzibar
Island

Lake
Malawi

Lake
Victoria

Lake
Tanganyika

Zambezi

Milumba Mountains

Lake
Kariba

Drakensberg

CONGO

BASIN

Katanga
Plateau

Victoria
Falls

Kalahari
Desert

Orange

Cape
Agulhas

São Tomé

Lower Guinea

Namib Desert

Cape of
Good Hope

SOUTH

ATLANTIC

OCEAN

INDIAN

OCEAN

AFRICA

STATUTE MILES
200   400   600   800   1000   1200   1400   1600
0
0   200   400   600   800   1000
KILOMETERS

Azimuthal Equidistant Projection

"Hail to you, O Nile! … Come to nourish Egypt! … Food provider, bounty maker, Who creates all that is good." So goes an ancient Egyptian paean to the Nile. For millions of contemporary Africans the river is still the "bounty maker." The enormous, north-flowing Nile encompasses a drainage basin of more than a million square miles and thousands of years of history. Its northern waters gave rise to one of the earliest and greatest civilizations. Even today, five millennia later, vestiges of ancient Egypt—unsurpassed pyramids, temples, and monuments—grace the riverscape.

In recent history, numerous explorers came in search of the Nile's source. But not until 1937 did a German adventurer, Dr. Burkhart Waldecker, discover that a spring in the Burundi hills formed the southernmost headwaters of the great river. From there, the Nile's waters twist through a web of tributaries, countries, cataracts, and the Aswan High Dam on their way to the Mediterranean Sea.

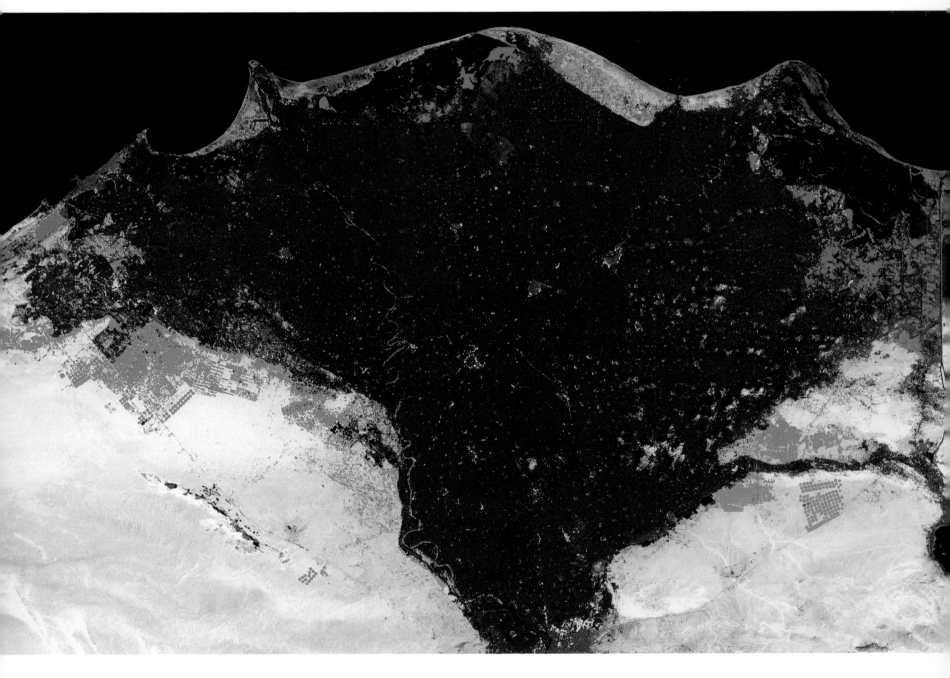

NILE DELTA

Scarlet cornucopia, the Nile Delta (above) fans out across 8,500 square miles of northern Egypt to create the most fertile lands in the country. Between Cairo and its conjunction with the Mediterranean, the Nile splits in two, with the Rosetta branch veining the western delta and the Damietta branch the east. This Landsat mosaic records land-use changes in the delta from 1972 to 1990. Yellow areas show the impact of urban expansion on agricultural lands. Light blue denotes now cultivated desert areas.

PYRAMIDS OF GIZA

A 1991 Russian image (left) looks down on the ancient glory of Giza—the Great Pyramid of Khufu (upper), Khafre's pyramid (middle), and Menkaure's pyramid (lower). Khufu's massive monument ranks as one of the Seven Wonders of the World. Built by Fourth Dynasty pharaohs at the edge of Egypt's Western Desert, the precisely constructed limestone monuments still stand after more than 4,500 years, fulfilling the ancient Egyptian entreaty to the gods: "May you cause to be enduring this pyramid … for ever and ever."

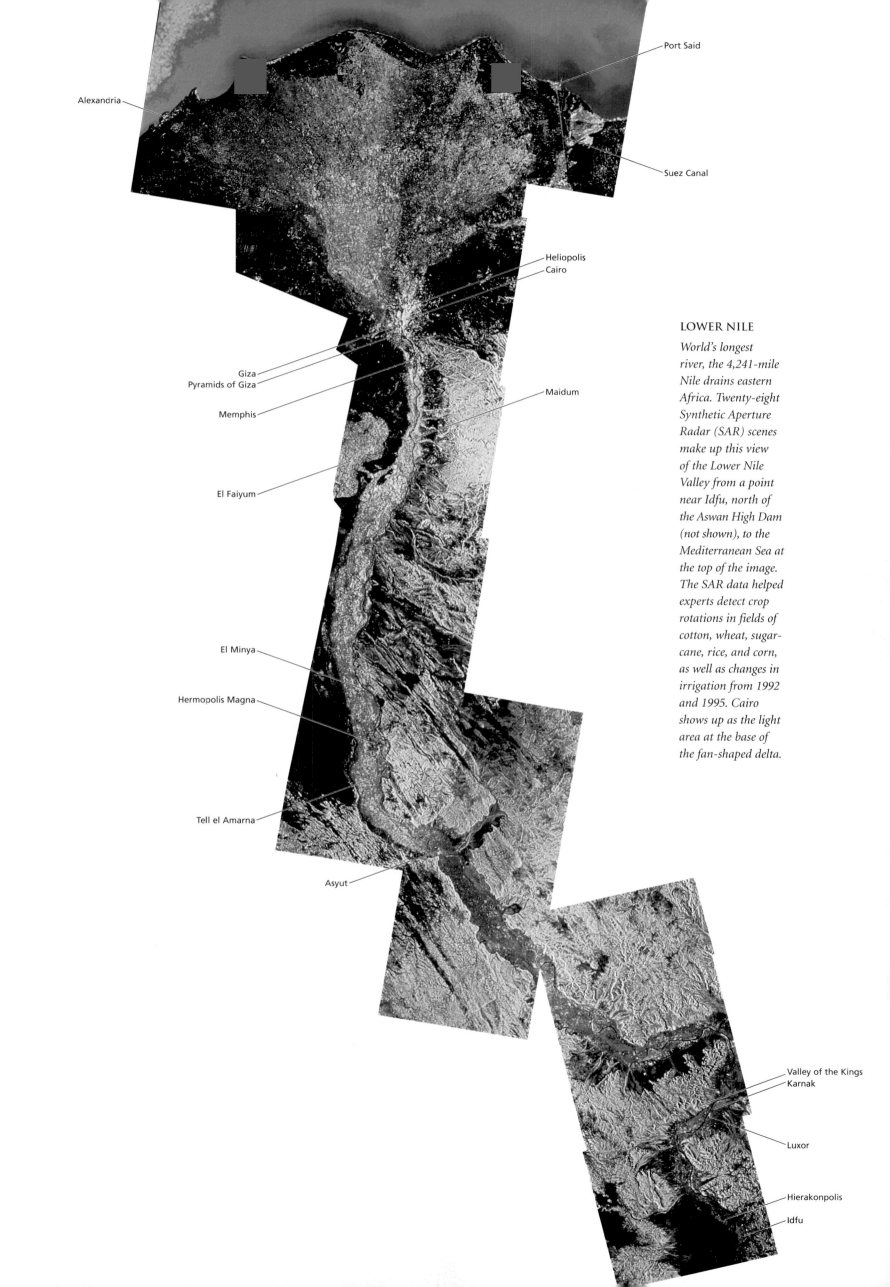

Alexandria

Port Said

Suez Canal

Heliopolis
Cairo

Giza
Pyramids of Giza

Memphis

Maidum

El Faiyum

El Minya

Hermopolis Magna

Tell el Amarna

Asyut

Valley of the Kings
Karnak

Luxor

Hierakonpolis

Idfu

LOWER NILE

World's longest river, the 4,241-mile Nile drains eastern Africa. Twenty-eight Synthetic Aperture Radar (SAR) scenes make up this view of the Lower Nile Valley from a point near Idfu, north of the Aswan High Dam (not shown), to the Mediterranean Sea at the top of the image. The SAR data helped experts detect crop rotations in fields of cotton, wheat, sugarcane, rice, and corn, as well as changes in irrigation from 1992 and 1995. Cairo shows up as the light area at the base of the fan-shaped delta.

Visitors to North Africa often find that the shifting sands of the Sahara evoke otherworldly visions. But East Africa, with its dramatic topography, also can claim some of the continent's most unforgettable landscapes. Africa's highest (below) and lowest (bottom) points are in the east. Its largest caldera (opposite) is here, too, along with impressive mountains, searing deserts, and great lakes.

The large number of extreme features and diverse landforms found in such a relatively small area results, in large part, from the East African Rift System, which extends from the Red Sea south to Mozambique. Active volcanoes rise in and near the rift, and earthquakes are common. Much of the rest of the continent is seismically quiet, as befits the enormous landmass that sat at the heart of the supercontinent Pangaea some 180 million years ago. Over eons, tectonic fracturing created today's other continental landmasses, leaving Africa as the only true relict of the ancient supercontinent.

KILIMANJARO

"As wide as all the world, great, high, and unbelievably white," Ernest Hemingway called Kilimanjaro (left), Africa's highest peak. The mountain's glaciated 19,340-foot western summit, Uhuru Peak, parallels a second summit, 16,889-foot Mawenzi, on the east. Actually a dormant volcano, Kilimanjaro lies near the Equator, its lower slopes cultivated by growers of coffee, vegetables, and grains. The mantle of sprawling savanna (red in this SPOT image) at its base has long been home to the pastoral Masai people.

NGORONGORO CRATER

Mosaic of East African diversity, this MSS image (opposite) centers around the great red spot of Ngorongoro Crater, Africa's largest caldera. The volcanic explosion that created the caldera, now a game preserve in northern Tanzania, occurred some three million years ago. But in 1966 its smaller, lake-filled neighbor to the north, Ol Doinyo Lengai, staged a violent outburst. To the west of Ngorongoro stretches the Serengeti Plain (blue-green). Lakes Eyasi and Manyara fill basins to the south; Lake Natron lies to north.

AFAR TRIANGLE

At a bend in the Horn of Africa, where the Gulf of Aden meets the Red Sea, the continent reaches its lowest point—Djibouti's Lake Assal, 512 feet below sea level (right). Known to geologists as the Afar Triangle, the pocket of Djibouti and Ethiopia shown in the image sits at the intersection of three faults in the Earth's crust. As the crust fractures and splits apart here, magma wells up and adds new land to the coast of Djibouti, making it, as one geologist quipped, "Africa's fastest growing nation."

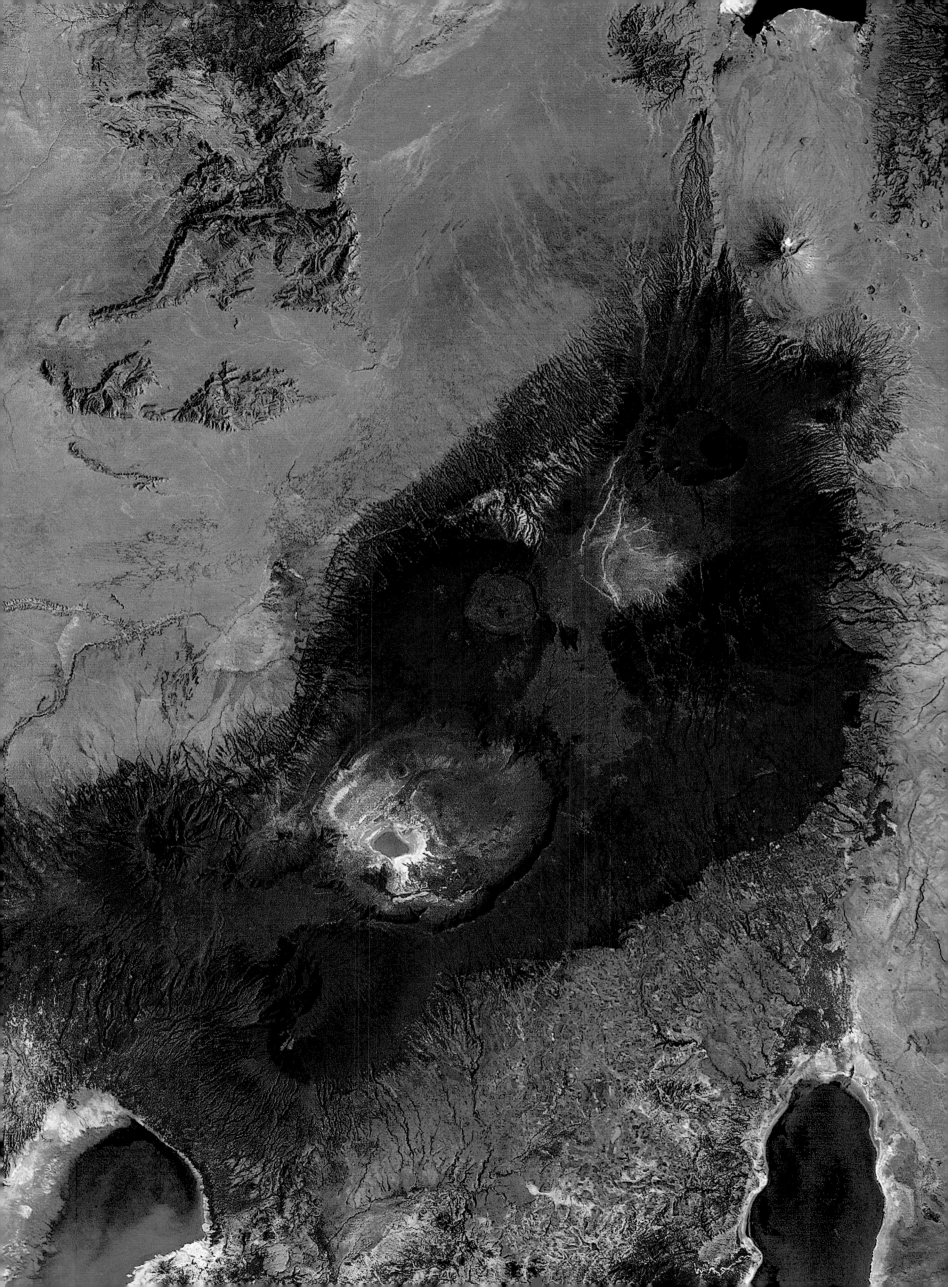

AFRICA · LANDFORMS

The Sahara's name comes from the Arabic word *sahra,* meaning "desert." The seemingly endless sands and the wild, austere beauty of the world's largest desert have long captivated the human imagination. Holding dominion over virtually all of northern Africa, the Sahara extends from the Atlantic Ocean, in the west, to the Red Sea, in the east.

Only an occasional oasis and the Nile regularly water this realm of sand.

When viewed from a space shuttle or from a satellite orbiting high above the continent, the desert becomes a composition as intricate as an Impressionist painting or a symphony with different movements. Great swaths of shifting dunes appear to float across vast, uninhabited wilderness;

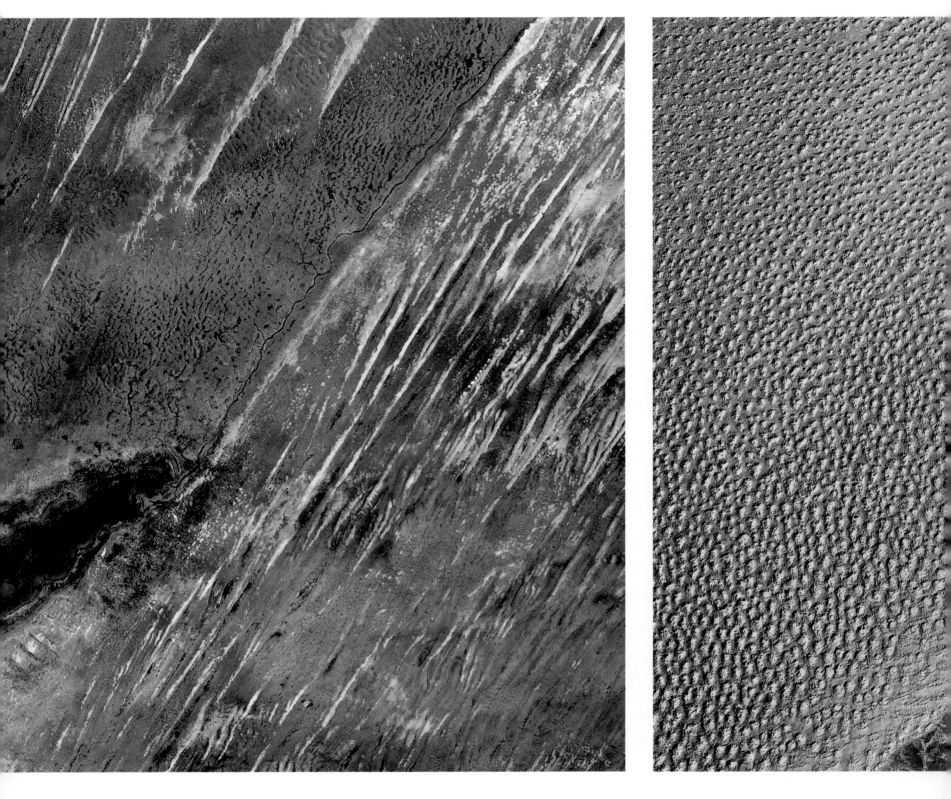

MAURITANIA

Ripples on the landscape of western Mauritania, linear dunes stencil a sand sea that stretches across this 1993 SPOT scene. Lake Rkiz forms the dark oval at lower left in the image. Southern Mauritania lies in a region known as the Sahel, a word meaning "shore" in Arabic. This semiarid belt marks the boundary between the Sahara and the southern part of the continent. Ranging from 200 to 700 miles wide, the Sahel grows and shrinks, responding to droughts, rains, and people-induced desertification.

ALGERIA, TUNISIA, AND LIBYA

In this MSS image, a golden quilt of star dunes spreads across three country borders in the Grand Erg Oriental, creating infinite patterns and endless barriers to travel. Throughout history, even intrepid nomads such as the camel-riding Tuareg have avoided these inhospitable spots by following trans-Sahara caravan routes like the one at lower right. Ergs contain merciless terrain, where sandstorms kick up suddenly, water appears mostly in mirages, daytime temperatures climb to deadly heights, and nights bring frigid discomfort.

a wind-patterned sand painting stretches to the horizon. While poets who gaze upon the desert might see exquisite abstractions, geologists can see identifiable formations. Earth scientists have classified the Sahara's landscapes into three major types: hamadas, or rocky wastelands; regs, or stretches of gravel and pebbles; and ergs, the sand seas featured below.

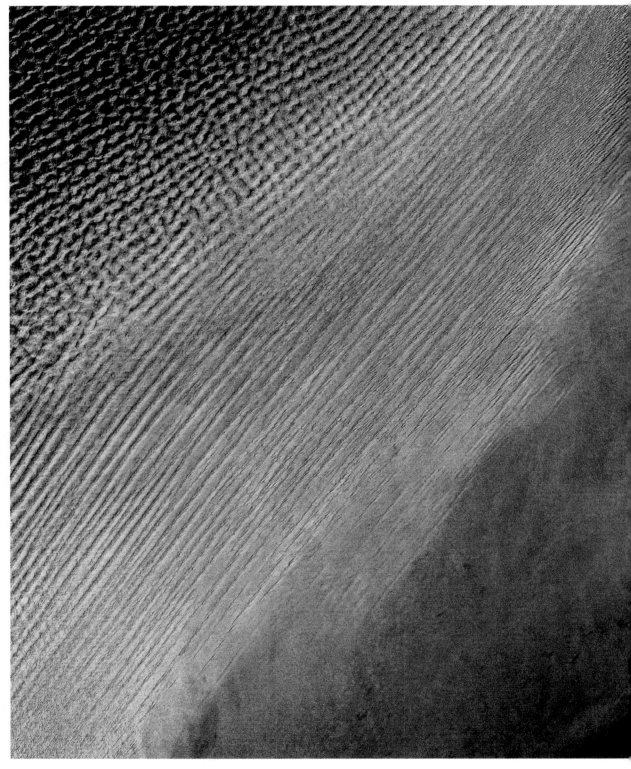

LIBYA

Long linear dunes stretch from lower left to upper right in this MSS image of the Sahra Marzuq, in southwest Libya. At lower right, dark bedrock appears beneath a thin layer of sand. Long-term analysis using satellite imagery helps scientists test the theory that linear dunes evolve into star dunes. Seasonal, multidirectional winds may have already begun shaping the field of dunes at upper left into star-shaped sand hills. In time, the dunes could measure a half mile to a mile across and reach heights of 300 to 650 feet.

AFRICA · LANDFORMS

Africa moves to very ancient rhythms. Seasonal winds rearrange its desert sands, and longed-for rains send herds of migratory animals moving back and forth across shrinking wildlands, searching for water holes and savannas still green with grasses. Water remains a prized commodity on this continent. The growing demands of an increasing human population exacerbate the water shortage and hasten desertification.

Ironically, the first humans in prehistoric Africa enjoyed a land and climate much more hospitable than Africans know today. In fact, both the Sahara and the Kalahari teemed with wildlife only 7,000 years ago. Will the forces of desertification that created them reverse? Or does the future hold more aridity?

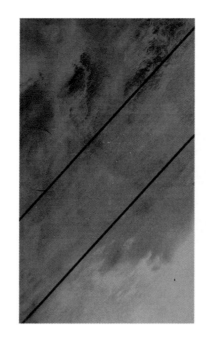

ANCIENT SAHARA RIVER SYSTEMS

Diagonals cutting across these images (left) outline the same 30-mile-wide, 180-mile-long area in the eastern Sahara. In the right-hand image, 1981 SIR-A radar penetrates some 16 feet below the sands to reveal ghostly marks in the subsurface rock. These remains of ancient river systems recall a wetter era in the Sahara.

LIBYA

Holding its own against the hot, intractable sands of the Sahara's Ubari Sand Sea, the Hamada Segher plateau (right) of southwestern Libya resembles an island in a windswept ocean of sand. A complex of rock— uplifted and exposed in places such as the plateau—underlies all of the Sahara. In fact, all of the Sahara's grains of sand formed when exposed rocks, over time, weathered to a fine texture. The dune formations in this image—linear dunes in the north and south, star dunes to the east and west—reflect prevailing wind patterns around the base of the plateau.

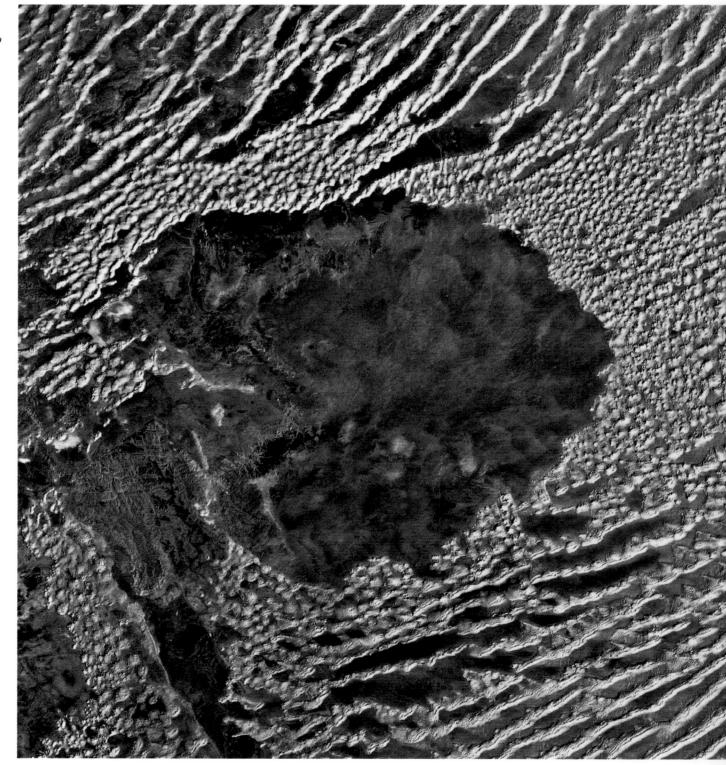

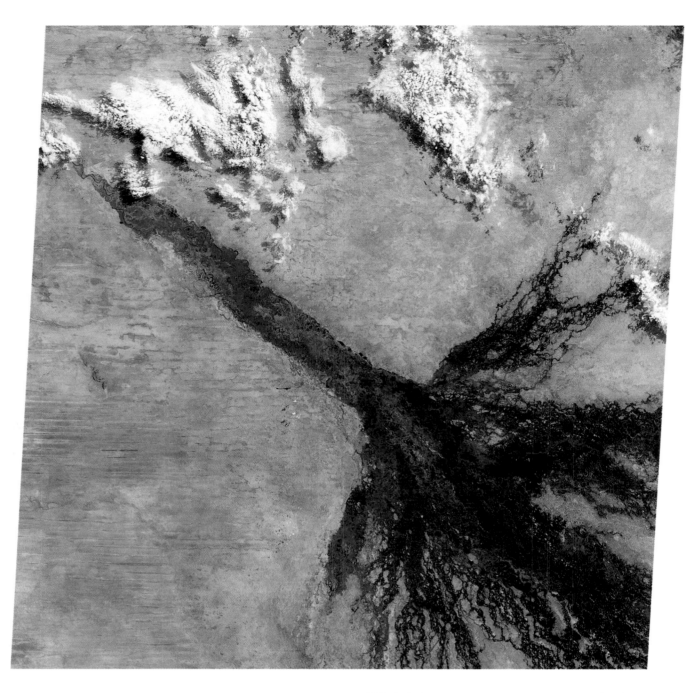

OKAVANGO DELTA

Creator of the world's largest inland delta, the Okavango River (above) ends in a 6,200-square-mile alluvial sprawl that covers Kalahari sands. Fed by October-to-March rains, the river rises in the Angola highlands to the north, weaves through Namibia, and terminates here in Botswana, where its waters inspire a seasonal celebration among wildlife. Great numbers of buffalo, elephants, zebras, antelope, and waterbirds materialize along the delta when the river's life-sustaining waters run high.

KALAHARI DESERT

Sands of the Kalahari (right) mark the border between Namibia and South Africa with an intricate, rarely changing pattern of dune fields, visible at upper right in this 1986 SPOT image. A longitudinal dune belt, deposited perhaps 10,000 years ago, lies farther to the west. Streambeds that run with water during seasonal rains weave through the lower left and upper right of the image. The highly reflective white areas indicate salt pans that fill briefly with the shallow waters of strongly saline lakes during the rainy season.

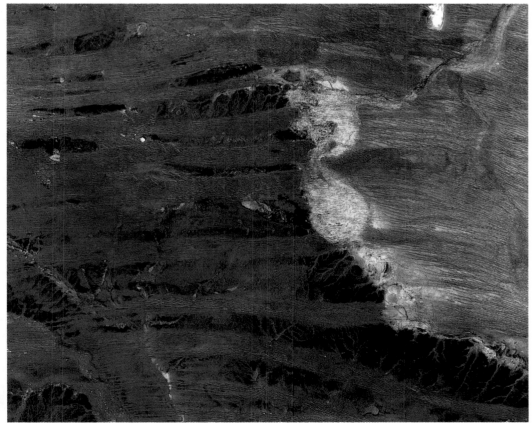

Africa's islands bear the clear imprint of both nature and humans: Most are volcanic; most fell under the sway of European colonialism. In the Atlantic, a number of island chains off the northwest coast were once under Portuguese dominion; a few still are.

The Portuguese presence in West Africa began in the 1400s with Prince Henry the Navigator. His sea captains ventured as far south as present-day Sierra Leone, establishing a lucrative trade in gold and slaves. Other Europeans followed, claiming islands and mainland territories as colonies of empire. Some claims remain, as in the case of Spain's Canary Islands.

Islands off East Africa's coast have had a somewhat different history. Here, the French exerted the strongest claim, controlling the rich spice and perfume islands of Réunion, Madagascar, and the Comoros. The French era, as well as colonialism in general, has died a slow death over the past few decades, and newly independent countries have often found themselves without the political or technological infrastructure they need to prosper.

GRAN CANARIA

This 1993 SPOT image shows 529-square-mile Gran Canaria (right), the third largest of Spain's seven Canary Islands. Volcanic in origin, like the rest of this chain off Africa's northwest coast, the island slopes precipitously to the Atlantic from mountains more than a mile high.

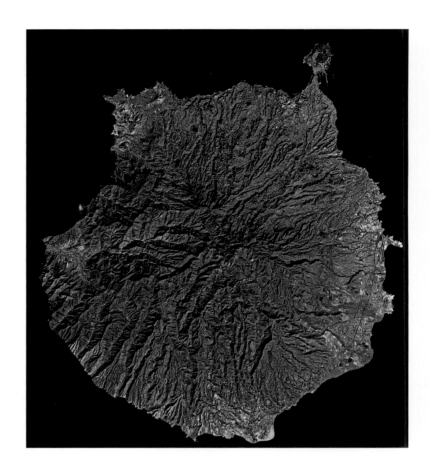

MAYOTTE, COMORO ISLANDS

One of the four Comoro Islands dotting the northern Mozambique Channel, independent-minded Mayotte (left) remains a French territory, although its sister islands declared independence from France in 1975. A volcanic mountain chain (red) runs across the interior of the island, creating fertile soil in which farmers grow vanilla beans, coffee beans, and ylang-ylang trees. These trees produce flowers used to make a perfume.

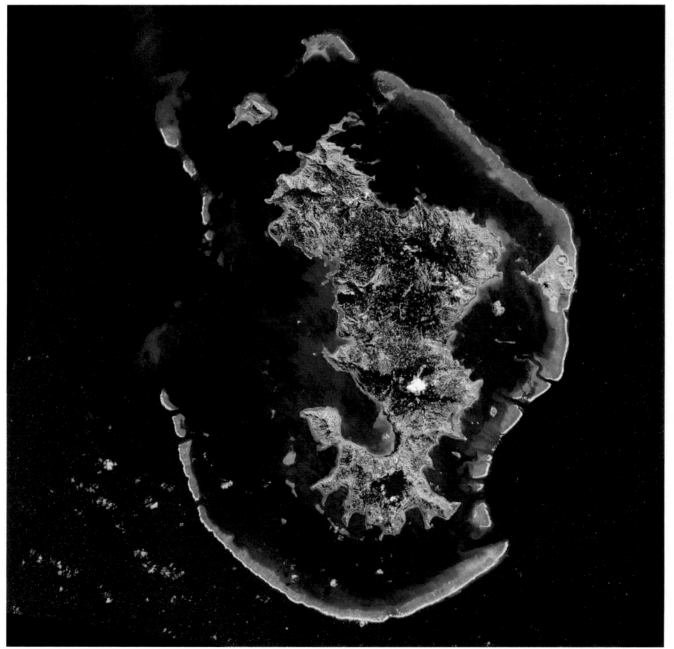

MADAGASCAR

Earth's fourth largest island, Madagascar broke away from the African mainland some 160 million years ago and now lies 250 miles to the southeast, in the Indian Ocean. Land of lemurs, the giant elephant bird (now extinct), and other exotic wildlife, the thousand-mile-long island holds unique fauna and flora. The Landsat mosaic at right provided information used to establish and manage a network of parks and reserves that will protect this great biological treasure.

Gran Canaria

Mayotte, Comoro Islands

Madagascar

AFRICA · FORCES OF NATURE

Though rich in natural resources, Africa remains the poorest continent in the world. The majority of its peoples endure perpetual poverty, undernourishment, and disease. A slight shift in the always precarious natural balance—frequent sandstorms or a major drought, such as the Sahel drought in the 1970s and '80s—can take an immense human toll, creating famine and more disease. Parasites, rickets, and beriberi threaten the malnourished; many Africans also suffer from widespread malaria and sleeping sickness, insect-borne diseases now targeted by satellite technology.

In the case of sleeping sickness, vegetation maps developed from satellite imagery can indicate areas where tsetse flies, carriers of the disease, are likely to live. For malaria, satellite monitoring helps to pinpoint flooded pastures and scrublands where mosquitoes often breed. Already under way, such applications remain experimental and, unfortunately, prohibitively expensive for the nations that need such help.

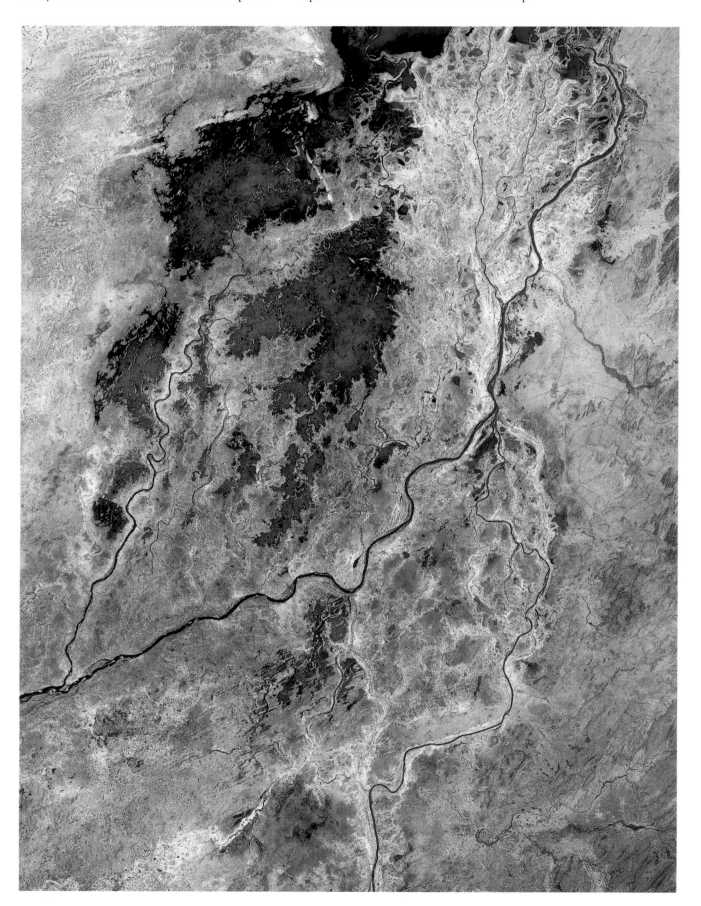

TSETSE FLIES

Longtime scourge of Africa and carrier of the dread sleeping sickness, the tsetse fly plagues central and southern sections of the continent. This 1986 TM image (left) shows an affected area in Mali, where the Niger and Bani Rivers meet.

Well-watered areas attract the animals whose blood the flies feed on, blood that may be infested with parasites that destroy red blood cells. The resulting anemia causes lack of energy, extreme drowsiness, and slow death.

Bites from flies transmit the parasites from host to host, infecting wild animals, cattle, and humans. Thousands of people succumb to the illness each year, but major outbreaks, such as one that hit southern Sudan in 1997, periodically occur. If doctors detect the disease before it enters the central nervous system, they can treat it. But in poverty-locked rural Africa, such detection remains rare.

A ban on cattle raising, a traditional preventive measure against the disease, has its own side effect. In malnourished Africa, it means even less protein on tables.

170

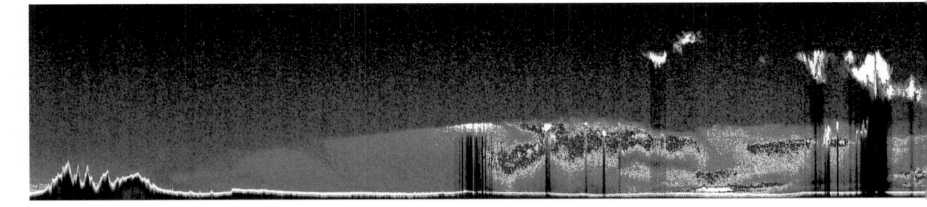

SAHARA DUST

Colorful plume of dust waves above the Sahara in an image showing activity in the Sahara dust layer (above). Hovering as much as four miles up, this layer carries dust over the Atlas Mountains, at left in the image, across the Atlantic Ocean, and to the Caribbean. As human activity creates more airborne dust, the phenomenon could spawn critical climatic changes.

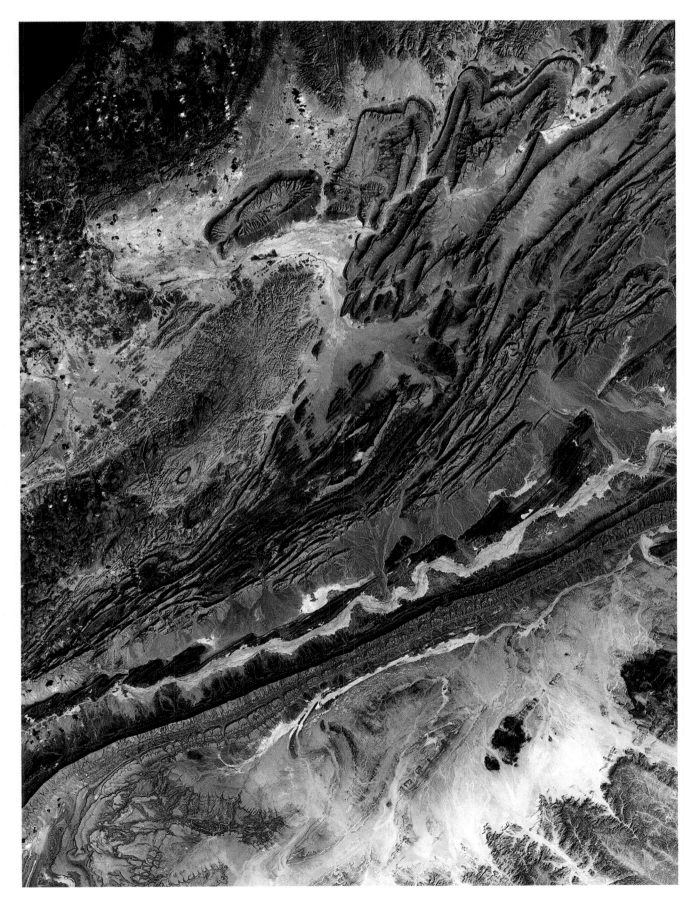

ATLAS MOUNTAINS

Colliding continents created the fantastic folds of the Atlas Mountain system (left). Millions of years ago, the tectonic plates carrying Africa and Eurasia began to converge, giving rise to Africa's Atlas and Spain's Baetic Mountains. The dry climate and the composition of the rock reduced erosion's impact in Morocco. The original fold belts of the Anti Atlas range show clearly in this Landsat MSS image. At the bottom of the image, the Sahara sweeps south.

AFRICA · FORCES OF NATURE

An enormous crack in the Earth's crust, the East African Rift System threatens to break the continent in two. Curving 3,500 miles along the eastern side of Africa, the Great Rift measures as much as 56 miles across and 6,500 feet deep. As tectonic activity continues to widen and lengthen it along parallel faults, its floor will steadily drop; in time, the rift may connect with the ocean and fill with water. Over millions of years, such crustal spreading caused the Arabian plate to separate from North Africa, creating the Red Sea.

Should the East African Rift be inundated, paleontologists would lose one of their most valuable laboratories, for it is in the rift that they are finding evidence of humankind's earliest ancestors. At such now legendary locations as Olduvai Gorge, between Lakes Natron and Eyasi (opposite), and Koobi Fora, at the northeast end of Lake Turkana (below), the Leakey family of paleontologists have uncovered some of the oldest skeletal fossils of human predecessors.

The rifting process itself helped preserve these vital remnants. As tectonic movements convulsed the surface of the Earth, African lakes were created, and their waters, in turn, fed streams that deposited layers of sediment. These sediments, particularly preserving calcium carbonate, encased whatever lay in their paths, including the now treasured remains of australopithecines—protohominids who inhabited the area at least 4.1 million years ago—and the first true hominids, who evolved here about 2.5 million years ago.

FEBRUARY 1, 1973

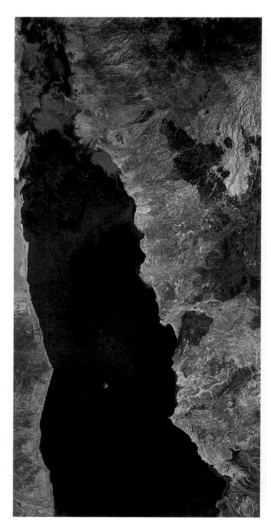

JANUARY 1, 1979

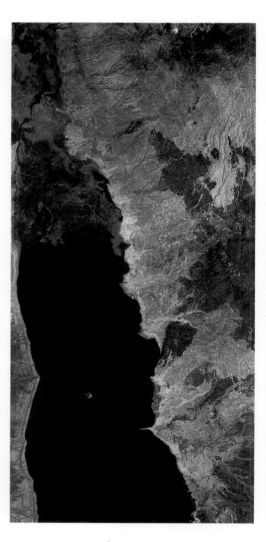

JANUARY 12, 1989

LAKE TURKANA

Situated in a basin sunk between parallel faults, northern Kenya's Lake Turkana lies along the eastern branch of Africa's rift system. The area's sparse vegetation allows satellite imagery to capture clearly the fault lines and to monitor the growing delta of the Omo River, feeding into the lake from the north. Normally the river provides the 154-mile-long lake with 80 percent of its fresh water, but dropping water levels have shrunk the lake and exposed more of the delta. Turkana has been shrinking for millions of years.

EAST AFRICAN RIFT SYSTEM

East Africa's Great Rift buckles, twists, and cleaves the landscape for 3,500 miles, from Mozambique in the south to the Red Sea and Gulf of Aden in the north. Commonly called the Great Rift, this long scar on Earth's face actually comprises an enormous system of rifts. Here in East Africa, tectonic forces cause the planet's crust, or outermost layer, to spread or split apart. As divergence occurs, blocks of crust sink between parallel faults and form depressions.

A complex system, the Great Rift divides into two branches. The western branch, marked by a dark blue-black line of lakes, curves south to Lake Malawi, along the borders of Mozambique, Malawi, and Tanzania. Northwest of Malawi, the 4,820-foot-deep Lake Tanganyika, second only to Russia's Lake Baikal in depth, fills a plunging depression caused by the rifting process. The rift's eastern branch, punctuated by shallow alkaline lakes and volcanoes such as Kilimanjaro, shows less definitively in this satellite image. But its remarkably pronounced escarpment perhaps forms the most famous part of the Great Rift.

In the north, Ethiopia's crumpled highlands and Afar Triangle also result from the rifting process. If spreading continues, the far eastern Horn of Africa, which occupies its own tectonic plate, could separate from the continent and become another island in the Indian Ocean, as Madagascar (visible in lower right corner) did some 160 million years ago.

War, pestilence, and drought have taken a heavy toll throughout humankind's long history on the African continent. And the creation of nations in recent decades has only exacerbated many of Africa's problems. In the semiarid Sahel, the cross-continental band that separates the Sahara from the rest of Africa, national borders have forced once nomadic populations into semi-sedentary lives. Now, their crops and cattle strip soils and abet the process of desertification going on throughout Africa.

Nationhood has also done little to quell age-old ethnic hatreds. Civil wars based more on hatreds than on political beliefs have ravaged populations in the last half century. In Rwanda and Burundi alone, more than a million people have died in such conflicts in less than four decades. The wars have caused displacement of people into massive refugee camps plagued by famine and disease. Such crises inevitably disrupt productivity, and with its growing population, Africa is losing ground in the effort to feed its people. Between 1961 and 1995, the continent's per capita food production dropped by 12 percent, despite better agricultural techniques.

The situation is far from hopeless, however. A wealth of mineral resources underlies Africa, much of it still awaiting an infrastructure that will support efficient mining. Growing environmental consciousness, another hopeful sign, has led to the creation of parks and preserves dedicated to protecting one of Africa's greatest natural resources: its unparalleled wildlife.

Virunga Mountains
Refugee Camps

REFUGEE CAMPS, 1994

Exodus of unprecedented proportions: In a 24-hour period in early August 1994, a quarter million Rwandan refugees fled into northwestern Tanzania's Ngara District. Their settlement, Benako, became the largest refugee camp in the world. Quickly deforested to meet the need for fuel and firewood, Benako shows up as the large light-colored patch in the top half of an August 1994 image (above). The ongoing genocide between rival Hutu and Tutsi forces fuels the ethnic unrest that has gripped the region for decades.

REFUGEE CAMPS, 1996

By 1996, regional unrest had swelled Tanzania's camps with refugees not only from Rwanda but also from neighboring Burundi and Zaire. Workers sent by the United Nations High Commissioner for Refugees helped Tanzania cope with the influx of refugees. Growing areas of deforestation make the impact of the makeshift "cities" obvious in this July 1996 image. Almost half a million refugees from Rwanda returned home in July, but Zaireans and Burundis continued to pour into the camps.

VIRUNGA MOUNTAINS

Surrounded by deforested lands (purple), central Africa's volcanic Virunga Mountains (right) curve through the center of a planimetric radar image. In the southern part of the range, the forests seethe with activity as endangered mountain gorillas, farmers, and war-ravaged exiles compete to survive. To get firewood for fuel and clear land for banana plantations, the people denude gorilla habitat. In the 3-D image (above) green areas indicate forests; brown, lava from an eruption; and blue, disturbed cultivated areas.

AGRICULTURAL FIRES

Red band made by slash-and-burn agriculture extends across the width of Africa and stains the continent's interior (above). The ancient technique of clearing forests for cropland by slashing trees, then burning them, quickly depletes the soil, requiring additional clearing. Overgrazing and cutting forests for firewood have also increased the desertification of sub-Saharan Africa. In the far south, climate changes may bring about a northward shift of the rain belt, increasing aridity at the continent's southern tip.

CASABLANCA, MOROCCO

Exotic Casablanca faces the Atlantic Ocean, as shown in this 1978 MSS image. Just 200 miles from the tip of Spain, in Europe, Morocco's largest city retains a rich mix of Berber, Arabic, Jewish, and French influences. Already a major commercial center by the 13th century, the North African city took its current shape in the middle of the 18th century. Along with much of the rest of Morocco, Casablanca came under French control in 1912. When the country gained its independence in 1956, Casablanca became the major exporter of Moroccan phosphate deposits.

TRIPOLI, LIBYA

Ancient by any standard, Tripoli (below) has occupied its rocky promontory in the Mediterranean Sea ever since Phoenicians founded it in the seventh century B.C. Now Libya's capital, largest city, and chief port, it overlooks a protected harbor less than 300 miles from Italian ports. Italians, in fact, ruled Tripoli in the first part of the 20th century. Following the Libyan oil boom of the 1950s and '60s, the city began to experience a rapid growth in population and development. This SPOT image made above northwestern Libya in 1993 reveals urban sprawl reaching from the sea into the desert. The breakwater protecting Tripoli's busy harbor appears at top center in the image.

ALGIERS, ALGERIA

Situated at the western edge of the Bay of Algiers (top center in this 1988 SPOT image), Algeria's capital city derives its name from the Arabic word for "island"—al'Jaza'ir—a reference to the outcroppings of rock in the bay. The Mitidja Plain, where Algeria concentrates almost half the country's industrial force, buffers the busy port on the southeast. Like Tripoli, in Libya, the city of Algiers owes its origins to Phoenician traders who colonized the coast of North Africa more than 2,000 years ago. In time, Romans also built a town on the strategic site. The Ottoman Turks ruled the region from the middle of the 16th century until the French invasion of 1830. The Turks built the city's famous old citadel, or Casbah. Today nearly two million people reside in Algiers.

CAIRO, EGYPT

Sea of humanity amid a great sea of sand, Cairo's 13 million souls live with the Sahara at their flanks (right). This Thematic Mapper image, made on July 2, 1984, shows the desert in light shades of brown. The deep reddish brown color shows vegetation along the Nile; the river itself appears as a long dark thread, which seems to unravel as it flows north through the wide delta. Since the time of the pharaohs, this strategic site at the junction of Upper Egypt's Nile Valley and the Nile Delta of Lower Egypt has held a major city. Modern Cairo traces its origins to the Fatimid Arabs who brought it to glory a little more than a thousand years ago. The largest city on the continent, Cairo founders under the weight of its own enormous size. And yet it remains the intellectual and cultural capital of the Arab world.

CAPE TOWN, SOUTH AFRICA

Wedged into the spectacular peninsula on the southwestern corner of the continent, Cape Town (at the center of this 3-D SPOT image) sweeps along the edge of Table Bay. Its signature peak—Table Mountain—rises 3,567 feet at its back, with the peaks of the Twelve Apostles extending along the Atlantic coast (upper left). Seat of South Africa's Parliament, the city of two million people owes its prosperity to its shipping facilities and ranks as the world's largest exporter of diamonds. The Dutch originally settled the Cape Town area in 1652, but the British occupied the town in 1795. In the mid to late 20th century, Cape Town, along with the rest of South Africa, suffered under the racially discriminatory policies of apartheid. When apartheid ended in 1994, so did the enforced segregation of the city.

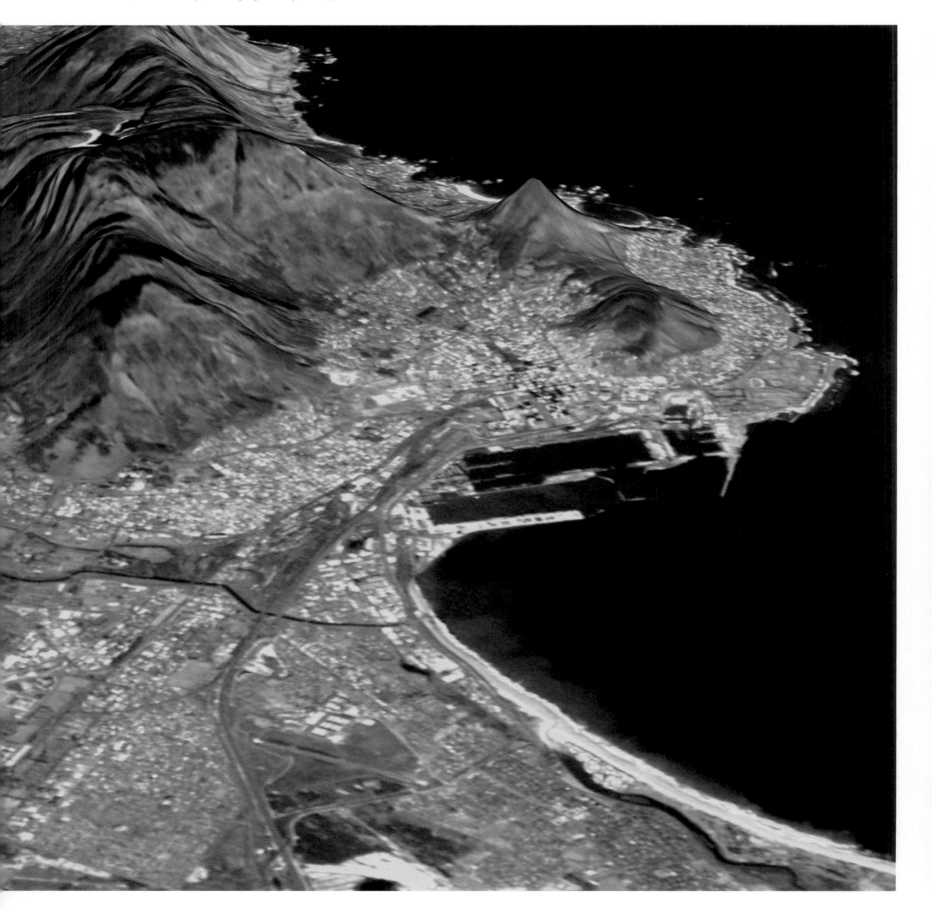

KINSHASA, DEM. REP. OF THE CONGO

Cupped by the Congo River's wide Pool Malebo, Kinshasa appears in the upper right corner of this 1997 TM image. Capital of the Democratic Republic of the Congo (formerly Zaire), the city sits at the nation's western border and just across the river from Brazzaville, the capital of neighboring Congo. Though Kinshasa's streets exhibit both wealth and poverty, and a military-based government claims power, the city nonetheless supports a vibrant popular and intellectual culture that influences much of the continent.

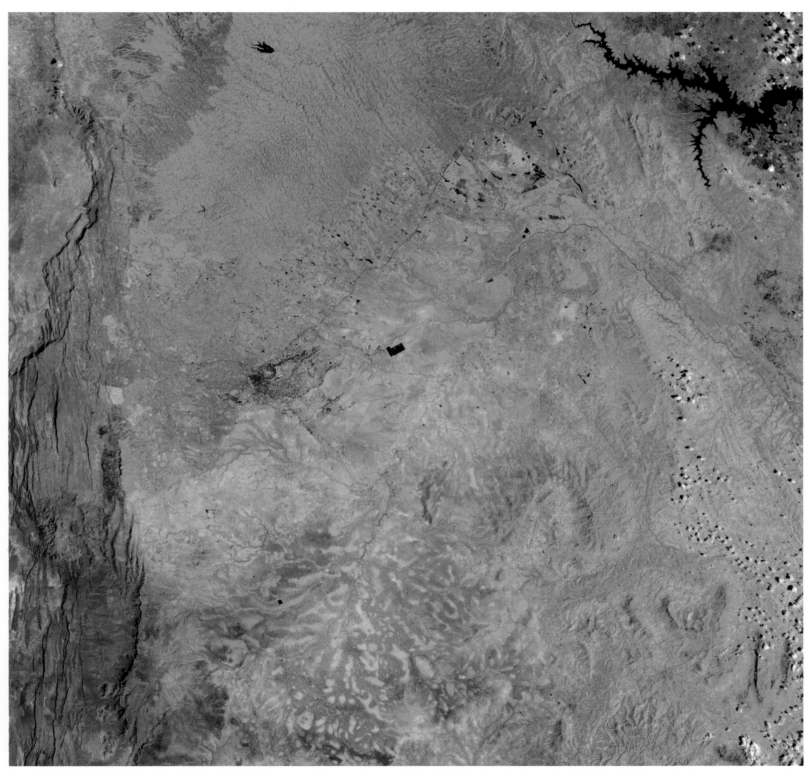

NAIROBI, KENYA

Kenya's capital city, Nairobi lies just a degree south of the Equator and at the edge of the country's agricultural heartland, which shows as a brown sprawl across the left center of this 1995 TM image. Less than ten miles to the south, wild animals roam Nairobi National Park. The city occupies two distinct topographies: In the west, it stretches across part of the eastern branch of the Great Rift Valley. The city's southern and eastern parts sprawl across the Athi Plains and River. No more than a British colonial railroad town at the beginning of the 20th century, Nairobi burgeoned into a major urban center after Kenya gained its independence in 1964.

AUSTRALIA & NEW ZEALAND

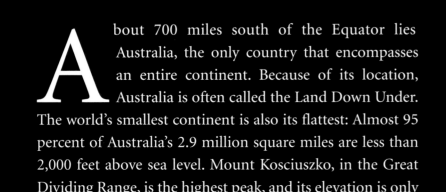

About 700 miles south of the Equator lies Australia, the only country that encompasses an entire continent. Because of its location, Australia is often called the Land Down Under. The world's smallest continent is also its flattest: Almost 95 percent of Australia's 2.9 million square miles are less than 2,000 feet above sea level. Mount Kosciuszko, in the Great Dividing Range, is the highest peak, and its elevation is only

7,310 feet—half the height of the Matterhorn, in Europe.

Australia is second to Antarctica as the world's driest continent. A third of it is desert, and another third is a vast steppe. Australians call this area the outback. It stretches across most of western Australia and portions of central Australia, then gradually fades away before reaching the Great Dividing Range in Queensland. The range is a chain of weathered mountains running along the east and southeast

coasts. Sandwiched between them and the Pacific Ocean is most of the country's fertile land.

By comparison, Australia's eastern neighbor is mountainous and relatively temperate. Sixteen peaks in New Zealand's Southern Alps reach above 10,000 feet. As much as 260 inches of rain drench the area around Milford Sound in Fiordland National Park, but the national average ranges

GREAT BARRIER REEF

Largest structure ever built by living creatures, the Great Barrier Reef lies off Australia's northeast coast. In the image above, turquoise identifies parts of the reef between Cape Bedford and Port Douglas, Queensland, at lower right. The 1,250-mile-long reef formed over millions of years from the skeletons of tiny marine animals. Some 400 coral species and 1,500 species of colorful fish

Great Barrier Reef

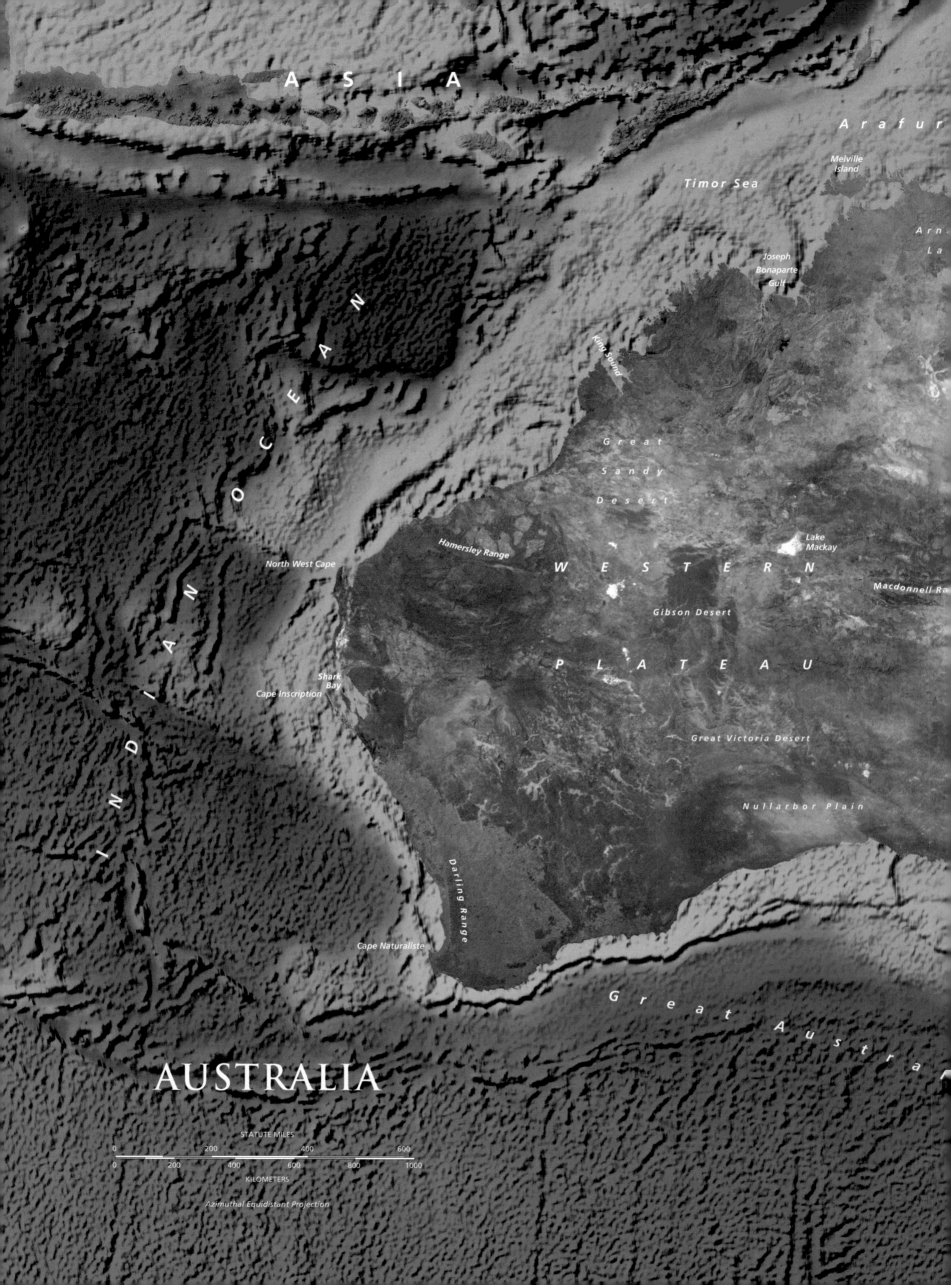

A S I A

Arafur

Timor Sea

Melville
Island

Arn
La

Joseph
Bonaparte
Gulf

King Sound

Great

Sandy

Desert

Lake
Mackay

Hamersley Range

W E S T E R N

Macdonnell Ra

North West Cape

Gibson Desert

P L A T E A U

Shark
Bay

Cape Inscription

Great Victoria Desert

Nullarbor Plain

Darling Range

Cape Naturaliste

G r e a t   A u s t r a

AUSTRALIA

I N D I A N   O C E A N

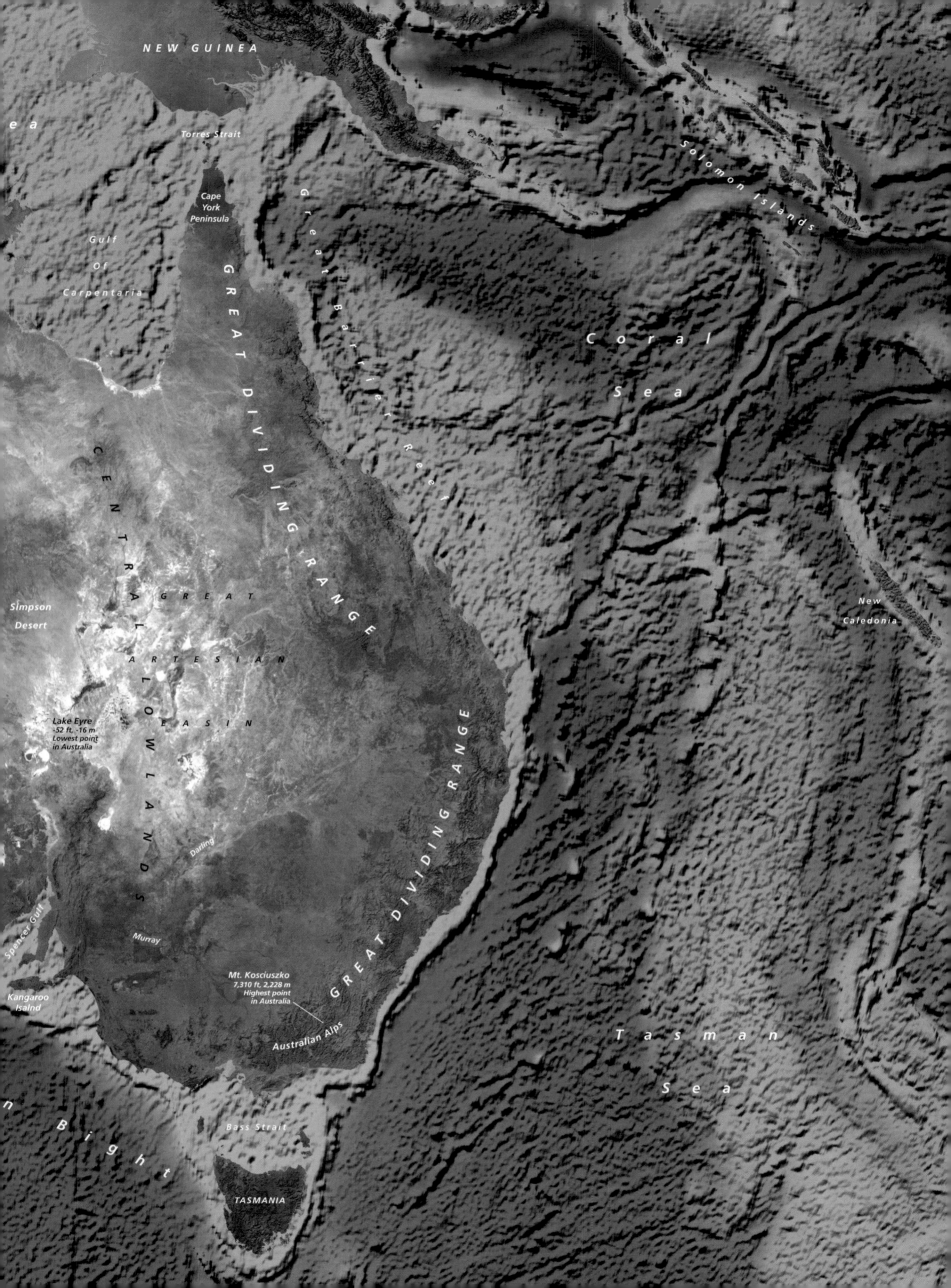

NEW GUINEA

Torres Strait

Cape
York
Peninsula

Gulf

Of

Carpentaria

GREAT DIVIDING RANGE

Great Barrier Reef

Solomon Islands

C o r a l

S e a

CENTRAL

G R E A T

Simpson
Desert

A R T E S I A N

New
Caledonia

Lake Eyre
-52 ft, -16 m
Lowest point
in Australia

L O W L A N D S

B A S I N

GREAT DIVIDING RANGE

Darling

Spencer Gulf

Murray

Mt. Kosciuszko
7,310 ft, 2,228 m
Highest point
in Australia

Kangaroo
Isalnd

Australian Alps

T a s m a n

S e a

Bass Strait

Bight

n

ea

TASMANIA

I N D O N E S *

Araf

Timor Sea

Darwin • Oenpelli
        • Jabiru

Pine Creek
        Daly • Katherine

                    Roper

Wyndham • Ord
    Kununurra   Victoria

                        Newc
                        Wate

• Derby
    Fitzroy • Fitzroy Crossing • Halls Creek

Broome •

Lagrange •   Tennant Cree

                                NORTHERN

Port Hedland •

Dampier • • Roebourne • Marble Bar
    Fortescue   DeGrey

                    Oakover   A U S T

• Onslow

Exmouth •   Alice Springs •

        • Tom Price
        Ashburton • Newman   A U S T

                • Savory Creek   • Yulara

Gascoyne   W E S T E R N   A U S T R A L I A

Carnarvon •

Denham •   • Meekatharra • Wiluna

Murchison

        • Mount Magnet   S O U T H

• Mullewa   Leonora • • Laverton

Geraldton •

Dongara •

• Wubin   Kalgoorlie •   • Rawlinna

        • Southern Cross Kambalda •   Eucla Motel •   Cedu
        • Merredin
Perth ⊛ • Northam
Rockingham • Kwinana   • Norseman
Mandurah
                Blackwood
Bunbury •   • Esperance

    • Manjimup

        • Albany

                        G r e a t   A u s t r a l i

AUSTRALIA

INDIAN OCEAN

STATUTE MILES

0   200   400   600

0   200   400   600   800   1000

KILOMETERS

Azimuthal Equidistant Projection

PAPUA NEW GUINEA

140°
150°
160°

A

Torres Strait

SOLOMON ISLANDS

10°

Nhulunbuy

Gulf
of
Carpentaria

Weipa

Alyangula

Aurukun

Coen

Coral Sea

CORAL SEA

Kowanyama

Cooktown

ISLANDS

Burketown

Cairns

Normanton

Innisfail

Georgetown

Camooweal

Townsville
Ayr

TERRITORY
(Australia)

TORY

Mount Isa

Cloncurry

Charters
Towers

Bowen

Dajarra

Hughenden

QUEENSLAND

Winton

Mackay

20°

ALIA

Longreach

Clermont

New
Caledonia
(France)

Emerald

Rockhampton
Mount Morgan

TROPIC OF CAPRICORN

Birdsville

Gladstone

Bundaberg

RALIA

Quilpie

Charleville

Maryborough

Roma

Gympie

Lake
Eyre
North

Cunnamulla

Toowoomba

Maroochydore
Caloundra

L. Eyre
South

Brisbane
Ipswich

Marree

Goondiwindi

Gold Coast

Leigh Creek

Collarenebri

Lismore

Port Augusta

NEW SOUTH WALES

Moree

Grafton

Whyalla

Broken Hill

Bourke

Walgett

Armidale

Coffs Harbour

Port Pirie

Tamworth

Wallaroo

Dubbo

Taree

Port Macquarie

Adelaide

Mildura

Cessnock
Kurri Kurri-Weston

Maitland
Newcastle

rt
coln

Orange

Bathurst

Budgewoi
Gosford

Griffith

Lithgow
Katoomba

Richmond

SYDNEY

Goulburn

Wollongong

Wagga Wagga

Canberra

Nowra

Horsham

Shepparton

Albury
Wodonga

AUSTRALIAN
CAPITAL
TERRITORY

Queanbeyan

Cooma

Mount
Gambier

VICTORIA

Bendigo

Wangaratta

Ballarat

Sunbury

Warrnambool

Melton

MELBOURNE

Colac

Geelong

Moe

Sale

Traralgon
Morwell

Bight

Bass Strait

Tasman Sea

30°

Burnie

Devonport

St. Helens

Launceston

Queenstown

TASMANIA

Hobart

40°

140°
150°
160°
170°

Several hundred million years ago Australia was one of the northernmost portions of a vast continent that covered much of the Southern Hemisphere. Geologists say that over the centuries the continent drifted across the South Pole and pulled much of what would later become Australia south of the Equator. When the continent began to break up about 160 million years ago, one of the pieces it spawned was Gondwana, a huge landmass that included Australia, Antarctica, South America, Africa, and India. More than 100 million years passed before Australia finally broke away to form today's island continent.

Relics from the ancient past are abundant here. In the south, the saltwater lakes of Frome, Torrens, Eyre, and Gairdner are vestiges of a vast inland sea that flowed south from the Gulf of Carpentaria. In the east, the Great Dividing Range spans the length of the country into the island state of Tasmania. Most of the mountains were formed several million years ago.

SHARK BAY AND DENHAM SOUND

Light blue in the image below, the shallow waters of Western Australia's Shark Bay provide a haven for fish and dugongs. To the west, Peron Peninsula separates the bay from Denham Sound.

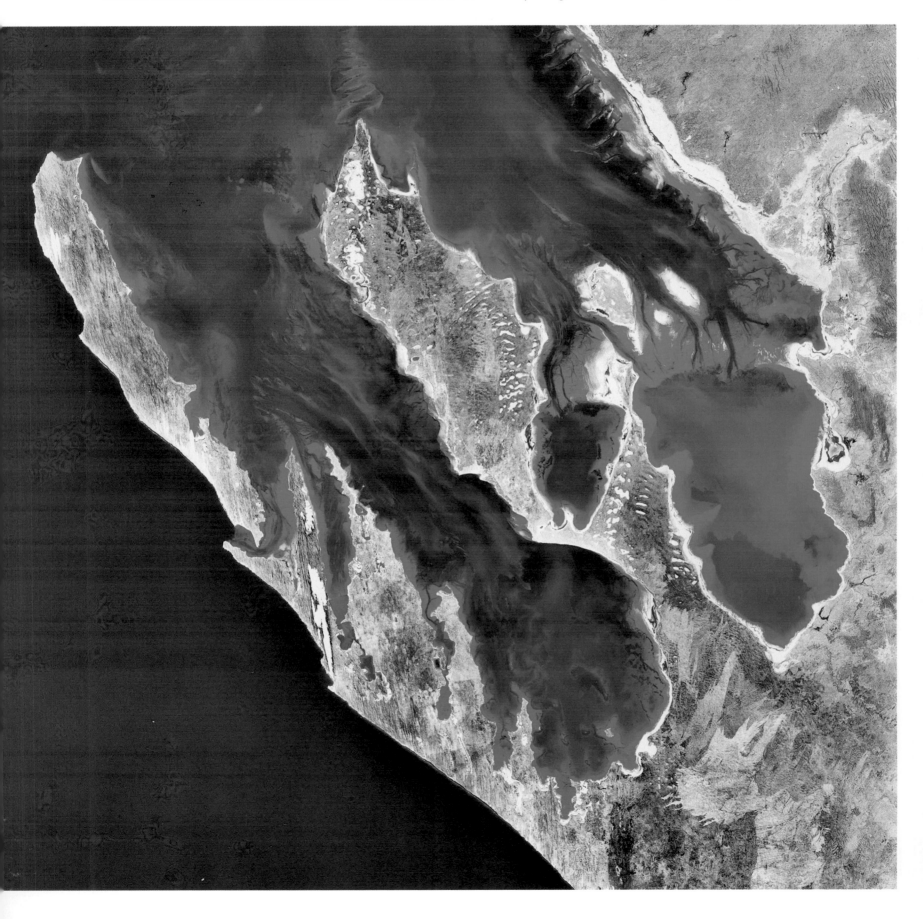

GIBSON DESERT

Western Australia's Gibson Desert (left) differs from some of the other deserts on the continent. Instead of sand, a reddish-tinted residue called laterite covers much of the surface. Because scientists also find this by-product of eroding rocks forming in tropical areas of Asia and Africa, some of them believe the Gibson once had a humid climate. In 1876, Englishman Ernest Giles led an expedition across the desert. His team named the desert for Alfred Gibson, a team member lost in the trek.

TASMANIA

More than 12,000 years ago, Tasmania (right) formed part of Australia's mainland. But rising sea levels over time created the Bass Strait, and Australia's southernmost region became an island. Today Tasmania resembles southeastern Australia. A mountainous, forested place three times as large as Massachusetts, it holds only a fraction of that state's population. Most of the settlements lie in the north, the east-central midlands, and along the south-central coast near Hobart, the capital city. Many of the people in these areas operate dairy farms or sheep ranches. In this Landsat MSS mosaic, the dark and light-green area in the southwest is Southwest National Park, which the UN designated a World Heritage Site in 1982. This lush wilderness—one of Earth's few virgin temperate rain forests—includes some of the world's tallest and oldest hardwoods.

Perhaps no climatic event underscored Australia's natural vulnerabilities as forcefully as the 1982-83 El Niño. The capricious weather system produced devastating droughts, bushfires, and floods; left 75 people and thousands of animals dead; and caused property damages amounting to about 2.5 billion dollars (U. S.).

Australia's climate is dominated by the dry, sinking air of the subtropical high-pressure belt that moves north or south with the seasons. As a result, rainfall is highly variable, with much of the continent averaging less than 20 inches a year. Such aridity, along with searing winds from the outback, can cause the mercury to soar, setting the stage for some of the world's most serious bushfires.

During a February 1983 drought, for example, a dust storm swept across portions of southern Victoria and caused the skies of Melbourne to turn almost black in the middle of the afternoon. The storm dumped 11,000 tons of dirt on the ground before it passed. Several days later, on February 16, bushfires went on a rampage in southeastern Australia. In the town of Macedon few structures were left standing.

Australia also suffers from floods and blistering heat waves. Monsoons can drench the tropical northern latitudes, and torrential rains occur occasionally throughout the rest of the continent. Hot spells are particularly bad in the north. In February 1998, the Western Australia town of Mardie broke the national record with a temperature of 122.9°F.

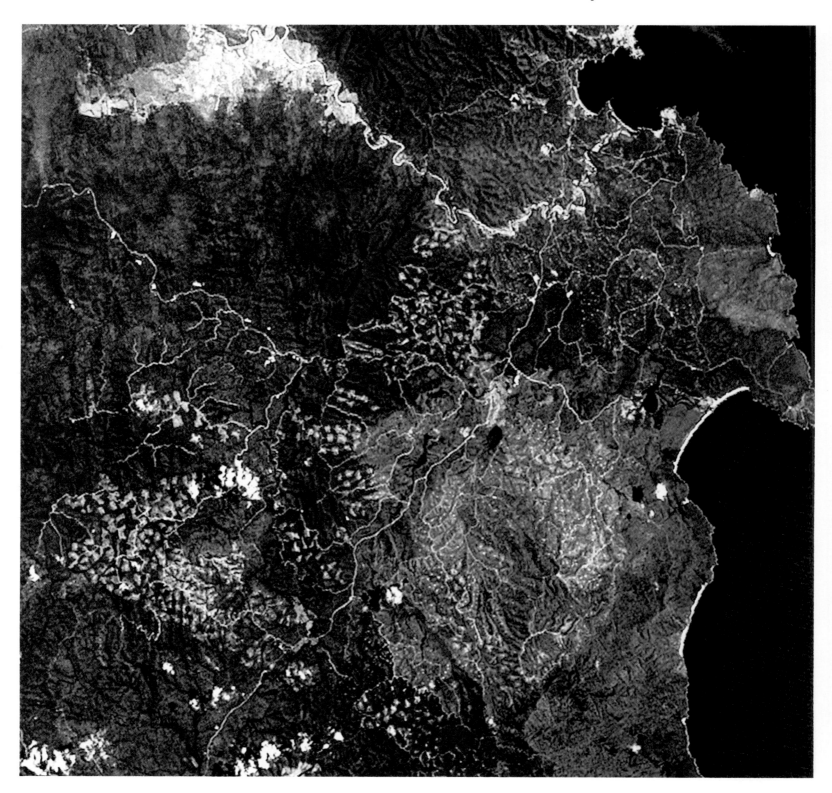

FIRE FOOTPRINT, 1980

South of Eden, New South Wales, lumber companies and environmentalists fought over the harvesting of old-growth forests (shown in red). Clearings left by loggers appear as small green patches. Just before a satellite imaged this area, a wildfire rippled through the region and left a green scar.

Fire Scars

Fire Footprint

FIRE SCARS

A satellite high above the Great Sandy Desert of Western Australia helps scientists measure fire tracks (left). Slashes of pale yellow in the image show where wind-driven blazes have scorched vegetation.

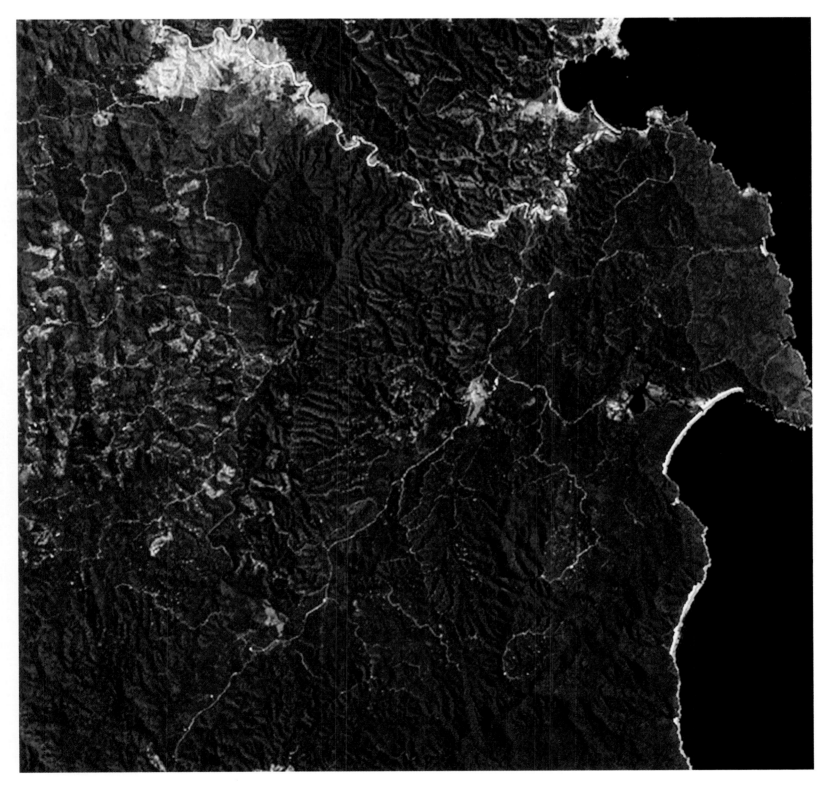

LOOKING BACK, 1988

Almost eight years after a fire ravaged the forest on the opposite page, its scar hardly shows in the image above. Vegetation grew back relatively quickly, and the woodland revived. Forestry managers aided the recovery process by adopting less destructive methods of tree harvesting.

189

AUSTRALIA · HUMAN IMPACT

Humans have left their mark on Australia ever since they first arrived more than 50,000 years ago. The nomadic Aborigines left their stamp on the land by using fire extensively to manage the vegetation. European settlers did not, however, and some people argue that the continent's problem with bushfires is a result of the discontinued use of controlled, regular fires.

Although Australia's soil was poor before the first people came, humankind has done little to improve it. Much of the farmland is considered degraded, partly because of agrichemicals, over-grazing, and recurring droughts. In places where hillsides have been cleared for pastures, rains have washed salts out of the soil and downhill, thereby increasing the salinity of the soils below.

Logging also has taken quite a heavy toll, although perhaps not as much as on other continents. Since Europeans first settled here, Australia has lost about 40 percent of its total forested area to clearing.

STIRLING RANGE NATIONAL PARK

This February 1988 MSS image of Stirling Range National Park, in Western Australia, shows the impact of agricultural overkill (below). Rectangular fields of cleared land engulf the protected area, which resembles a rippling scarlet and black island in a gray and white sea. Australia designated the 50-mile-long mountain range in the country's southwest corner a national park in 1957. It features rocky peaks and good views of the Indian Ocean coast less than 40 miles away. Few people live in the region around the park—less than one person per square mile, according to some statistics. Most residents live on large farms where they grow grain or raise sheep while coping with water shortages. The white circles in the image denote lakes that typically fill up in July and August, the winter rainy season.

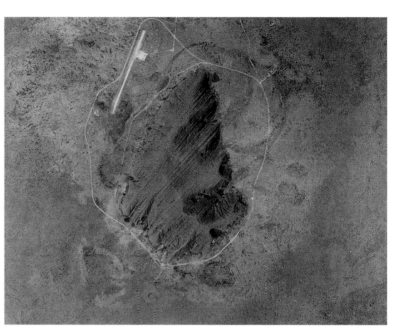

ULURU (AYERS ROCK)

Rising like a red giant in the deserts of central Australia, Uluru—formerly called Ayers Rock—has become the focal point of one of the country's most notable national parks. A planimetric view of the monolith (upper) gives no hint of topographical relief, but a 3-D perspective extracted from overlapping aerial photography shows how Uluru differs from the surrounding terrain (lower). Aborigines say their ancestors made the 1,142-foot rock, the world's largest monolith. Claiming descent from creatures who came out of the void at the dawn of time to breathe life into the Earth, Aborigines believe they must care for the land. They ask visitors not to climb the sacred Uluru, but many people ignore the request. With thousands of tourists a year, the potential for damage to the sandstone structure remains strong.

191

PERTH

For many years, Perth (left) remained a small, isolated town on Australia's west coast, 1,700 miles away from its closest urban neighbor, Adelaide. But the discovery of minerals lured thousands of people to Western Australia, and many of them opted to settle in Perth. Its population now stands at about 1.3 million. The main business district unfolds northeast of Kings Park, a thousand-acre parcel set aside in 1872. In this image the park appears as a patch of dark green and red adjacent to Melville Water, part of the Swan River.

SYDNEY

In 1788 ships carrying convicts and soldiers from England sailed to the site of present-day Sydney, establishing Australia's first European settlement (right, at right center in this merged SPOT and TM image). Today about 3.7 million people live in the country's largest city and its suburbs (purple), which stretch south of Botany Bay, lower right, and west beyond Prospect Reservoir, left center. Heathcote and Royal National Parks, in the south, and Ku-Ring-Gai Chase National Park, in the north, appear in shades of green.

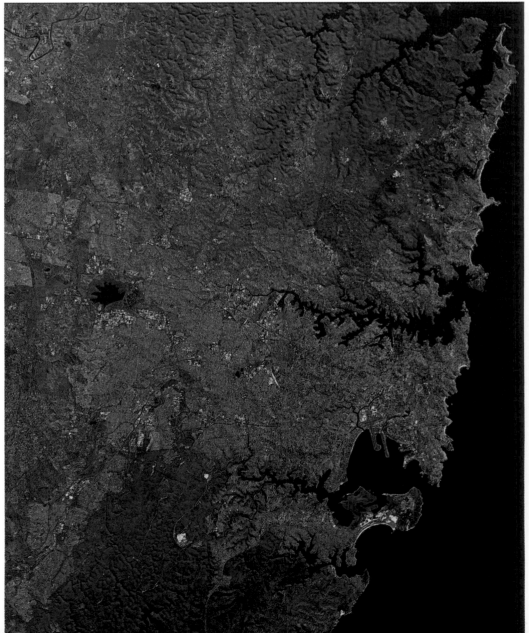

CANBERRA

Hills embrace Canberra, the meticulously planned national capital (at left, in shades of purple and blue) on the Molonglo River. In 1908, Australia chose this site for its capital instead of Melbourne or Sydney, rivals for the honor. The new city rose between them in the highlands west of the Great Dividing Range. American architect Walter Burley Griffin planned Canberra around a man-made lake that now bears his middle and last names. The thin white line running across the image traces the border of Australian Capital Territory.

MELBOURNE

Nestled around the topmost reaches of Port Phillip Bay in southeastern Australia, the city of Melbourne (right) maintains a European atmosphere. Deciduous trees, instead of the ubiquitous eucalyptus, line many of Melbourne's streets, along with buildings constructed in the classic Georgian style. In this TM image, the city and its neighbor Geelong appear blue at top center and lower left. East of Melbourne, dark green areas identify the fern-covered mountains of Dandenong Ranges National Park.

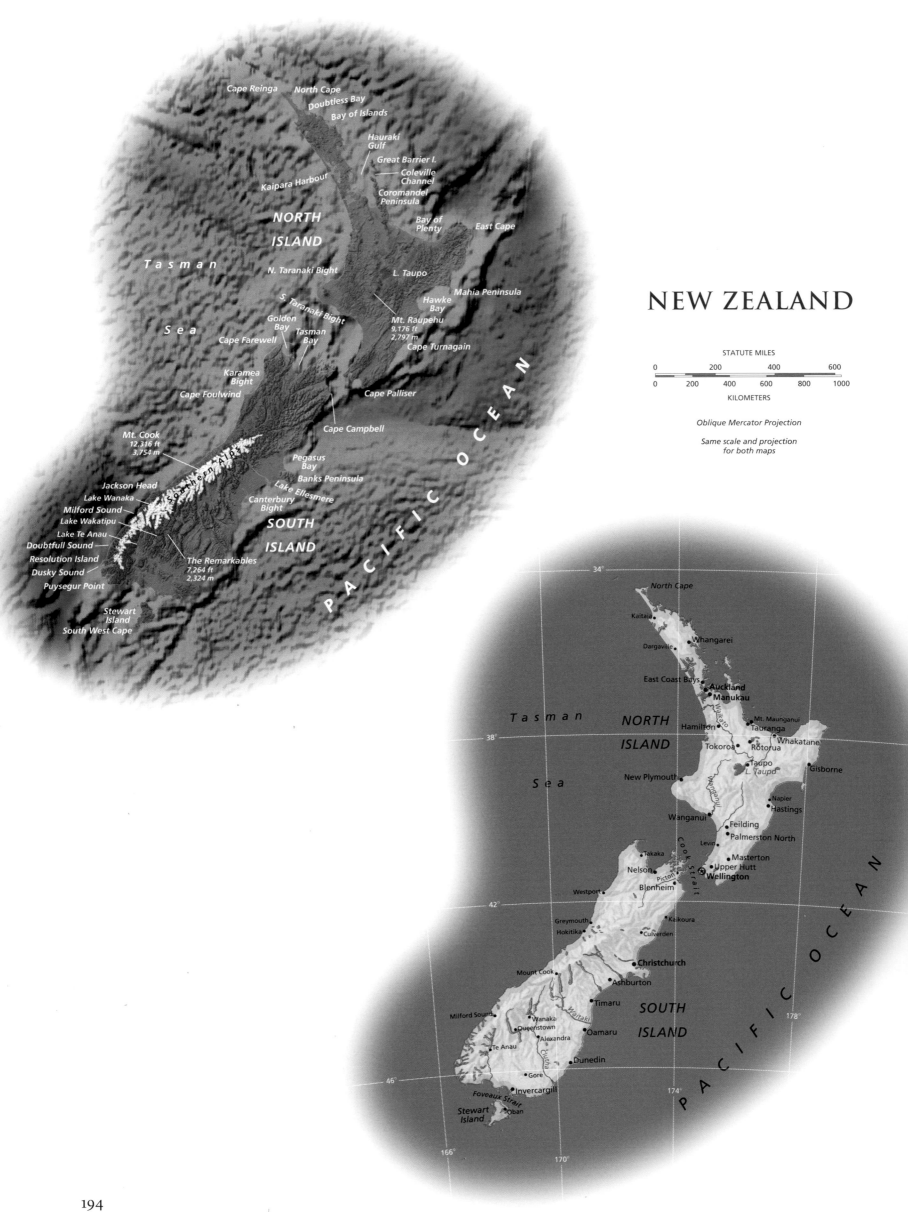

NEW ZEALAND

STATUTE MILES

| 0 | 200 | 400 | 600 |

| 0 | 200 | 400 | 600 | 800 | 1000 |

KILOMETERS

Oblique Mercator Projection

*Same scale and projection
for both maps*

Cape Reinga
North Cape
Doubtless Bay
Bay of Islands
Hauraki Gulf
Great Barrier I.
Coleville Channel
Coromandel Peninsula
Kaipara Harbour
NORTH ISLAND
Bay of Plenty
East Cape
Tasman
N. Taranaki Bight
L. Taupo
Mahia Peninsula
Sea
Hawke Bay
S. Taranaki Bight
Mt. Raupehu
9,176 ft
2,797 m
Golden Bay
Cape Turnagain
Cape Farewell
Tasman Bay
Karamea Bight
Cape Palliser
Cape Foulwind
Mt. Cook
12,316 ft
3,754 m
Cape Campbell
Pegasus Bay
Banks Peninsula
Jackson Head
Lake Wanaka
Southern Alps
Lake Ellesmere
Milford Sound
Canterbury Bight
Lake Wakatipu
SOUTH ISLAND
Lake Te Anau
Doubtfull Sound
The Remarkables
7,264 ft
2,324 m
Resolution Island
Dusky Sound
Puysegur Point
Stewart Island
South West Cape

PACIFIC OCEAN

34°
North Cape
Kaitaia
Whangarei
Dargaville
East Coast Bays
Auckland
Manukau
Tasman
NORTH ISLAND
Waikato
Mt. Maunganui
Hamilton
Tauranga
38°
Tokoroa
Rotorua
Whakatane
New Plymouth
Taupo
L. Taupo
Gisborne
Sea
Wanganui
Napier
Hastings
Feilding
Levin
Palmerston North
Takaka
Masterton
Nelson
Upper Hutt
Picton
Wellington
Westport
Blenheim
42°
Greymouth
Kaikoura
Hokitika
Culverden
Christchurch
Mount Cook
Ashburton
Waitaki
Timaru
SOUTH ISLAND
Milford Sound
Wanaka
Queenstown
Oamaru
Alexandra
Te Anau
Clutha
Dunedin
46°
Gore
Invercargill
Foveaux Strait
Stewart Island
Oban
Cook Strait
178°
174°
PACIFIC OCEAN
166°
170°

194

MOUNT COOK

The glacier-crowned glory of New Zealand's Southern Alps, Mount Cook thrusts 12,316 feet into the sky (above). The country's highest mountain rises as part of the steep, nearly continuous range that separates the South Island's fjords and rain forests from the drier eastern plains. The Maori call this mountain Aorangi, which means "cloud piercer." European settlers renamed it in honor of Capt. James Cook, the intrepid British explorer who came to the South Pacific in the 18th century. Using red to indicate vegetation, this 1987 3-D SPOT image reveals the large area of wilderness that forms Mount Cook National Park, a vast expanse of glaciers, lakes, and subalpine tussock—raised ground held together by plant roots in bogs or marshes.

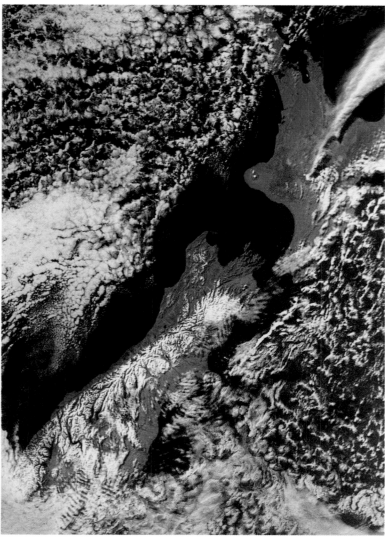

MOUNT RUAPEHU

In the early morning hours of June 17, 1996, Mount Ruapehu (left) began to rumble and shake. The tallest mountain on the North Island of New Zealand soon generated an ash plume that extended about four and a half miles into the atmosphere. The plume towers over the island in the upper right corner of this AVHRR image. The snowcapped Southern Alps, on the South Island, stretch toward the bottom left corner. In the 19th century, a Maori chieftain feared that Europeans would develop Ruapehu and two nearby volcanoes. To protect the mountains held sacred by his people, he gave them to the government in 1887. That same year, New Zealand honored the Maori's trust by creating Tongariro National Park, the first national park in the country. More than a century later, the United Nations designated Tongariro a World Heritage Site.

Mount Ruapehu

Mount Cook

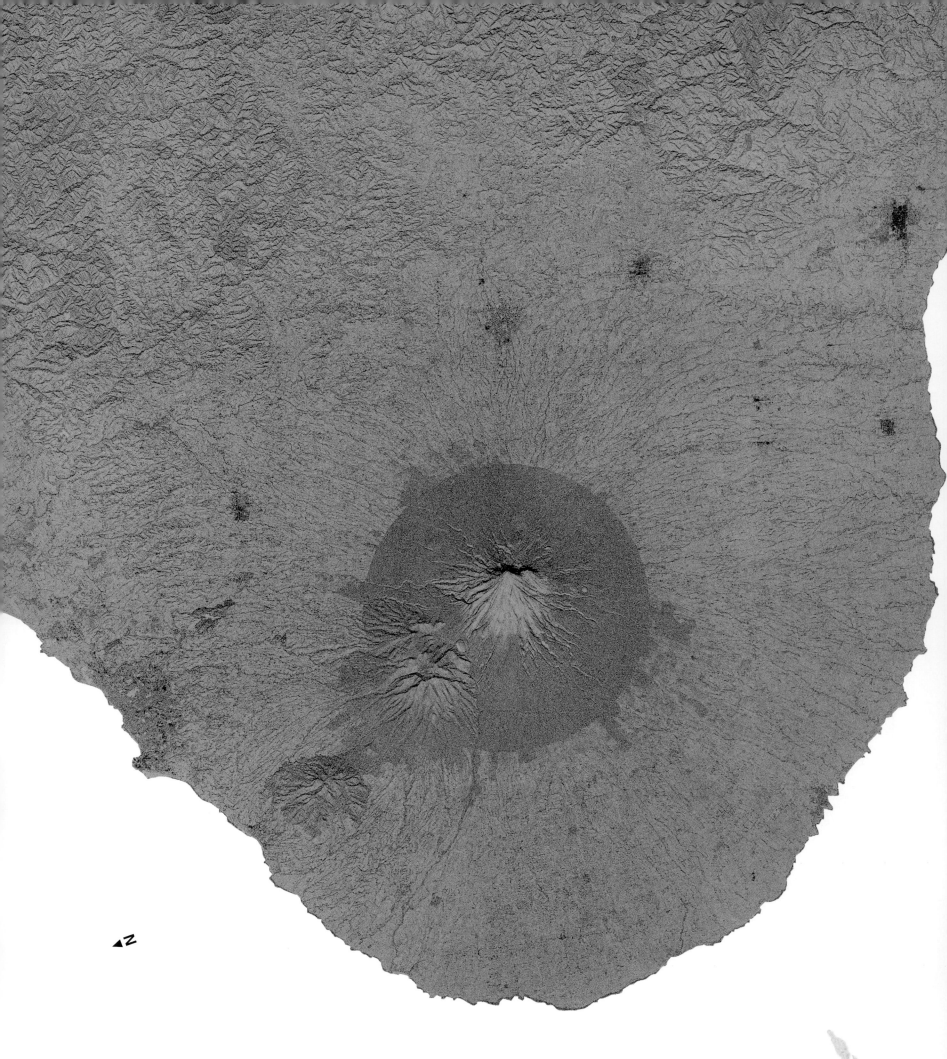

MOUNT TARANAKI

*Volcanic Mount Taranaki, quiet for almost 300 years, dominates a colorized
SAR image. Known as good farm country (shown in lighter purple), the area
around the 8,260-foot mountain enjoys a warm, sunny climate. Taranaki
itself attracts hikers, but crumbling rocks on steep slopes often pose a hazard.*

Mount Taranaki •

• Wellington

Christchurch •

WELLINGTON

Topography has played a major role in the growth of New Zealand's capital on the Cook Strait (above). Wellington's deep harbor helped make it a good port. In 1855 an earthquake on the Wairarapa Fault, east of town, raised the harbor about four feet, creating new land on which to construct buildings.

CHRISTCHURCH

Christchurch and the Canterbury plains of the South Island make up one of New Zealand's agricultural regions (below). The plains have developed over the past million years, a product of erosive activity in the Southern Alps. Rising to the west, the Alps grow 30 feet higher every 1,000 years.

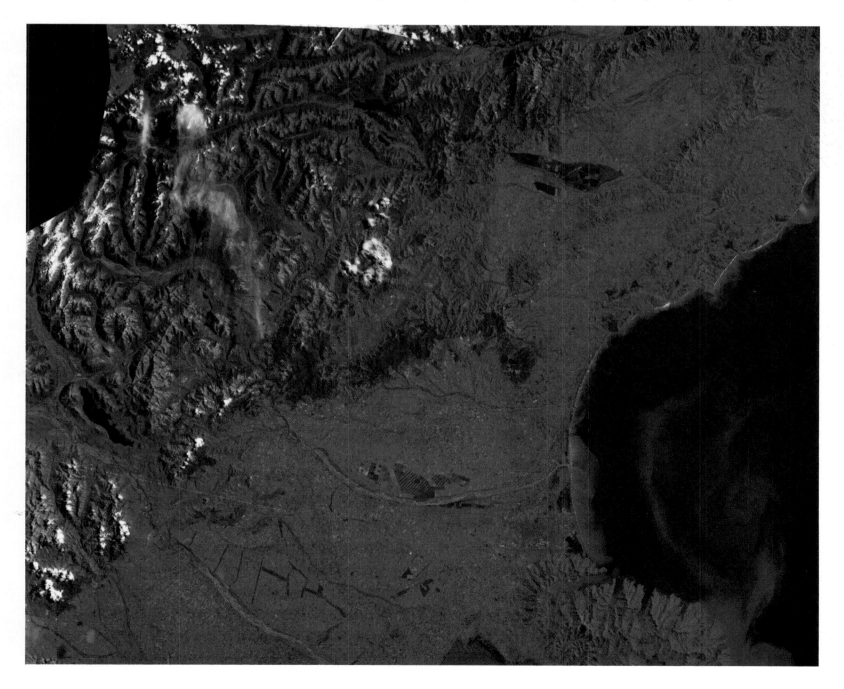

ANTARCTICA

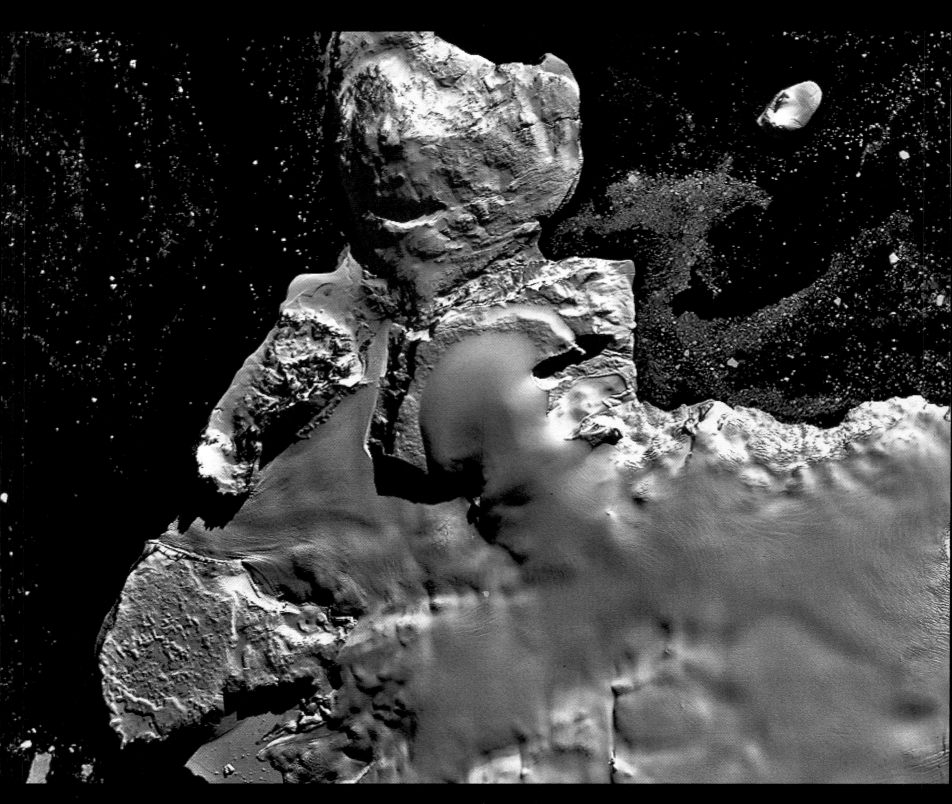

From the beginning of myth and time, Antarctica, like a shy and distant foreigner, has been reluctant to unveil her terrible beauty. "The risque one runs in exploring a coast in these unknown and icy seas, is so very great," wrote Capt. James Cook in the 1770s, "that I can be bold enough to say that no man will ever venture farther than I have done, and the lands which may lie to the South will never be explored." Captain Cook circumnavigated the continent but never saw it; ice and winds rebuffed his wooden ships and iron will. Yet others came after him, driven by human enterprise, and the veil parted.

Coastlines were mapped, mountain ranges named. The interior was unlocked through heroic hardship and costly miscalculation. Men trudged into a white nothingness to plant their flags and win their honors. "Great God, this is an awful place," wrote Capt. Robert Falcon Scott upon arriving

at the South Pole in January 1912. He never made it back home to England: Antarctica entombed him, leaving only his records and diaries to be found by a search party.

Exiled at the bottom of the world, this cold, high, dry, windy, and lonely continent is still full of secrets. But while it can shy away from many technologies, it cannot hide from satellites, eyes in the sky that can see through its veil and reveal what lies below.

JAMES ROSS ISLAND

James Ross Island embraces Erebus and Terror Gulf, in the northwest Weddell Sea near the eastern edge of the Antarctic Peninsula. This "banana belt" of Antarctica lies about 700 miles south of Tierra del Fuego, South America's tip. In the image above, the SPOT satellite sees the continent during the austral summer, when sunny days make it possible to acquire visible images. Shadows accentuate ice-covered mountains.

James
Ross
Island

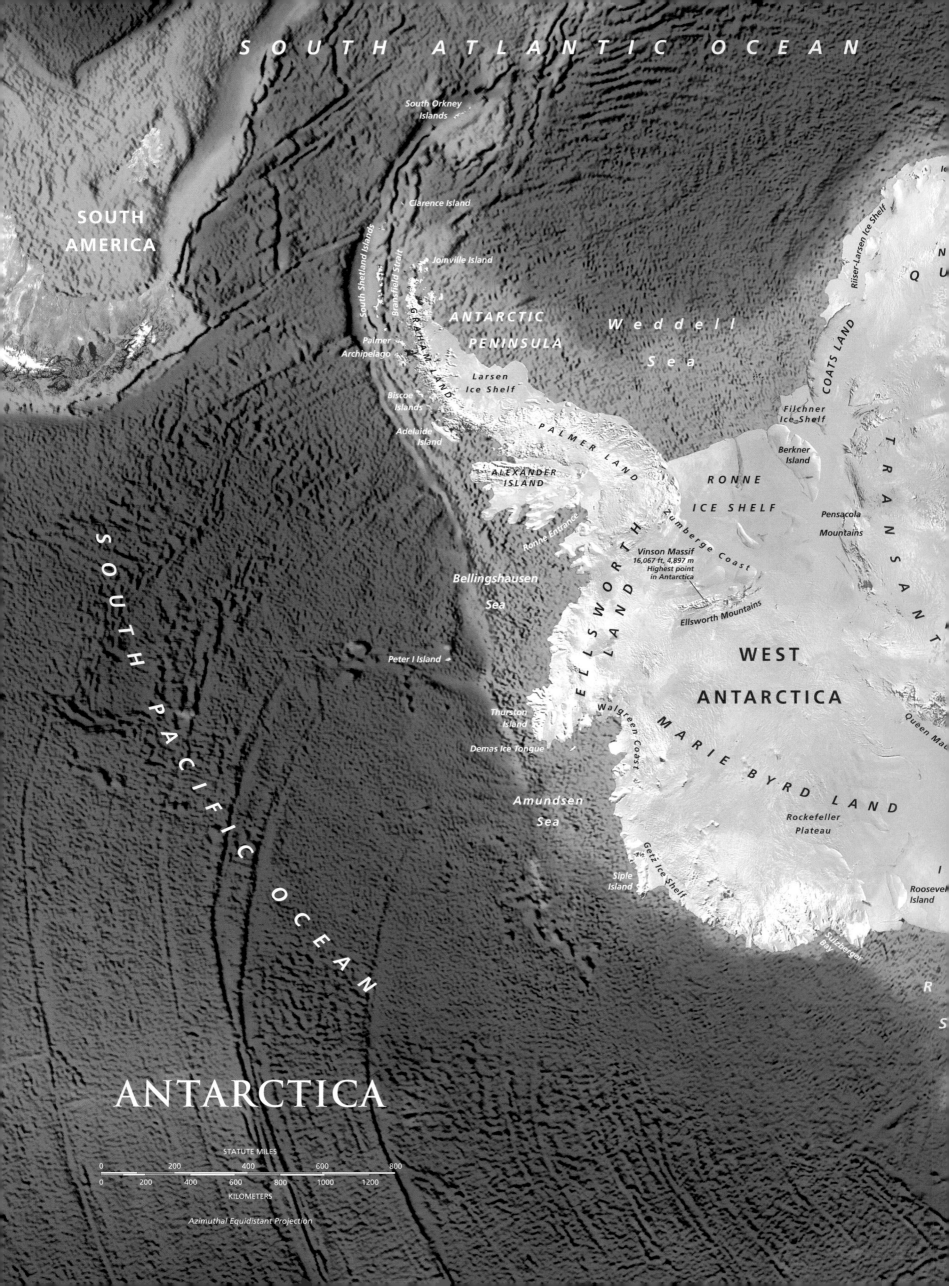

SOUTH ATLANTIC OCEAN

South Orkney
Islands

SOUTH
AMERICA

Clarence Island

South Shetland Islands

Bransfield Strait

Joinville Island

GRAHAM LAND

ANTARCTIC
PENINSULA

Weddell
Sea

Palmer
Archipelago

Larsen
Ice Shelf

Rüser-Larsen Ice Shelf

N
U
Q

Biscoe
Islands

COATS LAND

Filchner
Ice Shelf

Adelaide
Island

PALMER LAND

ALEXANDER
ISLAND

Berkner
Island

RONNE
ICE SHELF

TRANSANT

Ronne Entrance

Zumberge Coast

Pensacola
Mountains

Vinson Massif
16,067 ft, 4,897 m
Highest point
in Antarctica

SOUTH PACIFIC OCEAN

Bellingshausen
Sea

Ellsworth Mountains

ELLSWORTH LAND

WEST
ANTARCTICA

Queen Mau

Peter I Island

Thurston
Island

Walgreen Coast

MARIE BYRD LAND

Demas Ice Tongue

Amundsen
Sea

Rockefeller
Plateau

Getz Ice Shelf

Roosevel
Island

Siple
Island

Sulzberger
Bay

R

S

ANTARCTICA

STATUTE MILES

| 0 | 200 | 400 | 600 | 800 |

| 0 | 200 | 400 | 600 | 800 | 1000 | 1200 |

KILOMETERS

Azimuthal Equidistant Projection

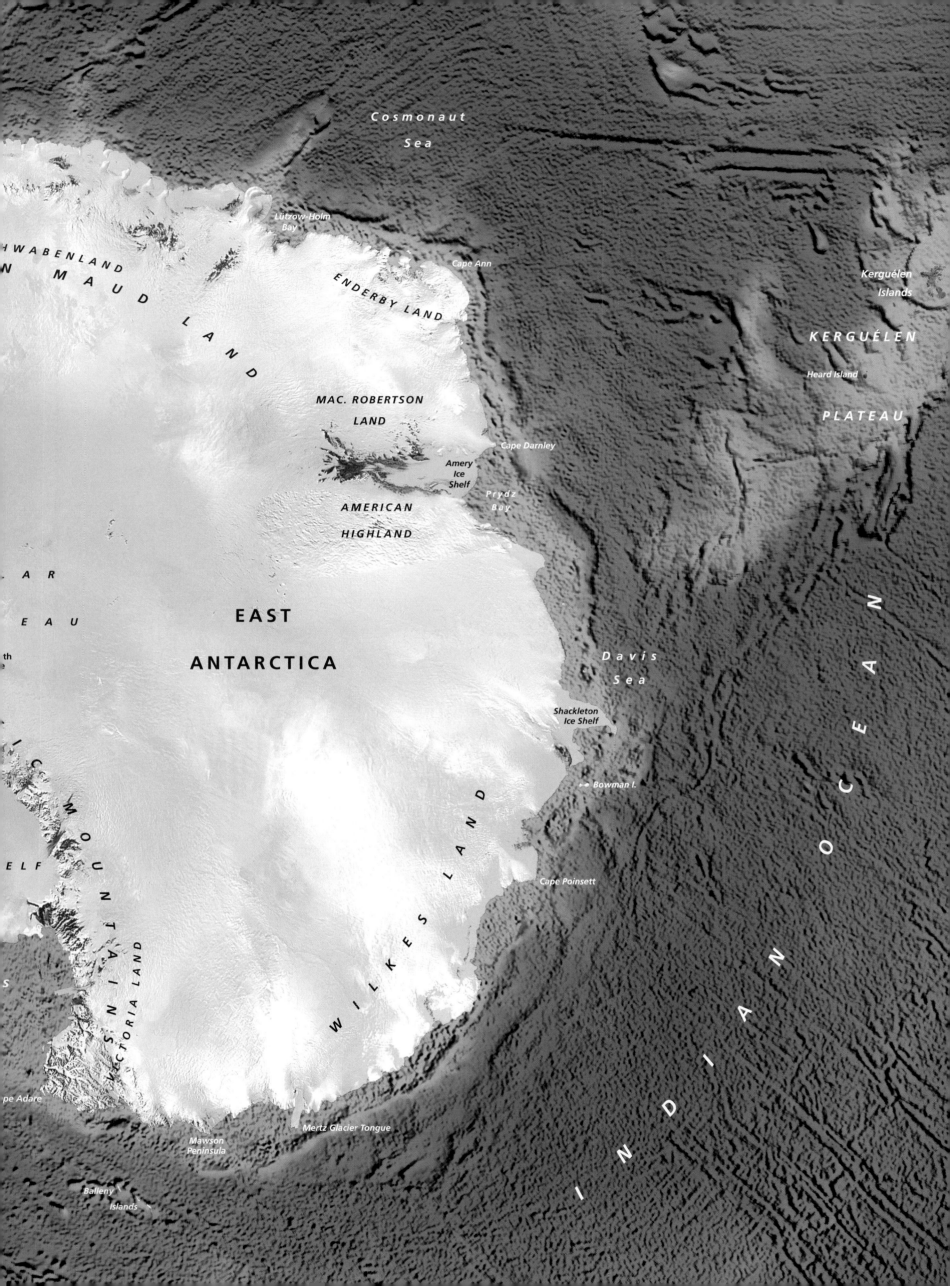

Cosmonaut
Sea

HWABENLAND

MAUD LAND

Lützow-Holm
Bay

Cape Ann

ENDERBY LAND

Kergélen
Islands

KERGUÉLEN

MAC. ROBERTSON
LAND

Cape Darnley

Heard Island

PLATEAU

Amery
Ice
Shelf

Prydz
Bay

AMERICAN

HIGHLAND

AR

EAU

EAST

th

ANTARCTICA

Davis
Sea

ELF

Shackleton
Ice Shelf

I
N
D
I
A
N

Bowman I.

Cape Poinsett

O
C
E
A
N

ROSS

MOUNTAINS

WILKES LAND

pe Adare

CTORIA LAND

Mertz Glacier Tongue

Mawson
Peninsula

Balleny
Islands

I
N
D
I
A
N

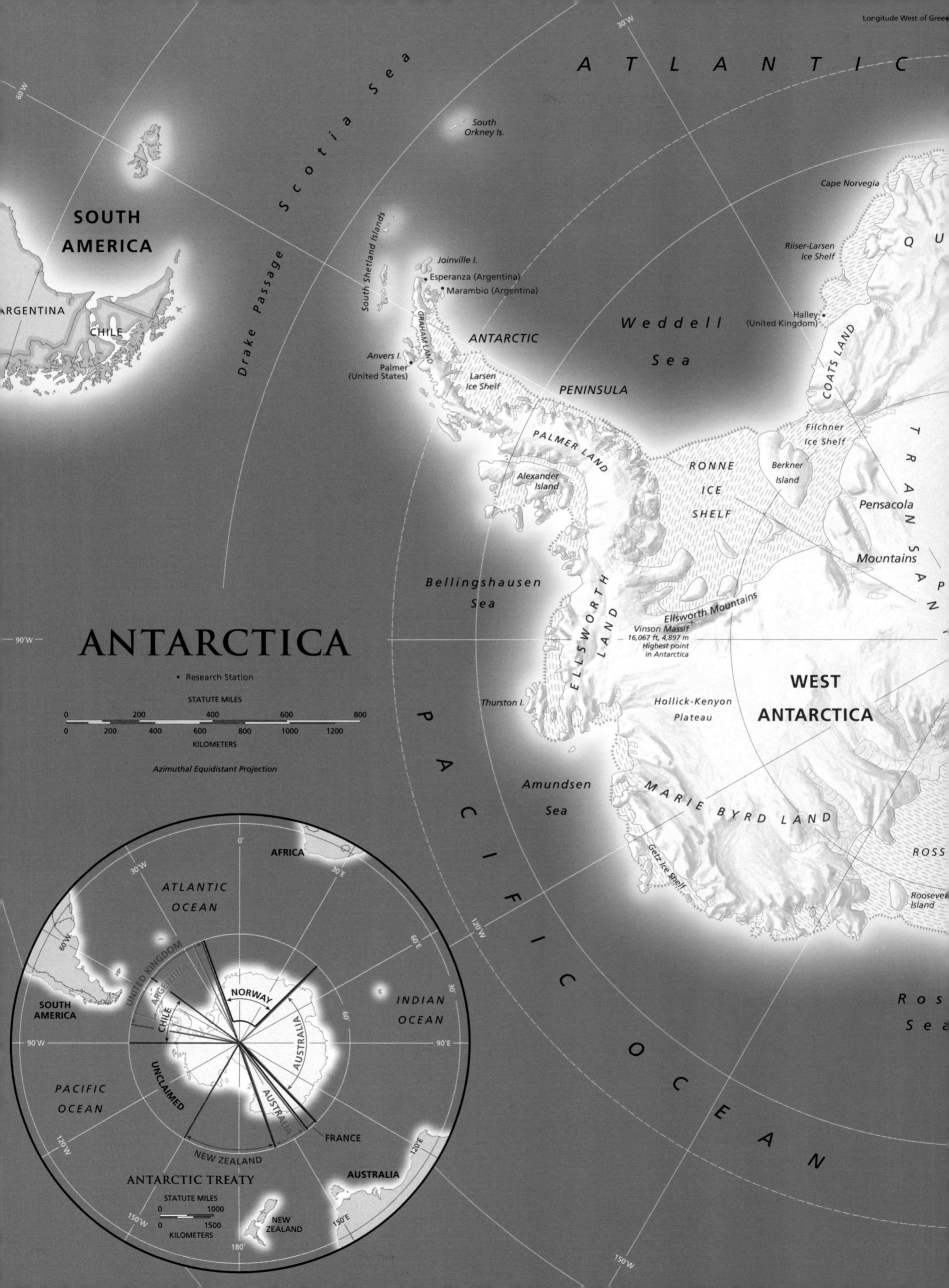

ATLANTIC

Scotia Sea

South
Orkney Is.

Cape Norvegia

SOUTH
AMERICA

Drake Passage

South Shetland Islands

Riiser-Larsen
Ice Shelf

QU

ARGENTINA

CHILE

Joinville I.
Esperanza (Argentina)
Marambio (Argentina)

GRAHAM LAND

ANTARCTIC

Weddell
Sea

Halley
(United Kingdom)

COATS LAND

Anvers I.
Palmer
(United States)

Larsen
Ice Shelf

PENINSULA

PALMER LAND

Filchner
Ice Shelf

T
R
A
N
S

Alexander
Island

RONNE
ICE
SHELF

Berkner
Island

Pensacola

A
N

Bellingshausen
Sea

ELLSWORTH
LAND

Ellsworth Mountains
Vinson Massif
16,067 ft, 4,897 m
Highest point
in Antarctica

Mountains

ANTARCTICA

Research Station

STATUTE MILES

0   200   400   600   800

0   200   400   600   800   1000   1200

KILOMETERS

Azimuthal Equidistant Projection

Thurston I.

WEST
ANTARCTICA

Hollick-Kenyon
Plateau

P
A
C
I
F
I
C

Amundsen
Sea

MARIE BYRD LAND

Getz Ice Shelf

ROSS

O
C
E
A
N

Roosevelt
Island

Ros

Sea

AFRICA

ATLANTIC
OCEAN

0°

30°E

NORWAY

UNITED KINGDOM

ARGENTINA

CHILE

60°E

INDIAN
OCEAN

SOUTH
AMERICA

60°W

AUSTRALIA

60

30

90°W

90°E

PACIFIC
OCEAN

UNCLAIMED

AUSTRALIA

FRANCE

120°W

NEW ZEALAND

120°E

ANTARCTIC TREATY

AUSTRALIA

STATUTE MILES

0   1000

0   1500

KILOMETERS

150°W

NEW
ZEALAND

150°E

180°

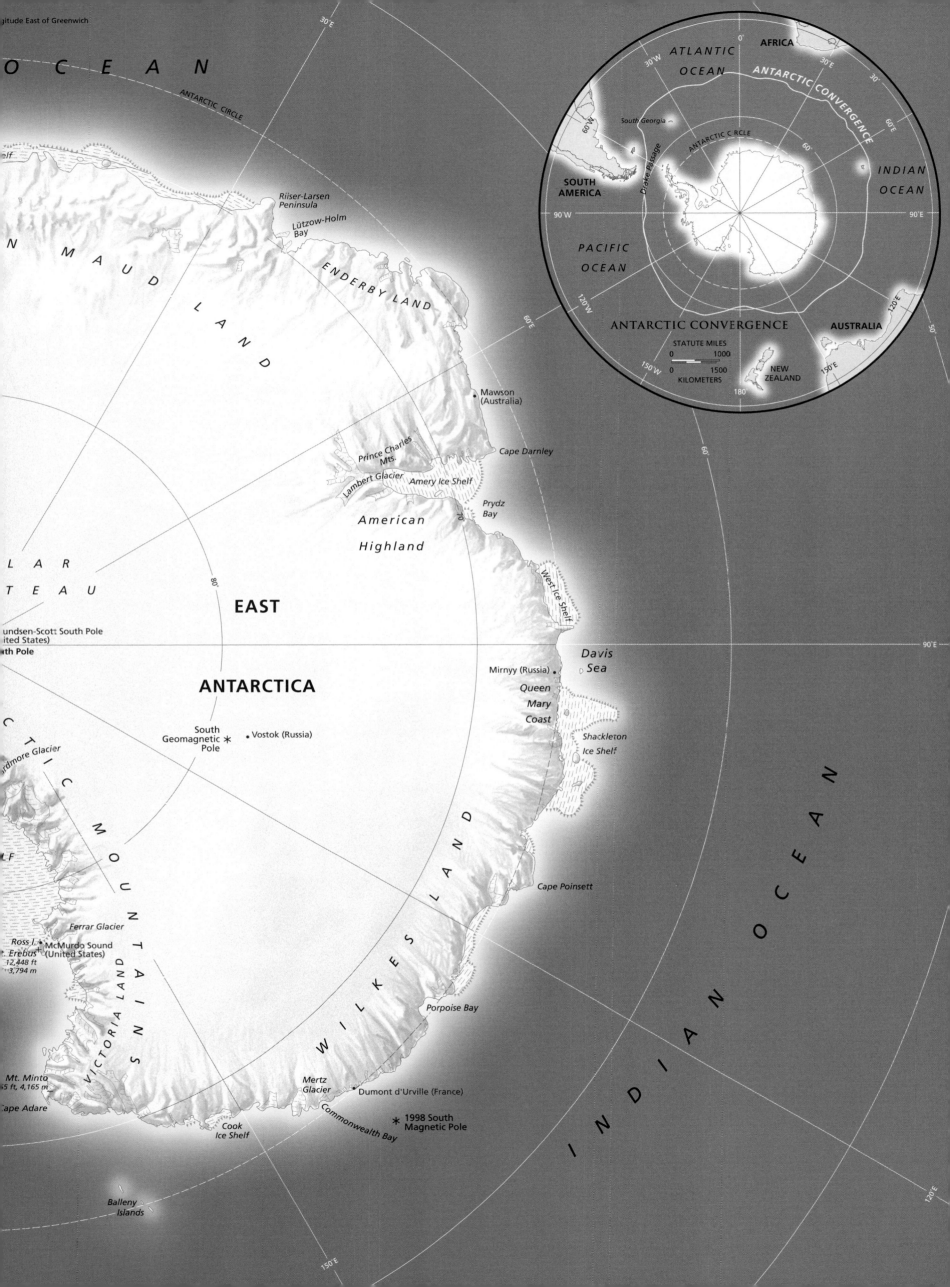

gitude East of Greenwich

O C E A N

ANTARCTIC CIRCLE

elf

N MAUD LAND

Riiser-Larsen
Peninsula

Lützow-Holm
Bay

ENDERBY LAND

Mawson
(Australia)

Prince Charles
Mts.

Lambert Glacier

Amery Ice Shelf

Cape Darnley

60°E

American

Highland

Prydz
Bay

70°

L A R
T E A U

80°

EAST

undsen-Scott South Pole
ited States)
th Pole

ANTARCTICA

90°E

West Ice Shelf

Davis
Sea

Mirnyy (Russia)

Queen
Mary
Coast

Shackleton
Ice Shelf

South
Geomagnetic
Pole * • Vostok (Russia)

T I C

rdmore Glacier

M O U N T A I N S

LF

Ferrar Glacier

Ross I.
Erebus
12,448 ft
3,794 m

McMurdo Sound
(United States)

VICTORIA LAND

W I L K E S   L A N D

Cape Poinsett

60°

I N D I A N   O C E A N

Mt. Minto
65 ft, 4,165 m

ape Adare

Mertz
Glacier

Porpoise Bay

Dumont d'Urville (France)

Commonwealth Bay

* 1998 South
Magnetic Pole

Cook
Ice Shelf

Balleny
Islands

150°E

120°E

ATLANTIC
OCEAN

0°

30°W

AFRICA

30°E

ANTARCTIC CONVERGENCE

60°W

60°E

South Georgia

ANTARCTIC CIRCLE

SOUTH
AMERICA

Drake Passage

60°

INDIAN
OCEAN

90°W

90°E

PACIFIC
OCEAN

120°W

120°E

ANTARCTIC CONVERGENCE

AUSTRALIA

STATUTE MILES

0   1000

0   1500

KILOMETERS

150°W

NEW
ZEALAND

150°E

180

ANTARCTICA · LANDFORMS

nlike the Arctic, an ocean surrounded by land, Antarctica is a continent surrounded by oceans. Two large seas, the Ross and Weddell, extend far inland and are fronted by massive ice shelves. One of them, the Ross Ice Shelf, covers an area about the size of France. Summits typically rise above 8,000 feet in the Transantarctic Mountains, and the highest mountain, Vinson Massif, reaches 16,067 feet in the Ellsworth Mountains.

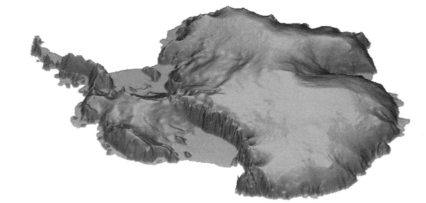

1997 RADAR MOSAIC

More than 3,000 images make up this preliminary radar mosaic (above). First detailed satellite coverage of the entire continent, it helps scientists study ice flow and stability, surface melting, and uplift of the Transantarctic Mountains.

1994-95 RADAR MOSAIC

Data collected by the ERS-1 satellite from April 1994 to March 1995 created this radar-altimeter mosaic of Antarctica (left). Yellow indicates higher and flatter regions of the Polar Plateau. Today ice covers about 98 percent of the land and reaches a thickness of more than 9,000 feet at the South Pole.

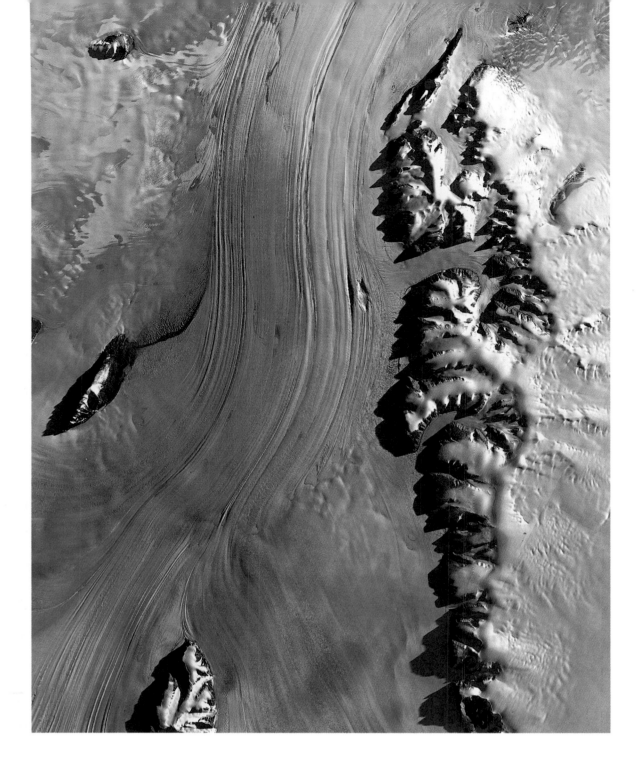

LAMBERT GLACIER

Landsat reveals the 25-mile-wide, 8,200-foot-thick Lambert Glacier (above), the largest glacier in the world. Shadows creep from Mawson Escarpment, rising 10,000 feet from an ice-shrouded base.

EREBUS VOLCANO

Earth's southernmost active volcano, 12,448-foot-high Mount Erebus reigns over Ross Island in this vertical-exaggeration image (below). The tongue of Erebus Glacier reaches into McMurdo Sound.

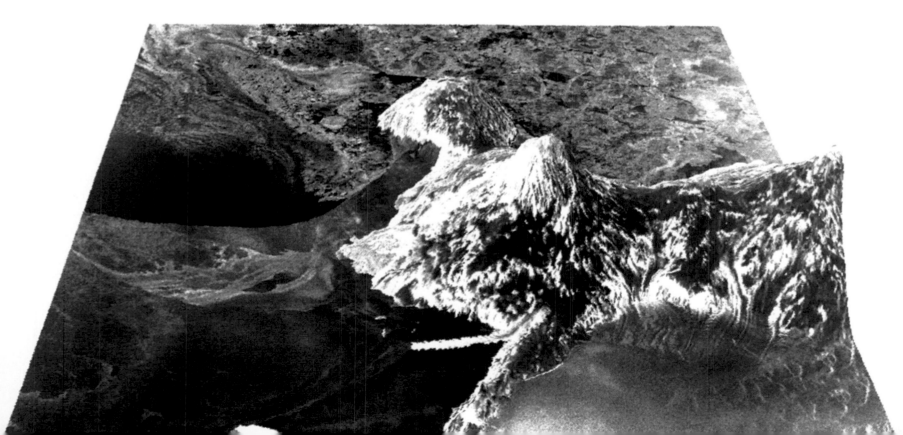

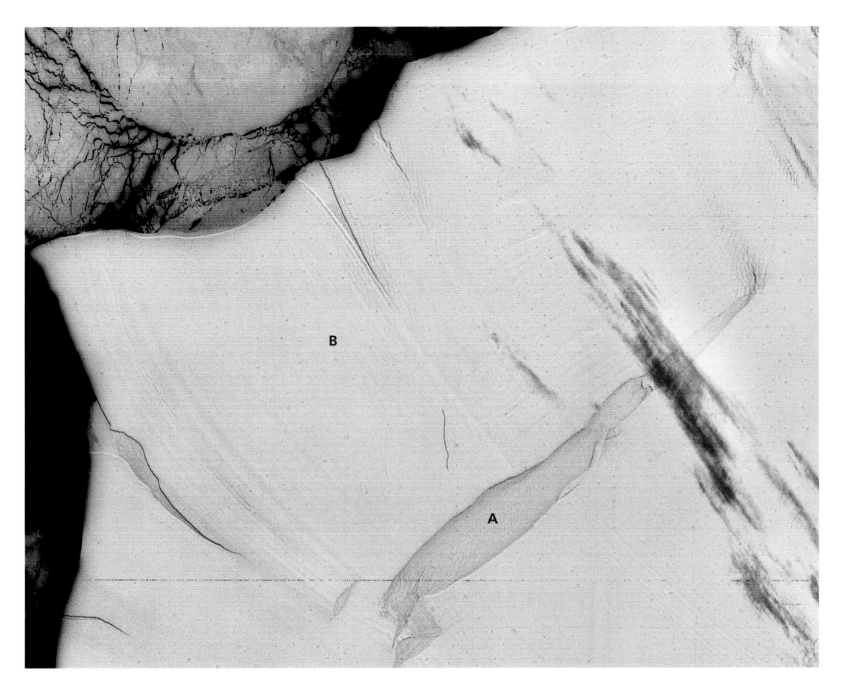

Antarctica contains 90 percent of all the ice in the world, and locked up in the ice is 70 percent of all the Earth's fresh water. Although ice may appear static, it moves, sculpts, cuts, and carves. It freezes and thaws and freezes again. Ice bends and breaks, thunders and grinds. It creates its own weather and climate, its own measure of time.

Each year about 480 cubic miles of new ice accumulate in Antarctica. And each year that same amount is lost to melting, evaporation, and calving—the discharge of ice from ice shelves and glaciers into the sea. Yet this amount is only one six-thousandth of one percent of the total 7,200,000 cubic miles of ice in Antarctica. All but 2 percent of the continent is covered in ice.

While the high and dry Polar Plateau is a crystal desert, coastal Antarctica is a place of transition, a realm of fierce katabatic winds, pitched seas, and castle-like icebergs. Slowly, inexorably, the continent's ice flows seaward, where powerful currents, gyres, and storms chew away at it.

FILCHNER ICE SHELF

Ice shelves occupy nearly one-third of Antarctica's coastline. Flowing ice from the high Polar Plateau feeds the shelves, extending their edges. In time, the sea undermines and weakens them; stresses and strains occur, causing pieces to break off and form icebergs. In the 1973 Landsat image above, a seven-mile-wide crevasse ("A") in the Filchner Ice Shelf indicates eventual calving. A large area of ice ("B" in the image) separated from the shelf and broke into three icebergs ("C"), as shown in the 1986 Landsat image (opposite, top).

South Atlantic
Sea Ice

Filchner
Ice Shelf

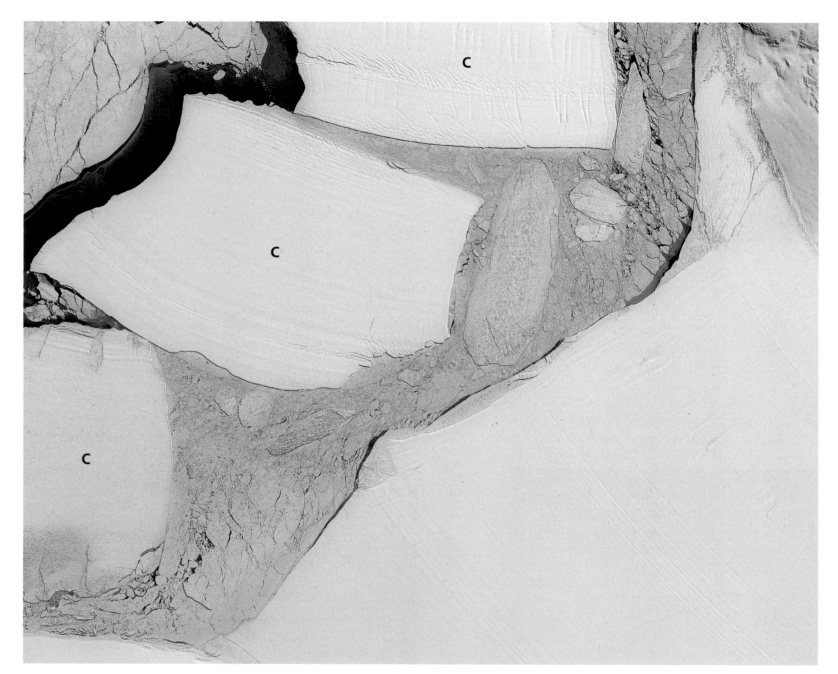

ANTARCTIC SEA ICE

Antarctica effectively doubles in size every austral winter, from April to October, growing a vast 7.3-million-square-mile protective shield of sea ice around its shores. Averaging only about 3 feet thick, contrasted with 10 feet thick for Arctic Sea ice, it shelters complex and mysterious worlds of algae and krill. The microwave image at right shows sea ice at its minimum extent on February 15, 1995, toward the end of the austral summer; the far right image, taken on September 15, 1995, shows the ice at its maximum reach.

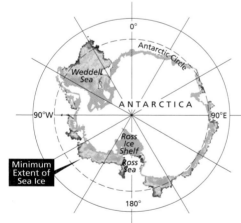

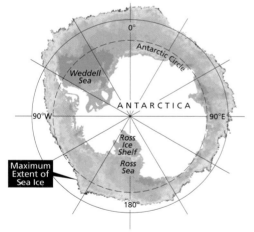

SOUTH ATLANTIC SEA ICE

On October 3, 1994, the space shuttle Endeavor made the first calibrated, multi-frequency, multipolarization spaceborne radar image of seasonal sea ice in the South Atlantic Ocean (left). Produced by overlaying three channels of radar data, each color denotes a different thickness of ice in an area measuring some 26 miles by 6 miles. The thickest areas appear red; newly formed ice, blue-gray. The blue lines indicate open leads of water between the ice floes.

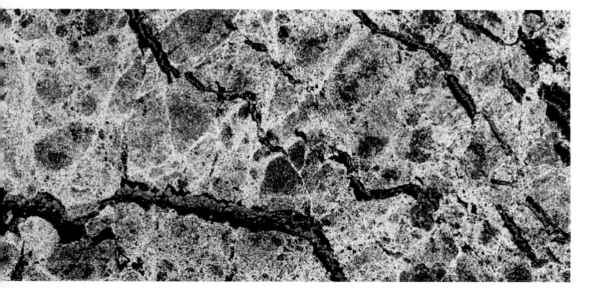

ANTARCTICA · HUMAN IMPACT

No place on Earth has escaped the influence of humankind, not even Antarctica. Capt. James Cook completed his circumnavigation of the continent in 1775, and by the 1820s sea hunters and whalers were visiting its waters. Their impact on penguins, seals, and whales was devastating. Hundreds of thousands of whales were slaughtered, and in just one season, from 1821 to 1822, hunters took 320,000 seals.

The heroic age spanned the early 1900s, witnessing the exploits of Amundsen, Scott, Shackleton, Mawson, and several other mind-over-matter legends. Then came the mechanized age with Byrd, Ellsworth, Dufek, and Fuchs. The Third Reich of Germany used airplanes to drop aluminum darts engraved with swastikas onto the ice. The U.S. Navy arrived a few years later,

bringing 4,700 men, 13 ships, and 23 aircraft. These impacts were minor at first. But with improved technologies came deeper intrusions.

The Antarctic Treaty of 1959, although a progressive document in many respects, inspired rampant construction as interested nations saw science stations as vehicles to establish and hold their territorial claims. Unfortunately, most of the roughly three dozen government-funded stations in Antarctica were built and managed with little regard for their surroundings. Toxins were spilled and penguins were displaced. The 1991 Protocol on Environmental Protection, which was appended to the Antarctic Treaty and ratified by every member nation in 1998, calls for the strict policing of science, exploration, and tourism; this approach could turn the tide on decades of poor practices.

McMURDO SOUND

Cutting a long line in the pack ice, a ship makes its way from McMurdo Sound to Antarctica's largest research facility, the U.S. McMurdo Research Station on Ross Island (below). Mount Erebus, the active volcano crowning the island, appears at top center in this Landsat MSS mosaic. The north side of Ross Island, at left, faces the open sea; the south side fuses with the McMurdo Ice Shelf, which forms part of the Ross Ice Shelf. Seemingly on an intercept course with the vessel's track, Erebus Glacier descends the island's slopes and flows onto the shelf.

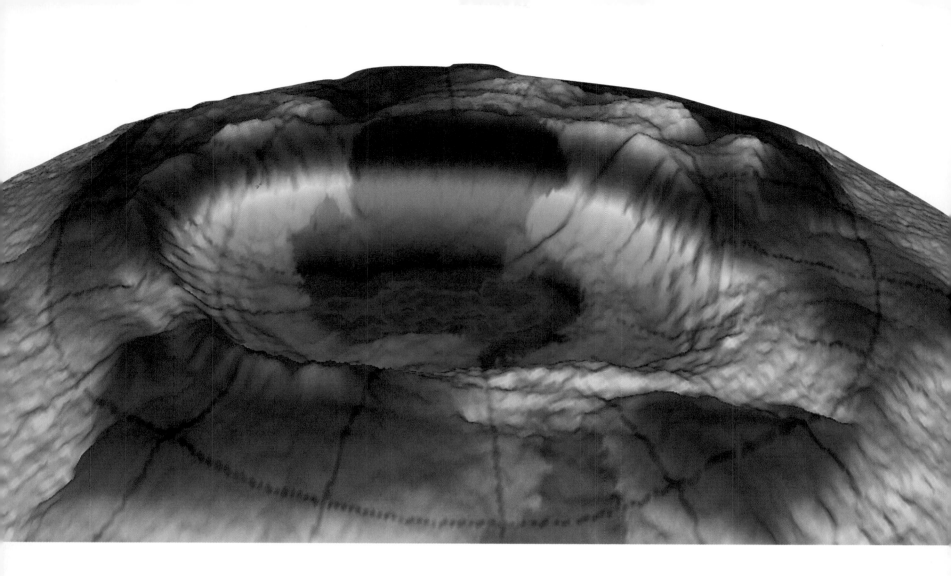

OZONE HOLE

Using a mapping spectrometer, NASA's Goddard Space Flight Center rendered this 3-D image of the hole in the ozone layer high above Antarctica (above). Scientists discovered the hole in the 1980s, and every austral spring the phenomenon reappears. When chlorofluorocarbons (CFCs) first entered international consumerism and people hailed them as wonder compounds, nobody expected that CFCs would rise into the upper atmosphere and destroy the ozone that protects Earth from harmful ultraviolet radiation.

SOUTH POLE

In December 1911, Roald Amundsen and four fellow Norwegians traveled by dogsleds and skis across the Polar Plateau, becoming the first men to reach the South Pole. Today as many as 100 researchers spend the summer there. A 165-foot-wide aluminum geodesic dome, built in the 1970s, forms the centerpiece of the U.S. Amundsen-Scott South Pole Research Station, visible in a RADARSAT image (below) from 496 miles up. A long "highway" to an abandoned antenna site extends from the station toward the upper right.

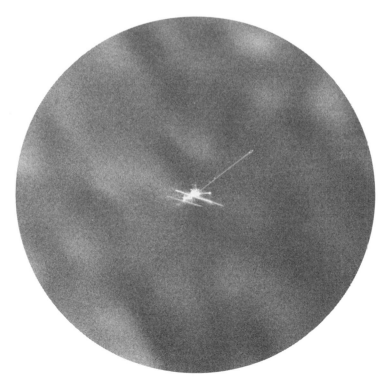

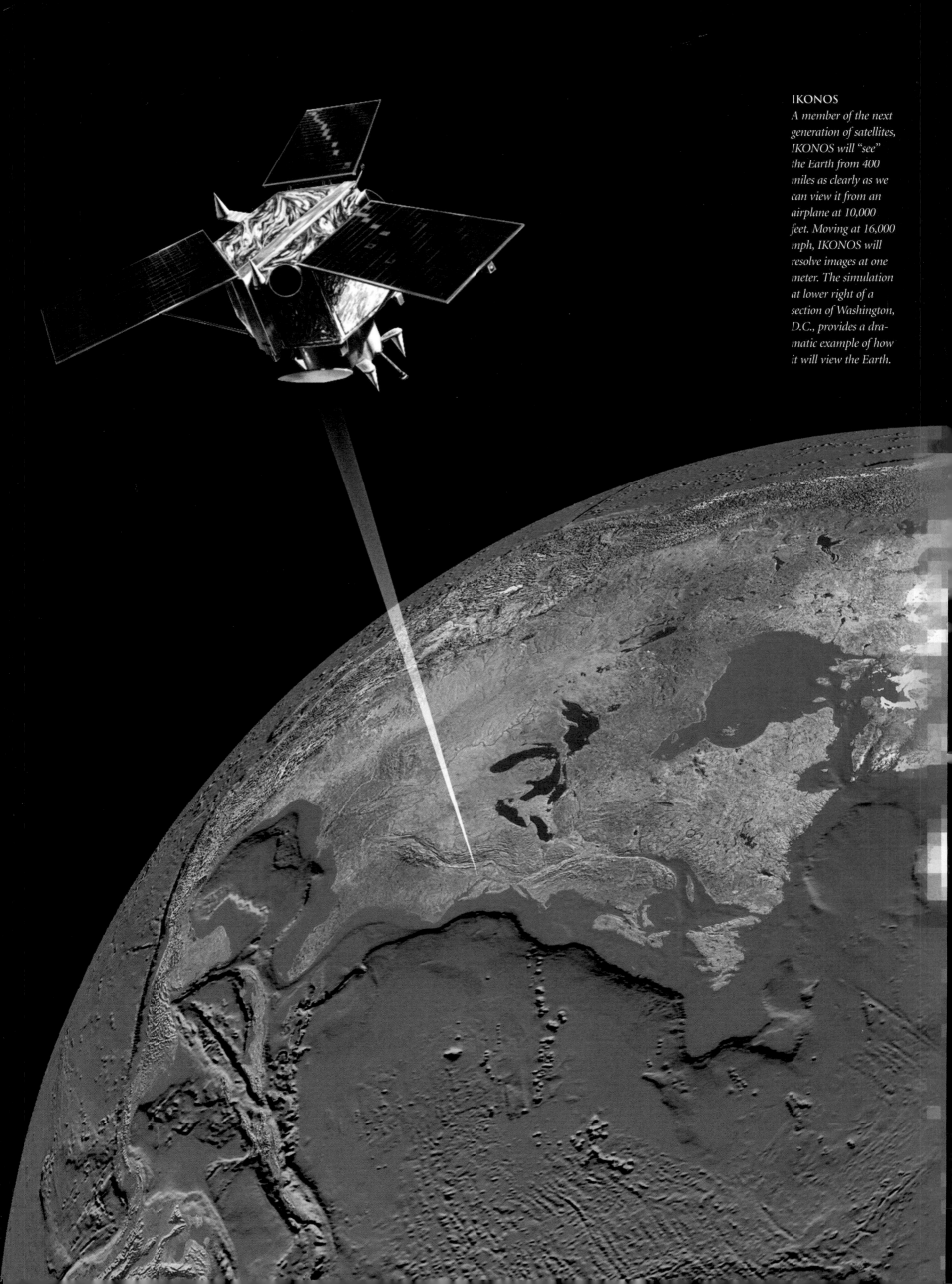

IKONOS
A member of the next generation of satellites, IKONOS will "see" the Earth from 400 miles as clearly as we can view it from an airplane at 10,000 feet. Moving at 16,000 mph, IKONOS will resolve images at one meter. The simulation at lower right of a section of Washington, D.C., provides a dramatic example of how it will view the Earth.

A s we turn the corner on the 21st century, we enter a new phase in the information age, the age of transparency, as Sir Arthur Clarke called it, by using vantage points in space to look back to Earth.

In reviewing milestones of the past, we note that technology brought television to the world of radio communication. It produced imaging systems like the Hubble Space Telescope that provide new insights into the universe. And the Internet ties us together in a state of increasingly global consciousness.

Now another technological leap forward: High-resolution Earth imaging from space at unprecedented levels of detail is becoming a global commercial reality, a new source of valuable information that is available for the first time to the public. Very sharp Earth images reveal information about our world—spatially, spectrally, and temporally—in ways that were never before possible, or even imagined. Satellite sensors hold steady to displacements measured in the range of a few microns, determining our position in orbit to a few meters with the aid of the Global Positioning System, establishing our line of sight to a fraction of a

meter on the ground using precision stellar referencing, and finally transmitting data to the ground at rates comparable to watching nearly 50 digital TV channels at once. Within minutes, high-speed ground processing systems view and analyze this "firehose" of image data harvested from space.

And what do we see? Orbiting the Earth north to south 14 times a day, these new sensors are able to see any spot on the planet, spatially, at one-meter resolution. By monitoring natural and man-made disasters, they enable faster human responses that may save lives. Spectrally, high-resolution near-infrared and multispectral imaging capabilities reveal objects on the ground in ways the human eye cannot. Temporally, the digital nature of the information allows us to map changes over time, thus helping predict growth trends, plan urban development, and assess the evolution of environmental conditions. New imaging technology can aid us in better informing ourselves of where we live and of what is changing around us, because of us—and in spite of us. Putting the technology of commercial high-resolution Earth imaging to good use may even help ensure humanity's survival.

SPACE AGENCIES AND CONTRIBUTORS

The Book Division and National Geographic Maps are grateful to the following agencies, companies, organizations, and universities for their assistance in the planning and preparation of the National Geographic Satellite Atlas of the World.

AEROPAN AERIAL PHOTOGRAPHY
25 Keren Hayesod, Jerusalem 94188, Israel
Specialization: Aeropan produces color, black-and-white, and infrared aerial photography, and orthophotography.

ALASKA SAR FACILITY (ASF)
Geophysical Institute, University of Alaska, Fairbanks
P.O. Box 757320, Fairbanks, AK 99775-7320
http://www.asf.alaska.edu
Specialization: ASF acquires, processes, archives, and distributes SAR data for the U.S. government and research and educational communities. SAR data are from ERS-1, ERS-2, JERS-1, and RADARSAT polar-orbiting satellites.

AUSTRALIAN CENTRE FOR REMOTE SENSING (ACRES)
SURVEYING AND LAND INFORMATION GROUP
DEPARTMENT OF INDUSTRY, SCIENCE, AND TOURISM
P.O. Box 28, Belconnen, ACT 2616, Australia
http://www.auslig.gov.au/acres/index.htm
Specialization: ACRES acquires, archives, and processes satellite remote sensing data for Australia, Papua New Guinea, and New Zealand. It is collaborating on the ARIES project, which plans to launch an Australian hyperspectral remote sensing satellite.

BYRD POLAR RESEARCH CENTER
THE OHIO STATE UNIVERSITY
108 Scott Hall, 1090 Carmack Road, Columbus, OH 43210
http://www-bprc.mps.ohio-state.edu
Specialization: A world leader in remote sensing of polar regions, the center has a strong program in the physics of remote sensing, emphasizing the interaction of broad spectral electromagnetic waves with sea ice and glacial ice.

CANADA CENTRE FOR REMOTE SENSING (CCRS)
NATURAL RESOURCES CANADA
588 Booth Street, Ottawa, Ontario, Canada K1A 0Y7
http://www.ccrs.nrcan.gc.ca
Specialization: CCRS receives, processes, and archives remotely sensed data for Canada. CCRS demonstrates the effective use of RADARSAT data and of high-resolution and hyperspectral airborne and satellite data for environmental monitoring. CCRS conducts research in scene physics radiometry, sensor calibration and validation, and data fusion.

CANADIAN SPACE AGENCY (CSA)
John H. Chapman Space Centre, 6767, Route de l'Aéroport, Saint-Hubert, Quebec J3Y 8Y9
http://www.space.gc.ca
Specialization: CSA coordinates Canada's Space Program, including Canada's first Earth observation satellite, RADARSAT-1, which has provided coverage of the whole of Antarctica, most notably through the Antarctic Mapping Mission.

CENTRE FOR REMOTE IMAGING, SENSING, AND PROCESSING (CRISP)
NATIONAL UNIVERSITY OF SINGAPORE
Lower Kent Ridge Road, Singapore 119260
http://www.crisp.nus.edu.sg
Specialization: CRISP specializes in remote sensing, ground station operation, image product generation and distribution, research in remote sensing applications, and data processing techniques. It has archived more than 135,000 SPOT, 13,500 ERS, and 7,000 RADARSAT images.

CENTRE NATIONAL D'ÉTUDES SPATIALES (CNES)
18 Avenue Edouard BELIN, 31055 Toulouse Cedex, France
http://www.cnes.fr
Specialization: CNES defines, designs, develops, and operates, in collaboration with national research programs, the space systems, ground segments, and certain airborne experiments conducted by the scientific community. SPOT Image in Toulouse was set up to distribute imagery returned by the SPOT Earth-observation satellite. (See SPOT Image Corporation profile)

CSIRO OFFICE OF SPACE SCIENCE AND APPLICATIONS
EARTH OBSERVATION CENTRE
GPO BOX 3023, Canberra, ACT 2601, Australia
http://www.cossa.csiro.au (and) http://www.eoc.csiro.au
Specialization: With cooperation from laboratories located throughout Australia, CSIRO helps create standards for formats, calibration and validation, and application of remotely sensed data.

DEPARTMENT OF LAND ADMINISTRATION (DOLA)
SATELLITE REMOTE SENSING SERVICES
65 Brockway Road, Floreat, Western Australia 6014
http://www.rss.dola.wa.gov.au
Specialization: DOLA acquires and processes Earth observations from satellites for public and private sector clients. It maps changes in vegetation cover and salt-affected areas in Western Australia; produces regional mosaics of satellite imagery to assist geological mapping; and monitors bushfires, vegetation growth, crop yields, and fire scars.

EARTH SATELLITE CORPORATION (EARTHSAT)
6011 Executive Boulevard, Suite 400, Rockville, MD 20852
http://www.earthsat.com
Specialization: This international consulting firm deals with the application and development of remote sensing and GIS technologies for the exploration, development, monitoring, and management of the Earth's resources. EarthSat has completed over 450 studies in forestry, land use, environmental analysis, change detection, GIS, military applications, water, mineral and petroleum exploration, and agriculture. It has processed more than 25,000 satellite and other images and has been selected by NASA to create a multidate global Landsat data set.

EARTHDATA INTERNATIONAL OF MARYLAND, LLC
(FORMERLY PHOTO SCIENCE, INC.)
45 West Watkins Mill Road, Gaithersburg, MD 20878
http://www.earthdata.com
Specialization: EarthData offers experience and expertise in spatial data acquisition, processing, development, and analysis. It uses airborne sensors developed specifically for digital aerial mapping and GIS applications.

ERIM INTERNATIONAL, INC.
P.O. Box 134008, Ann Arbor, MI 48113-4008
http://www.erim-int.com
Specialization: ERIM (Environmental Research Institute of Michigan) flew the first SAR and the first multifrequency and multipolarization SAR for remote sensing applications. It expanded SAR technology to include the first commercial interferometric SAR for extraction of terrain elevation. ERIM continues to innovate by using multispectral aerial and satellite data, SAR, LIDAR and ground-penetrating radar in combination with advanced GIS and other fusion technologies.

EURIMAGE, S.P.A.
Viale E. D'Onofrio, 212, Roma 00155 Italy
http://www.eurimage.it
Specialization: This multimission, remote sensing data distributor has a portfolio including low-resolution AVHRR, mid-resolution Landsat and ERS radar, and future high-resolution data from satellites such as QuickBird. Through links with the ESA, providers around the world, and major users such as the EU and the UN, Eurimage, S.p.A. offers service and support for those using satellite data to solve geo-information problems.

EUROPEAN SPACE AGENCY (ESA)
Headquarters, 8-10 Rue Mario Nikis, F-75738 Paris Cedex 15, France
http://www.esa.int (and) http://earthnet.esrin.esa.it
Specialization: The 14 Member States of this intergovernmental organization participate in programs on astronomy, astrophysics, Earth observation, telecommunications, launcher development, manned spaceflight, and research in a microgravity environment. ESA developed and launched METEOSAT and ERS, a series of satellites monitoring climactic and environmental conditions and helping to manage Earth resources. A new generation of Earth-observation satellites, ENVISAT and METOP, is planned for the end of the century.

GEOCARTO INTERNATIONAL CENTRE
GPO Box 4122, Rooms 16 and 17, 2nd floor, Wah Ming Centre,
421 Queen's Road West, Hong Kong
http://www.geocarto.com/geocarto.html
Specialization: Geocarto promotes multidisciplinary research in and application of remote sensing, GIS, geoscience, and cartography. It publishes books, periodicals, images, and maps; markets satellite data for research projects and practical applications; and provides technical advice on the application of remote sensing technologies.

GEOFORSCHUNGZENTRUM POTSDAM
(GFZ POTSDAM)
Telegrafenberg, D-14473 Potsdam, Germany
http://www.gfz-potsdam.de
Specialization: GFZ Potsdam specializes in GPS networks, SAR interferometry, mini-satellites (GFZ-1, CHAMP) for gravity field measurements, high resolution gravity models of the earth, altimetry, hyperspectral, and multispectral remote sensing.

GEOGRAPHICAL SURVEY INSTITUTE (GSI)
MINISTRY OF CONSTRUCTION, JAPAN
Kitasato-1, Tsukuba-shi, Ibaraki-ken, 305-0811 Japan
http://www.gsi-mc.go.jp
Specialization: Established in 1869, the institute is Japan's primary survey administration based upon the Survey Act. Its work includes the implementation of basic surveys, research and development, and international cooperation for survey and mapping activities.

GEOIMAGE, PTY., LTD.
13/180 Moggill Road, Taringa Brisbane, Queensland 4068, Australia
http://www.geoimage.com.au
Specialization: GEOIMAGE specializes in multiple-image mosaicing. It has produced regional Landsat TM and MSS mosaics of Australia and overseas areas, as well as high-resolution Landsat TM and SPOT panchromatic merges of Australian capital cities.

GEOSPACE BECKEL-SATELLITENBILDDATEN, GMBH
Jakob-Haringer-Str. 1, A-5020 Salzburg, Austria
http://geospace.co.at
Specialization: As the Austrian remote sensing Data Centre, GEOSPACE distributes Earth-observation satellite data to its customers in Austria. Globally, it works on applied research and on customer-tailored data evaluation for feasibility studies and applications in remote sensing. Featured studies include administration, land use, agriculture, forestry, archaeology, environment, and physical planning, in combination with GIS.

GERMAN AEROSPACE CENTER (DLR)
GERMAN REMOTE SENSING DATA CENTER (DFD)
DFD at DLR Oberpfaffenhofen, 82234 Wessling, Germany
http://www.dfd.dlr.de
Specialization: The center specializes in the reception, processing, archiving, distribution, and application of data from Earth-observation satellites. It designs and operates satellite ground stations; conceives, develops, implements, and validates data-processing algorithms; develops archiving and management systems for large quantities of data; and makes a variety of products available on-line and off-line.

HAMMON, JENSEN, WALLEN, AND ASSOCIATES, INC.
(HJW) IMAGING THE EARTH
8407 Edgewater Drive, Oakland, CA 94707
http://www.hjw.com
Specialization: HJW specializes in aerial photography, photogrammetry, digital orthophotography, image processing, remote sensing, and spatial data integration. It leads in digital orthorectification, multispectral image processing, airborne GPS, and soft-copy photogrammetry.

IMAGERIE STÉRÉO APPLIQUÉE AU RELIEF (ISTAR)
Les Espaces de Sophia, Bât. F-80, Route des Lucioles,
Sophia Antipolis, F-06560 Valbonne, France
http://www.istar.com
Specialization: ISTAR has automated the gathering of geographic data to create unique perspective mapping solutions for the wireless industry. ISTAR has processed over 2,500 SPOT satellite images, covering more than 3,000,000 square kilometers of urban areas in 100 countries.

INFOCARTO, S.A.
Gobelas, 25. Planta 3, Edificio Eulen A, 28023 La Florida, Madrid, Spain
http://www.infocarto.es
Specialization: Infocarto specializes in remote sensing analysis; applications to engineering, agriculture, and forest fire control; ERDAS IMAGING distribution; and SMARTECH NOAA antennas. It has developed various research and technology projects under EU contracts, providing services for forest fire management, estimating atmospheric emissions, and conducting the Medium Scale Surface Temperature Mission (MUST).

INSTITUTE FOR APPLIED GEOSCIENCES (IFG)
Odenwaldring 38, D-63069 Offenbach, Germany
E-mail: IFG VERLAG@aol.com
Specialization: IFG specializes in development planning, rural resource development, resource-potential mapping, and regional planning using digital image processing, thematic mapping, and digital cartography. It also conducts regional inventories of natural and socioeconomic sectors.

INSTITUTO DE INGENIERÍA
PO Box 40200, Caracas 1040-A, Venezuela
http://www.fii.org
Specialization: The institute is a pioneer in the application of remote sensing for GIS development in Venezuela. It is Venezuela's first large user of remotely sensed data in digital format, the first contributor in the teaching of remote sensing, and the main center for applications development for remote sensing. The Petróleos de Venezuela, S.A., also contributed to this atlas.

INSTITUTO NACIONAL DE PESQUISAS ESPACIAIS
(INPE) BRAZILIAN NATIONAL INSTITUTE
FOR SPACE RESEARCH, REMOTE SENSING DIVISION
MINISTRY OF SCIENCE AND TECHNOLOGY
Astronautas Ave. 1758, 12227-010 São Jose Campos SP, Brazil
http://www.inpe.br
Specialization: INPE specializes in space science, space technology, remote sensing, and meteorology. INPE also monitors the Amazon rain forest.

ISTITUTO NAZIONALE DI GEOFISICA (ING)
Via di Vigna Murata, 605, 00143 Rome, Italy
http://www.ingrm.it
Specialization: ING specializes in geophysical research and conducts a 24-hour earthquake surveillance of Italy. It utilizes remote sensing and image analysis for tectonic and geomorphological interpretation. ING has developed algorithms for atmospheric data as well as volcanic data (gas emissions and lava) and employs SAR in interferometry studies.

LANDCARE RESEARCH NEW ZEALAND, LTD.
P.O. Box 69, Lincoln 8152, Canterbury, New Zealand
http://www.landcare.cri.nz
Specialization: Landcare's image-processing team were principal investigators on Landsat 2, SIR-B, JERS-1, SPOT 1, and many other missions. Current research concentrates on SAR, especially multipolarization, multiband SAR from the NASA/JPL AirSar-Topsar PacRim Mission of 1996, along with SIR-C/X-SAR, ERS-1 and -2 data, JERS-1 SAR, and RADARSAT.

LUNAR AND PLANETARY INSTITUTE
3300 Bay Area Blvd., Houston, TX 77058
http://cass.jsc.nasa.gov/lpi.html
Specialization: The institute specializes in planetary geoscience, impact cratering, astronomy, and astrophysics. It detects and characterizes Earth's buried impact structures and documents impact craters on Venus and the moon using orbital radars.

M-SAT EDITIONS
Rue Jean Claret, 63063, Clermont-Ferrand, France
http://www.imsat.com
Specialization: M-SAT publishes and distributes high-quality satellite maps in full natural color of cities and states, and is currently building natural-color mosaics of the continents. In 1996, using Landsat 5 TM data with a resolution of 30 meters, M-SAT made the 250-image mosaic covering Western Europe. In 1997, it completed the mosaic of the continental U.S. using 432 Landsat 5 TM images.

NATIONAL AERONAUTICS AND SPACE
ADMINISTRATION (NASA)
Headquarters, 300 E. St., S.W., Washington, DC 20546-0001
http://www.nasa.gov
Specialization: With primary specializations in aeronautics, the exploration and development of space, Earth science, and space science, NASA has pioneered the field of remote sensing by developing, launching, and operating satellites since 1958. Data from several satellites and NOAA buoys have been combined to produce images of the sea surface and sea thermocline.

NASA/AMES RESEARCH CENTER
AIRBORNE SENSOR FACILITY
MS 240-6, NASA Ames Research Center, Moffett Field, CA 94035
http://asapdata.arc.nasa.gov
Specialization: This facility has promoted the development of airborne remote sensing imaging instruments through the calibration and validation of the EOS satellite and airborne platform imaging systems. It contributed to the ozone hole investigations over Antarctica in 1987 and participated in disaster-assessment responses for the Yellowstone fires, the Oakland fire, Hurricane Iniki, the St. Louis flood, and California floods.

NASA/GODDARD INSTITUTE FOR SPACE STUDIES (GISS)
2880 Broadway, New York, NY 10025
http://www.giss.nasa.gov
Specialization: NASA's GISS is the global processing center for the World Climate Research Program's International Satellite Cloud Climatology Project. It also participates in the analysis of other NASA and NOAA satellite data sets. Researchers at GISS are also using cloud and temperature-humidity data sets to diagnose the radiation budget of the Earth.

NASA/GODDARD SPACE FLIGHT CENTER (GSFC)
Code 935, Greenbelt, MD 20771
http://pao.gsfc.nasa.gov
Specialization: As the lead center in NASA's Mission to Planet Earth (MTPE) program, Goddard manages the Earth Observing System (EOS). To develop a better understanding of the environment, MTPE will rely on the EOS Data and Information System (EOSDIS), designed to archive, manage, and distribute MTPE data worldwide. Goddard also procures, develops, and verifies testing of the Geostationary Operational Environmental Satellite (GOES). Images from the SeaWiFS program and Scientific Visualization Studio (SVS) are featured in this atlas.

NASA/JET PROPULSION LABORATORY (JPL)
CALIFORNIA INSTITUTE OF TECHNOLOGY (CALTECH)
4800 Oak Grove Drive, Pasadena, CA 91109
http://jpl.nasa.gov
Specialization: JPL pioneered developments in digital image processing; initiated civilian spaceborne radar; and became a leader in placing imaging spectrometers on aircraft and satellites. JPL is renowned for contributions to geologic mapping, satellite oceanography, altimetry, scatterometry, SAR, and research in the applications of multispectral thermal-infrared data with airborne and spaceborne sensors. ASTER, AVIRIS, SIR-C/X-SAR, and TOPEX/Poseidon Projects are represented in this atlas.

NASA/JPL/CALTECH's AVHRR Project, Cartographic Applications Group

(CAG): *This group manipulated over 500 NOAA weather satellite images acquired by the Advanced Very High Resolution Radiometer (AVHRR) instrument to create satellite coverages for this atlas. Using hundreds of multidate NOAA AVHRR satellite scenes and imaging in the visible and near-infrared wavelengths, the mosaics were created in a rapid fashion using semiautomated software procedures based on JPL's VICAR/IBIS image processing and GIS software.*

NASA/LANGLEY RESEARCH CENTER
100 NASA Road, Hampton, VA 23681
http://www.larc.nasa.gov
Specialization: The center specializes in aeronautics, atmospheric science, and space technology. Its contributions include the development of the first LIDAR for atmospheric sensing from space; global mapping of aerosols and clouds; and high-resolution profiling of the atmosphere.

NASA/LYNDON B. JOHNSON SPACE CENTER (JSC)
2101 NASA Road 1, Houston, TX 77058-3696
http://www.images.jsc.nasa.gov
Specialization: JSC is NASA's primary center for planning and conducting human space flight missions. Photography from manned space flights is available in their extensive archive of 35mm, 70mm, and 4 x 5-inch transparencies of the earth from Space Transportation System (STS), missions.

NASA/MARSHALL SPACE FLIGHT CENTER (MSFC)
GLOBAL HYDROLOGY AND CLIMATE CENTER (GHCC)
977 Explorer Blvd., Huntsville, AL 35806
http://thunder.msfc.nasa.gov
Specialization: This center conducts lightning and thunderstorm research, climate variability studies, and remote sensing and instrument development. A three-year global lightning database, developed from the EOS Optical Transient Detector, is the most comprehensive such database ever produced.

NATIONAL OCEANIC AND ATMOSPHERIC ADMINISTRATION (NOAA)
Headquarters, 14th and Constitution Avenue, Washington, DC 20233
http://www.noaa.gov
Specialization: NOAA's historical role has been to predict environmental changes, protect life and property, provide decision makers with reliable scientific information, and foster global environmental stewardship. The world's largest civil operational, environmental space organization, it operates geostationary and polar-orbiting environmental satellites.

NOAA/NATIONAL WEATHER SERVICE (NWS)
Office of Meteorology, 1325 East-West Hwy., Silver Spring, MD 20910
http://www.nws.noaa.gov
Specialization: NWS provides weather, hydrologic, and climate forecasts and warnings for the United States, its territories, adjacent waters and ocean areas. NWS data and products form a national information database that can be used by other governmental agencies and the private sector.

NOAA/NESDIS/NATIONAL CLIMACTIC DATA CENTER (NCDC)
151 Patton Avenue, Asheville, NC 28801-5001
http://www.ncdc.noaa.gov
Specialization: NCDC retains the national archive of meteorological data.

NOAA/NESDIS/NATIONAL GEOPHYSICAL DATA CENTER (NGDC)
325 Broadway, Boulder, CO 80305
http://www.ngdc.noaa.gov
Specialization: NGDC distributes data on geophysics, bathymetry, and the ionosphere. It develops data visualization techniques and conducts research using data fusion technologies. The establishment of the archive and distribution center for data from the Defense Meteorological Satellite Program (DMSP) led to the generation of DMSP-derived products, such as the global map of human settlements.

NOAA/NESDIS/NATIONAL OCEANOGRAPHIC DATA CENTER (NODC)
1315 East-West Hwy., Silver Spring, MD 20910
http://www.nodc.noaa.gov
Specialization: NODC maintains and distributes the world's largest collection of publicly available oceanographic data and operates major research libraries. By international agreement, NODC is the World Data Center A for oceanography.

NOAA/NESDIS/OFFICE OF RESEARCH AND APPLICATIONS (ORA)
4700 Silver Hill Road, Stop 9909-EIRA, Washington, DC 20233-9909
http://orbit-net.nesdis.noaa.gov/ora
Specialization: NESDIS is responsible for the development and application of retrieval algorithms used with passive microwave satellite measurements to monitor land, sea, and atmospheric processes. Activities of its Office of Research and Applications include the development of products and services using both polar and geostationary satellite systems.

NATIONAL REMOTE SENSING AGENCY (NRSA)
DEPARTMENT OF SPACE, GOVERNMENT OF INDIA
Balanagar, Hyderabad 500037, A.P., India
http://www.nrsa.org
Specialization: The main activities include satellite data acquisition; archiving, processing, and disseminating data products; training; and the application of remote sensing for the mapping, monitoring, and management of natural resources and the environment.

NATIONAL REMOTE SENSING CENTRE, LTD. (NRSC)
Delta House, Southwood Crescent, Southwood, Farnborough, Hampshire, GU14 ONL, U.K.
http://www.nrsc.co.uk
Specialization: NRSC is a leading supplier of satellite and aircraft imagery. Its specialists cover many disciplines—geology, environment, agriculture, water resources, and cartography. Through its sister company, Air Reconnaissance Ltd., NRSC operates aerial instruments such as optical cameras, hyperspectral imagers, and thermal and laser imagers.

NATIONAL SPACE DEVELOPMENT AGENCY OF JAPAN (NASDA)
World Trade Center Bldg., 2-4-1, Hamamatsu-cho, Minato-ku, Tokyo 105-60
http://www.nasda.go.jp (and) http://www.miti.go.jp
Specialization: Under the umbrella organizations of MITI and the Japanese Space Development Program, NASDA is responsible for the development, launching, and tracking of satellites and spacecrafts.

ORBIMAGE
World Trade Center Bldg., 2-4-1, Hamamatsu-cho, Minato-ku, Tokyo 105-60
http://www.orbimage.com
Specialization: Orbital Imaging Corporation (ORBIMAGE) provides satellite-based imaging products and services for use in environmental monitoring, mapping, and surveying.

RADARSAT INTERNATIONAL (RSI)
3851 Shell Rd., Suite 200, Richmond, British Columbia, Canada V6X 2W2
http://www.rsi.ca
Specialization: Owned and operated by the Canadian Space Agency, RADARSAT is the first radar satellite entirely dedicated to operational applications. RADARSAT International is the North American distributor of ERS data and the Canadian distributor of SPOT, Landsat, and JERS data. Equipped with a powerful SAR, RADARSAT offers high-quality data to resource management and environmental-monitoring professionals.

REMOTE SENSING TECHNOLOGY CENTER OF JAPAN (RESTEC)
Roppongi First Bldg., 1-9-9, Roppongi, Minato-ku, Tokyo 106-0032, Japan
http://www.restec.or.jp/restec_e.html
Specialization: RESTEC collects and distributes remotely sensed data and supports the data acquisition and processing activities of the Earth Observation Center (EOC), NASDA.

ROHR PRODUCTIONS, LTD.
6 Michalaki Karaolis Street, Suite 402, PO Box 3312, 1681 Nicosia, Cyprus
E-mail: rohrprod@spidernet.com.cy
Specialization: RGHR developed one of the first mergers of Landsat 5 and SPOT, covering all of Israel and western Jordan. It collaborated on the first civilian digital model covering the same area and on 3-D animation software suitable for databases of unlimited size.

RUTHERFORD APPLETON LABORATORY (RAL)
Chilton, Didcot, Oxfordshire, United Kingdom, OX11 0QX
http://www.eiscat.rl.ac.uk
Specialization: The laboratory develops and builds remote sensing instrumentation for missions that monitor chemicals in the atmosphere and on the surface. It built ERS-1 and -2, and ATSR, featured in this atlas.

SCRIPPS INSTITUTION OF OCEANOGRAPHY
La Jolla, CA 92093-0225
http://sio.ucsd.edu
Specialization: The Institute of Geophysics and Planetary Physics at Scripps is a co-contributor with NOAA for various oceanography-related topics in this atlas. Using global relief data, several topographic models from the ocean floor to the peaks of the Himalaya were created.

SHASHIN KAGAKU CO., LTD.
436-5 Tatetomita-cho Ichijou agaru, Higashihorikawa dori Kamigyo-ku, Kyoto-si kyoto-pref, Japan
http://www.shashin-kagaku.co.jp
Specialization: As demonstrated by the dramatic portrayal of Mount Fuji, Shashin Kagaku has mastered satellite imaging, mosaics, and visualization.

SOVINFORMSPUTNIK INTERBRANCH ASSOCIATION
47, Leningradskiy Prospect, 125167, Moscow, Russia
http://www.sovinformsputnik.com
Specialization: Sovinformsputnik is the primary distributor of high-resolution remote sensing data with two-meter ground resolution. Orthorectified digital imagery and terrain models, combined with high-resolution satellite imagery processing, expanded upon conventional visualization capabilities to present today's highest resolution images from space of cities, archaeological sites, and physical features.

SPACE IMAGING
12076 Grant Street, Thornton, CO 80241
http://www.spaceimaging.com
Specialization: Space Imaging provides information for environmental and agricultural monitoring, mapping, infrastructure management, and oceanographic and atmospheric research. It collects and distributes information from a constellation of aerial platforms and satellites; a one-meter-resolution imaging satellite will be added in the near future. Space Imaging maintains space-based and aerial imagery in its CARTERRA archive.

SPOT IMAGE CORPORATION
1897 Preston White Drive, Reston, VA 22091-4326
http://www.spot.com
Specialization: The SPOT satellite system consists of three operational remote-sensing spacecraft: SPOT 1, 2, and 4. This commercial Earth-observation system gathers detailed and up-to-date imagery. It specializes in digital panchromatic (black-and-white) and multispectral (color) satellite imagery for myriad applications. The corporation is the U.S. office of the worldwide SPOT system, headquartered in Toulouse, France (5, rue des Satellites, BP 4359, F 31030, Toulouse Cedex 4, France).

SWEDISH SPACE CORPORATION (SSC) SATELLITBILD
P.O. Box 4207, SE-981 28 Kiruna, Sweden
http://www.ssc.se/sb
Specialization: The corporation specializes in the direct reception, processing, and delivery of satellite data. Located north of the Arctic Circle, its receiving station can see polar-orbiting satellites on almost every orbit; a satellite's recorded data can be downloaded on virtually every pass.

SWISSPHOTO VERMESSUNG, AG
Dorfstrasse 53, CH-8105 Regensdorf-Watt, Switzerland
http://www.swissphoto.ch
Specialization: Swissphoto specializes in surveying services, mapping and charting, and photogrammetric production services.

SYSTEMS FOR WORLD SURVEILLANCE, INC. (SWS)
P.O. Box 528 , Camden, ME 04843
http://www.rsat.com
Specialization: In addition to coastal and forestry studies, SWS specializes in thermal mapping of urban landscapes. Its products translate satellite imagery into intuitive and informative image maps. SWS provides environmental solutions to stresses on our natural resources.

TELESPAZIO, S.P.A.
DIVISIONE TELERILEVAMENTO E INFORMAZIONI AMBIENTALI, SERVIZIO COMMERCIALE PRODOTTI
Via Tiburtina, 965, 00156 Roma
http://www.telespazio.it
Specialization: Telespazio is a distributor of Eurimage and SPOT Image.

UNITED NATIONS HIGH COMMISSIONER FOR REFUGEES (UNHCR)
Casa Postale 2500, CH-1211 Geneva , 2 Dépôt, Switzerland
http://www.unhcr.ch
Specialization: UNHCR provides assistance to refugees. Environmental assessments of refugee-hosting areas and logistical analysis for humanitarian operations have relied upon data from satellite imagery.

UNITED STATES GEOLOGICAL SURVEY
Headquarters, 12201 Sunrise Valley Drive, Reston, VA 20192
http://www.usgs.gov
Specialization: USGS specializes in earthquake and volcanic hazard information, water supply and quality information, global change and climate history studies, biological resource studies, topographic and geologic mapping, and mineral resource assessments. It has mapped and analyzed change in the Antarctic ice sheet and produced the first satellite image map of the entire Antarctic continent.

USGS/EROS DATA CENTER
Sioux Falls, SD 57198
http://edcwww.cr.usgs.gov
Specialization: USGS contributions to this atlas were obtained from the EROS Data Center. The center is the national archive for land remote sensing data.

USGS/FLAGSTAFF
2255 North Gemini Drive, Flagstaff, AZ 86001
http://wwwflag.wr.usgs.gov
Specialization: The Astrogeology Program specializes in Earth and planetary geology, has produced hundreds of image mosaics and maps of other planets, and was the first to apply image-processing techniques to Landsat images of Antarctica.

U. S. NAVAL SPACE COMMAND
NAVAL SPACE SURVEILLANCE SYSTEM
5280 Fourth Street, Dahlgren, VA 22448-5300
http://www.navspace.navy.mil
Specialization: Operated by the U.S. Naval Space Command, this system has seen the number of detectable earth-orbiting objects triple in 30 years.

UNIVERSIDAD DE ALCALÁ, MADRID
Colegios 2, 28801 Alcalá de Henares, Madrid, Spain
http://www.alcala.es/departam/geogra/depgeo.htm
Specialization: The university provided the principal research on EU projects that applied remote sensing and mapping to the analysis of forest fires to examine burned areas and estimate plant water content and fire risk.

UNIVERSITY OF BRISTOL, CENTRE FOR REMOTE SENSING
SCHOOL OF GEOGRAPHICAL SCIENCE
University Road, Bristol BS8 1SS, England, U.K.
http://www.ggy.bris.ac.uk
Specialization: The Centre has generated the best available digital elevation models of Antarctica and Greenland, and a new global DEM at five-arc minutes from radar altimeter data. A 20-year climatology study of the northeast Atlantic and the Mediterranean is in production.

UNIVERSITY OF MIAMI, ROSENSTIEL SCHOOL OF MARINE AND ATMOSPHERIC SCIENCE (RSMAS)
4600 Rickenbacker Causeway, Miami, FL 33149-1098
http://www.rsmas.miami.edu
Specialization: RSMAS conducts applied research in marine and atmospheric science within its facilities including the Gilbert Hovey Grosvenor Laboratory. Its specialization includes AVHRR-infrared processing and analysis using the NOAA/NASA AVHRR Pathfinder data set, the utilization of Coastal Zone Color Scanner (CZCS) processing system, and the fusion of ocean color and infrared observations.

UNIVERSITY OF MUNICH, WORKING GROUP REMOTE SENSING (AGF)
INSTITUTE FOR GENERAL AND APPLIED GEOLOGY
Ludwig-Maximilians-Universität, Luisenstr, 37, 80333 Munich
http://www.iaag.geo.uni-muenchen.de/agf
Specialization: AGF specializes in the processing of multispectral, hyperspectral, and microwave data; digital image processing; data fusion and synergetic data evaluation; and definition of remote sensors.

UNIVERSITY OF NEW HAMPSHIRE
COMPLEX SYSTEMS RESEARCH CENTER (CSRC)
INSTITUTE FOR THE STUDY OF EARTH, OCEANS, AND SPACE
Morse Hall, 39 College Road, Durham, NH 03824-3525
http://eos-www.sr.unh.edu/csrc.html
Specialization: CSRC specializes in stress detection and damage assessment in trees affected by air pollutants. It used satellite and hyperspectral data to assess and monitor forest health caused by acid rain in Eastern Europe.

UNIVERSITY OF WISCONSIN, ENVIRONMENTAL REMOTE SENSING CENTER (ERSC)
INSTITUTE FOR ENVIRONMENTAL STUDIES
1225 W. Dayton Street, Madison, WI 53706
http://www.ersc.wisc.edu/ERSC
Specialization: ERSC has made significant contributions in large-area, satellite-based, land-cover mapping, soft-copy photogrammetry, regional monitoring of lake ice as a global climate indicator, and environmental and commercial applications of high-resolution satellite data.

VARGIS, LLC
208 Elden Street, Suite 204, Herndon, VA 20170
http://www.vargis.com
Specialization: VARGIS specializes in the commercial distribution of image map products. Aerials featured in this atlas were produced by the National Capital Planning Commission for the Washington GIS.

VIRTUOZO SYSTEMS INTERNATIONAL
21 Buchanan St., West End, P.O. Box 3797, South Brisbane BC, Queensland 4101, Australia
http://www.virtuozo.com.au
Specialization: VirtuoZo's expertise in digital photogrammetry software and visualization has been applied to 3-D terrain modeling using overlapping aerial photography or SPOT imagery. Vexcel Imaging Corporation also contributed to this atlas.

WORLDSAT INTERNATIONAL, INC.
211 Watline Avenue, Mississauga, Ontario, L4Z 1P3, Canada
http://www.worldsat.ca
Specialization: WorldSat produces natural-color satellite and airborne-image mosaics and 3-D perspectives. Images are used in applications and productions that include the publication of atlases and the creation of prints, posters, maps, globes and multimedia products. WorldSat offers a unique approach to remote sensing by blending the art instrinsic in the natural beauty of the Earth with the science used in resource management and environmental monitoring.

ABBREVIATIONS AND IMAGERY CREDITS

ABBREVIATIONS

ACRES *Australian Centre for Remote Sensing*
AMM *Antarctic Mapping Mission*
ANGAP *National Association for the Management of Protected Areas (Madagascar)*
ASTER *Advanced Spaceborne Thermal Emission and Reflection Radiometer*
ATSR *Along-Track Scanning Radiometer*
AVHRR *Advanced Very High Resolution Radiometer*
AVIRIS *Airborne Visible/Infrared Imaging Spectrometer*
CalTech *California Institute of Technology*
CCRS *Canada Centre for Remote Sensing*
CERES *Clouds and Earth's Radiant Energy System*
CIMSS *Cooperative Institute for Meteorological Satellite Studies*
CNES *Centre National d'Études Spatiales (French Space Agency)*
CRISP *Centre for Remote Imaging, Sensing, and Processing*
CSA *Canadian Space Agency*
CSIRO *Commonwealth Scientific and Industrial Research Organisation*
DEM *Digital Elevation Model*
DLR *German Aerospace Center*
DMSP *U.S. Air Force Defense Meteorological Satellite Program*
DOLA *Department of Land Administration (Western Australia)*
DoSLI *Department of Survey and Land Information*
EarthSat *Earth Satellite Corporation*
EOS AM *Earth Observing System AM (morning)*
ENSO *El Niño/Southern Oscillation*
EROS *Earth Resources Observation Systems*
ERS *Earth Resources Satellite*
ESA *European Space Agency*
GIS *Geographic Information System*
GISS *Goddard Institute for Space Studies*
GMS *Geostationary Meteorological Satellite*
GOES *Geostationary Operational Environmental Satellite*
GSFC *Goddard Space Flight Center*
HRV *High Resolution Visible*
IFG *Institute for Applied Geosciences*
INPE *National Institute for Space Research (Brazil)*
IRS *Indian Remote Sensing Satellite*
ISTAR *Imagerie Stéréo Appliquée au Relief*
JERS *Japanese Earth Resources Satellite*
JPL *Jet Propulsion Laboratory*
LISS *Linear Imaging Self-scanning Sensor*
MESSR *Multispectral Electronic Self-Scanning Radiometer*
MODIS *Moderate Resolution Imaging Spectroradiometer*
MOMS *Modular Optoelectronic Multispectral Scanner*
MOS *Marine Observation Satellite*
MSFC *Marshall Space Flight Center*
MSS *Multispectral Scanner*
MSU *Microwave Sounding Unit*
NASA *National Aeronautics and Space Administration*
NASDA/MITI *National Space Development Agency of Japan/Ministry of International Trade and Industry*
NCDC *National Climatic Data Center*
NESDIS *National Environmental Satellite, Data, and Information Service*
NGDC *National Geophysical Data Center*
NGS *National Geographic Society*
NOAA *National Oceanic and Atmospheric Administration*
NODC *National Oceanographic Data Center*
NRSC *National Remote Sensing Centre, Ltd.*
NSCAT *NASA Scatterometer*
NTDLPE *Northern Territory Department of Lands, Planning, and Environment (Australia)*
OLS *Operational Linescan System*
ORA *Office of Research and Applications*
RAL *Rutherford Appleton Laboratory*
RESTEC *Remote Sensing Technology Center of Japan*
RSGS *Remote Sensing Satellite Ground Station (China)*
RSI *RADARSAT International*
RSRU *Remote Sensing Research Unit, University of California*
SAC *Satellite Applications Centre (Pretoria, South Africa)*
SAR *Synthetic Aperture Radar*
SeaWiFS *Sea-viewing Wide Field-of-view Sensor*
SIR-C/X-SAR *Spaceborne Imaging Radar-C/X-band Synthetic Aperture Radar*
SMMR *Scanning Multichannel Microwave Radiometer*
SOVZOND *Soviet Association for Earth Remote Sensing*
SPOT *Satellite Pour l'Observation de la Terre*
SSC *Swedish Space Corporation*
SSM/I *Special Sensor Microwave Imager*
TIMS *Thermal Infrared Multispectral Scanner*
TIROS *Television and Infrared Observation Satellite*
TM *Thematic Mapper*
TOMS *Total Ozone Mapping Spectrometer*
UNHCR *United Nations High Commissioner for Refugees*
USAID *United States Agency for International Development*
USGS *United States Geological Survey*
VTIR *Visible and Thermal Infrared Radiometer*

IMAGERY CREDITS

The list below gives the page number and a brief description for each image in this atlas, followed by the name of the company or companies providing the imagery; the names of the spacecraft and sensor; and a description of the spatial resolution. The band (wavelength) combinations, when available, are given in parentheses, and the date of acquisition follows. Entries that name several companies include the companies that processed the data and the original source of the satellite data used to create the published version.

COVER (front) *BIOSPHERE,* NASA/GSFC, ORBIMAGE: OrbView-2 SeaWiFS 1km (derived geophysical value), ocean September 1997–July 1998, land June 1998.

COVER (back) *GLOBAL COMPOSITES* (top to bottom, left to right), *EL NIÑO SEA SURFACE TEMPERATURE AND HEIGHT ANOMALIES,* NASA/GSFC, CNES: TOPEX/Poseidon Radar altimeter, NOAA AVHRR, and NOAA TAO buoys, November 1997; *NATURAL COLOR,* WorldSat International, Inc., NOAA: NOAA AVHRR 1km, 1991-94; *SEA SURFACE TEMPERATURE,* NASA/GSFC, Naval Oceanographic Office/Oceanographic Applications Branch, Northrop Grumman/DSSD, NASA/Stennis Space Center: NOAA AVHRR; *LIGHTS AT NIGHT,* NASA/GSFC, NOAA/NESDIS/NGDC: U.S. Air Force DMSP OLS, October 1994-October 1997; *BIOSPHERE,* NASA/GSFC, ORBIMAGE: OrbView-2 SeaWiFS 1km (derived geophysical value), ocean September 1997-July 1998, land June 1998; *ATMOSPHERIC WATER VAPOR,* NASA/GSFC: GOES-8 Imager 16km (thermal infrared), summer 1995; *EARTHQUAKES,* NASA/GSFC, USGS/National Earthquake Information Center, U.S. Naval Research Laboratory, Smithsonian Institution's Global Volcanism Program: NOAA AVHRR, earthquakes 1960-1985; *THERMAL-INFRARED WEATHER,* NOAA/NESDIS/CIMSS: GOES-8 Imager 12km (thermal infrared), 8/11/98; *ORBITAL PATHS OF THE FUTURE EOS AM-1 SATELLITE,* NASA/GSFC: NOAA AVHRR.

2-3 *EASTERN MEDITERRANEAN,* NASA/GSFC: OrbView-2 SeaWiFS 1km (6, 5, 1), 4/6/98.

4-5 *MOUNT ST. HELENS, 1996,* WorldSat International, Inc., Space Imaging: Landsat TM 30 m (1, 2, 4), 8/21/96.

8 *THE EARTH,* WorldSat International, Inc., NOAA: NOAA AVHRR 1km, 1991-94.

10 *FIRST TELEVISION IMAGE,* NOAA/NESDIS/NCDC, NASA: TIROS-1 Vidicon camera, 1960; *TIROS,* NOAA/NESDIS/Headquarters; *LANDSAT,* Space Imaging; *GOES,* NOAA/NESDIS/Headquarters; *SPOT,* © CNES, SPOT Image; *RADARSAT,* Illustration by Paul Fjeld, CSA; *EOS AM-1,* NASA/GSFC.

11 *COLD WAR, COSMOS* (left inset) and *U.S. CAPITOL* (left), Sovinformsputnik: Cosmos KVR-1000 2m, 5/31/88; *CORONA* (right inset), National Reconnaissance Office photograph (National Archives collection) as published in *CORONA: Between the Sun and the Earth* (Robert A. McDonald, ed.), 1997; *KREMLIN* (right), USGS/EROS Data Center: Corona KH-4B 2m, 5/22/70; *SPACE JUNK, 1965, 1988,* U.S. Naval Space Command.

12 *CAPE COD,* Space Imaging: Landsat TM 30m (4, 3, 2), 8/3/97.

14 *THE PENTAGON* (left to right), EarthData International of Maryland, LLC: Piper Navajo Chieftain Wild RC30 Aerial Film Camera 30m, 10m, 1m, 3/25/95; *CAPE CANAVERAL* (left to right), Space Imaging: Landsat TM 30m (3, 2, 1; 4, 3, 2; 7, 4, 3), 1/26/97; *POINT BARROW* (left to right), Alaska SAR Facility, NOAA/NWS (Alaska Region): NOAA AVHRR 1km (thermal infrared); ERS-1 SAR 100m (C-band), 2/4/92, 2/7/92, 2/10/92.

15 *GEOGRAPHIC INFORMATION SYSTEM,* USGS/Headquarters, Russian Ministry of Natural Resources, Russian Federal Service for Geodesy and Cartography: Landsat TM 30m (2, 4, 5), 8/21/89.

WORLD

16-17 *PARADE OF STORMS,* NOAA/NESDIS/NCDC: GOES-8 Imager 8km (thermal infrared), 8/23/95.

18-19 *THE WORLD,* NASA/JPL/CalTech/Cartographic Applications Group (CAG), NGS: NOAA AVHRR 1km (2, 2, 1), 1990-94.

20 *PROJECTIONS* (top to bottom), *MOLLWEIDE, BARTHOLOMEW, MERCATOR, INTERUPTED GOODE HOMOLOSINE,* WorldSat International, Inc., Jim Knighton, NOAA: NOAA AVHRR 1km, 1990-94.

23 *NORTH POLAR REGION* (top) and *SOUTH POLAR REGION* (bottom), NASA/JPL/CalTech/CAG, NGS: NOAA AVHRR 1km (2, 2, 1), 1990-94.

24-25 *BIOSPHERE,* NASA/GSFC, ORBIMAGE: OrbView-2 SeaWiFS 1km (derived geophysical value), ocean September 1997–July 1998, land June 1998; (bottom to top) *TOPOGRAPHY/BATHYMETRY,* NOAA/NESDIS/NGDC: GEOSAT Radar altimeter 3km (derived geophysical value), 1997; *CLOUD AMOUNT,* NASA/GISS: GOES, NOAA-7, METEOSAT, GMS (derived geophysical value), July 1983; *PRECIPITATION,* NASA/GSFC, NASA/JPL/CalTech: NOAA-11 HIRS/MSU 17km (derived geophysical value), June 1988; *SNOW DEPTH AND SEA ICE,* NASA/GSFC: NIMBUS-7 SMMR 27 and 55km (derived geophysical value), February 1983 and March 1980; *DAY/NIGHT TEMPERATURE DIFFERENCE,* NASA/GSFC, NASA/JPL/CalTech: NOAA HIRS/MSU 17km (derived geophysical value), June 1979; *WIND SPEED,* NASA/GSFC: GEOSAT Radar altimeter 9km (derived geophysical value), 1987; *WAVE HEIGHT,* NASA/GSFC: GEOSAT Radar altimeter 9km (derived geophysical value), 1987; *SEA LEVEL VARIABILITY,* NASA/GSFC: GEOSAT Radar altimeter 9km (derived geophysical value), 1987-88; *SEA SURFACE TEMPERATURE,* University of Miami: NOAA-9 AVHRR 18km (derived geophysical value), July 1984.

26-27 *TOPOGRAPHY/BATHYMETRY,* NOAA/NESDIS/NGDC: GEOSAT, ERS-1 and GTOPO30 Radar altimeter 3km, 1985-86, 1994-95.

28-29 *PHYSICAL EARTH,* NASA/JPL/CalTech/CAG, NGS: NOAA AVHRR 1km (2, 2, 1 with thematic overlays), 1990-94.

30-31 *LAND COVER ANNUAL* (top) and *SEASONAL ONSET, PEAK, AND END* (bottom), USGS/EROS Data Center: NOAA AVHRR 1km, April 1992-March 1993.

32 *CLOUDS,* NASA/GISS: NOAA, GOES, GMS, METEOSAT, Imaging radiometers 55km (thermal infrared), 10/15/83; *PRECIPITATION,* NOAA/NESDIS/ORA: DMSP SSM/I 2.5 degrees, July 1987–May 1998.

33 *LIGHTNING,* NASA/MSFC: MicroLab-1 NASA's Optical Transient Detector 8km, 1997; *HURRICANES* (Hurricane Erin), *RAINFALL* (left) and *WIND* (right), NOAA/NESDIS/NCDC: WSR-880 Doppler radar .54 nautical miles, 8/2/95.

34-35 *OCEAN FLOOR*, NOAA/NESDIS/NODC, Scripps Institution of Oceanography: GEOSAT, ERS-1, and GTOPO30 Radar altimeter 3km, 1985-86, 1994-95; *GEOID*, ESA/D-PAF (GFZ Potsdam): ERS Radar altimeter, 1993.

35 *SHIP TRACKS*, NOAA/NESDIS/NODC, Scripps Institution of Oceanography, Lamont-Doherty Earth Observatory: post-World War II to present.

36-37 *GLOBES*, NASA/JPL/CalTech, CNES: TOPEX/Poseidon Radar altimeter 1km (KU-band), 1/15/97, 6/25/97, 11/10/97, 5/3/98; *CUTAWAYS*, NASA/GSFC, CNES: TOPEX/Poseidon Radar altimeter, NOAA AVHRR, and NOAA TAO buoys, sea depth temperature 5 feet vertical, sea depth and sea height 60 miles horizontal, land 1km, January 1997, June 1997, November 1997, May 1998.

38-39 *POPULATION PORTRAIT*, NOAA/NESDIS/NGDC: U.S. Air Force DMSP OLS 1km, 10/1/94–3/31/95.

NORTH AMERICA

40-41 *GRAND CANYON*, M-SAT, © Eurimage, Space Imaging: Landsat TM 30m (3, 2, 1), 6/22/91–9/22/93.

42-43 *NORTH AMERICA*, NASA/JPL/CalTech/CAG, NGS: NOAA AVHRR 1km (2, 2, 1), 1990-94.

46-47 *THE LOWER 48 STATES*, M-SAT, © Eurimage, Space Imaging: Landsat TM 30m (3, 2, 1), 1991-93.

48 *DIOMEDE ISLANDS*, USGS/EROS Data Center: Corona KH-4B 2m, 4/30/65.

48-49 *MOUNT McKINLEY, ALASKA*, USGS/EROS Data Center Field Office (Anchorage, Alaska): Landsat MSS 60m (4, 5, 7), 8/24/79.

49 *GREENLAND* (left), University of Bristol: ERS-1 Radar altimeter 2.5km x 350m, 4/94–3/95; (right) NASA/JPL/CalTech: ERS-1 SAR 20m, 2/25/92, 2/28/92, 3/2/92.

50 *MAPPING DEATH VALLEY*, NASA/JPL/CalTech: Aircraft TIMS 10m (3 thermal-infrared bands), 6/11/91.

51 *VALLEY OF EXTREMES*, NASA/JPL/CalTech: Landsat TM 28.5m (5/7, 5/4, 3/1), 11/4/86.

52 *CHESAPEAKE BAY*, EarthSat: Landsat TM 30m (3, 2, 1), 5/93-6/93.

53 *MACKENZIE RIVER, CANADA*, GEOSPACE, Space Imaging: Landsat TM 30m (3, 2, 1), 8/7/85; *MISSISSIPPI RIVER, LOUISIANA*, © CNES, SPOT Image: SPOT HRV 20m (3, 2, 1), 10/6/95; *GULF OF MEXICO "DEAD ZONE,"* NASA/GSFC, ORBIMAGE: OrbView-2 SeaWiFS 1km, 2/23/98.

54 *MANICOUAGAN CRATER, QUEBEC*, CCRS: Landsat TM 30m (3, 4, 5), 8/19/86; *METEOR CRATER, ARIZONA*, NASA/JPL/CalTech: Aircraft TIMS 6m (3 thermal-infrared bands), 8/22/94; *CHICXULUB CRATER, YUCATÁN*, Lunar and Planetary Institute: DEM 7.2 x 7.2km, 8/1/93.

55 *GREAT LAKES*, University of Wisconsin: NOAA-9 AVHRR 1km, 7/21/86.

56 *COLUMBIA ICEFIELD, CANADA*, WorldSat International, Inc., SSC Satellitbild, ©CNES, SPOT Image: Landsat TM 30m (1, 2, 4), 8/23/96; SPOT HRV 10m (panchromatic), 9/9/95.

57 *CORAL REEF, BELIZE*, WorldSat International, Inc., SSC Satellitbild, © CNES, SPOT Image: SPOT HRV 20m (1, 2, 3), 3/2/97.

58 *MISSISSIPPI, 1988* and *MISSISSIPPI, 1993*, Space Imaging: Landsat TM 30m (7, 4, 3), 7/4/88, 7/18/93.

59 *HURRICANE FRAN*, NASA/GSFC: GOES-8 Imager 1km (1, 4, 4), 9/12/96.

60 *MOUNT ST. HELENS* (top and middle), WorldSat International, Inc., USGS/EROS Data Center: Landsat MSS 60m (1, 2, 4), 7/29/72, 8/23/85; (bottom) WorldSat International, Inc., Space Imaging: Landsat TM 30m (1, 2, 4), 8/21/96.

61 *OAKLAND HILLS, CALIFORNIA*, NASA/Ames Research Center: NASA C-130 N5001 TM Simulator 4.6m (6, 7, 5), 10/21/91.

62 *CANADA/UNITED STATES*, CCRS: Landsat MSS 80m (4, 5, 7), 7/26/78.

63 *UNITED STATES/MEXICO*, Space Imaging: Landsat TM 30m (5, 4, 3), 5/24/90; *MEXICO/GUATEMALA*, NASA/MSFC: Landsat TM 30m (2, 4, 3), 5/20/88.

64 *TRANS-ALASKA PIPELINE*, NASA/Ames Research Center: NASA U-2 Wild-Heerbrugg RC-10 Camera 2m (color infrared), 8/2/81.

65 *GREAT SALT LAKE, UTAH*, M-SAT, © Eurimage, Space Imaging: Landsat TM 30m (3, 2, 1), 7/18/92–7/27/93; *PANAMA CANAL*, RADARSAT International, CSA, CCRS, Resource GIS and Imaging, Ltd.: RADARSAT-1 SAR 50m (C-band), 4/7/97.

66 *VANCOUVER, BRITISH COLUMBIA*, CCRS: Landsat TM 30m (3, 4, 5), 9/5/87; *LOS ANGELES, CALIFORNIA*, Rise Geotechnics: Landsat TM 50m (7, 4 and 3, 1), 11/11/86.

67 *SAN FRANCISCO BAY AREA, CALIFORNIA*, M-SAT, © Eurimage, Space Imaging: Landsat TM 30m (3, 2, 1), 6/12/93.

68 *NEW YORK, NEW YORK*, Hammon, Jensen, Wallen, and Associates, Inc.: Twin Engine Piper Aztec Zeiss LMK 1015 Aerial Survey Camera 1:24,000 (natural color), 7/11/96.

69 *QUÉBEC, QUEBEC*, CCRS: Landsat TM 30m (3, 4, 5), 8/6/87; *CHICAGO, ILLINOIS*, ERIM International, Inc.: Landsat TM 30m (3, 2, 1), 10/5/92, 9/10/92.

70 *NEW ORLEANS, LOUISIANA*, © CNES, Spot Image: SPOT HRV 20m (3, 2, 1), 5/12/86.

71 *WASHINGTON, D.C.*, Space Imaging: Landsat TM 30m (5, 4, 3), 10/23/93; IRS-1C Panchromatic 25m, 10/18/96; *MEXICO CITY*, NASA/JPL/CalTech: Landsat TM 30m (4, 3, 7), 1/31/85.

SOUTH AMERICA

72-73 *THE AMAZON BASIN*, NASA/JPL/CalTech, NASDA, Alaska SAR Facility: JERS-1 SAR 100m (classification map), September–October 1995.

74-75 *SOUTH AMERICA*, NASA/JPL/CalTech/CAG, NGS: NOAA AVHRR 1km (2, 2, 1), 1990-94.

78 *LAKE TITICACA*, EarthSat: Landsat TM 30m (7, 4, 1), 8/3/85, 8/2/87; *ATACAMA DESERT*, © CNES, SPOT Image: SPOT HRV 20m (3, 2, 1), 9/7/86.

79 *MOUNT ACONCAGUA*, Universidad de Alcalá: Landsat TM 30m (4, 5, 3), 1/31/87.

80-81 *AMAZON AND RIO NEGRO CONFLUENCE*, GEOSPACE, Space Imaging: Landsat TM 30m (3, 2, 1), 6/7/85.

81 *MOUTH OF THE AMAZON*, INPE: Landsat TM 30m (5, 4, 3), 8/4/85–8/24/95.

82 *MOUNT GUAIQUINIMA*, Instituto de Ingeniería, Petróleos de Venezuela, S.A.: Landsat MSS 80m (5, 6, 4), 1/8/79.

83 *ANGEL FALLS*, USGS/EROS Data Center: Landsat MSS 80m (4, 2, 1), 1/1/79.

84 *TIERRA DEL FUEGO*, ESA: ERS-1 SAR 25m (bands 12/9/92, 2/17/93, 1/13/93).

85 *THE FALKLAND ISLANDS*, NRSC, BP Exploration, Ltd.: Landsat TM 30m (land 4, 5, 3; water 3, 2, 1), 5/10/87, 5/3/87.

86 *ANDEAN GLACIERS*, Universidad de Alcalá: Landsat MSS 80m (7, 5, 4), 1/14/86; *ANDEAN PERSPECTIVE*, Scripps Institution of Oceanography, NOAA/NESDIS/NODC: GEOSAT, ERS-1, and GTOPO30 Radar altimeter 3km, 1985-86, 1994-95.

87 *VOLCANIC SOILS*, Space Imaging: Landsat TM 30m (7, 4, 3), 8/19/85.

88 *BEFORE DEFORESTATION*, NASA/GSFC: Landsat MSS 60m (4, 2, 1), 6/17/75.

89 *AFTER DEFORESTATION*, NASA/GSFC: Landsat TM 30m (4, 5, 3), 6/11/96.

90 *DRUG FIELDS*, EarthSat: Landsat TM 30m (4, 7, 3), 9/7/85, 8/28/87; *PANTANAL*, NASA/JPL/CalTech: NASA ER-2 AVIRIS 20 x 20m (224 bands in 370-2,500nm), 8/20/95.

91 *IGUAÇU FALLS AREA*, EarthSat: Landsat TM 30m (5, 4, 3), 6/28/94.

92 *CARACAS, VENEZUELA*, Instituto de Ingeniería, Petróleos de Venezuela, S.A.: Landsat TM 30m (7, 5, 2), 3/14/91; *BOGOTÁ, COLOMBIA*, © CNES, SPOT Image: SPOT HRV 20m (3, 2, 1), 6/24/94.

93 *LIMA, PERU*, © CNES, SPOT Image: SPOT HRV 20m (3, 2, 1), 3/2/86.

94 *BRASÍLIA, BRAZIL*, Universidad de Alcalá: Landsat TM 30m (4, 5, 3), 9/21/86.

95 *SÃO PAULO, BRAZIL*, GEOSPACE, Space Imaging: Landsat TM 30m (3, 2, 1), 8/6/86; *RIO DE JANEIRO, BRAZIL*, Systems for World Surveillance, Inc., INPE: Landsat TM 30m (3, 2, 1), 4/29/96.

96 *LA PAZ, BOLIVIA*, © CNES, SPOT Image: SPOT HRV 10m (3, 2, 1), 5/1/91; *SANTIAGO, CHILE*, © CNES, SPOT Image: SPOT HRV 10m (3, 2, 1), 6/9/90.

97 *BUENOS AIRES, ARGENTINA*, Space Imaging: Landsat TM 30m (4, 5, 3), 6/16/87.

EUROPE

98-99 *ALETSCH GLACIER*, GEOSPACE, Space Imaging: Landsat TM 30m (3, 2, 1), 9/28/85.

100-101 *EUROPE*, NASA/JPL/CalTech/CAG, NGS: NOAA AVHRR 1km (2, 2, 1), 1990-94.

104 *STRAIT OF GIBRALTAR*, ESA: ERS-1 SAR 30m (yellow-green, cyan-magenta), 1/7/92.

105 *BOSPORUS*, © CNES, SPOT Image: SPOT HRV 10m (3, 2, 1), 6/13/93.

106 *PYRENEES*, WorldSat International, Inc., SSC Satellitbild, SOVZOND: Resurs-01-03 MSU-SK 160m (1, 2, 4), 1996-97.

107 *ALPS* (top), M-SAT, © Eurimage, Space Imaging: Landsat TM 30m (3, 2, 1), 8/31/89–7/10/94; (bottom) WorldSat International, Inc., SSC Satellitbild, SOVZOND: Resurs-01-3 MSU-SK 160m (1, 2, 4), 1996-97.

108 *ICELAND*, RAL, ESA, Natural Environment Research Council: ERS-2 ATSR-2 1km (3.7µm), 9/8/97; *NORWEGIAN FJORDS*, © Eurimage, ESA, Telespazio: Landsat TM 30m (3, 2, 1), 6/21/86.

109 *SCANDINAVIA*, SSC Satellitbild, NOAA, SOVZOND, WorldSat International, Inc.: NOAA AVHRR 1km; Resurs-01-3 MSU-SK 160m.

110 *MOUNT ETNA* (left), © CNES, SPOT Image: SPOT HRV 20m (3, 2, 1), 11/3/89; (middle) © Eurimage, ESA: Landsat TM 30m (4, 5, 3), 6/3/95, 7/21/95; (right) Instituto Nazionale di Geofisica, ESA, © Eurimage: Landsat TM 30m (2, 5, 7), 6/20/84; *MOUNT VESUVIUS*, © CNES, SPOT Image: SPOT HRV 10m (3, 2, 1), 10/8/95.

111 *BOOT OF ITALY*, DLR: NOAA AVHRR 1km (1, 2, 4), 1990-95.

112 *NETHERLANDS*, Space Imaging: Landsat TM 30m (7, 5, 1), 7/5/87.

113 *SCANDINAVIA'S "ØRESUND LINK."* WorldSat International, Inc., SSC Satellitbild, © CNES, SPOT Image: SPOT HRV 20m (1, 2, 3), 8/18/97.

114 *JET CONTRAILS*, GEOSPACE, NOAA: NIMBUS AVHRR 1km (4, 3, 1), October 1989; *VOLGOGRAD, RUSSIA*, © CNES, SPOT Image: SPOT HRV 20m (3, 2, 1), 7/26/96, 8/14/96.

115 *CHORNOBYL, UKRAINE*, EarthSat: Landsat TM 30m (4, 7, 3), 5/24/86.

116 *SPANISH COAST OIL SPILL*, Infocarto, S.A.: ERS-1 SAR 30m, 12/13/92.

117 *FROM AIR TO WATER POLLUTION*, University of New Hampshire: Landsat TM 30m (6, 5, 2), 9/30/85; *ADRIATIC SEA*, GEOSPACE, Space Imaging: Landsat TM 30m (3, 2, 1, and special algae enhancement), 7/9/89.

118 *LONDON, ENGLAND*, Wildgoose Publications, WorldSat International, Inc.: Airborne Zeiss RMK TOP Camera 25cm (natural color), summer 1994.

119 *PARIS, FRANCE*, © CNES, SPOT Image: SPOT HRV 10m (3, 2, 1), 8/10/95; *BERLIN, GERMANY*, M-SAT, © CNES, SPOT Image: SPOT HRV 10m (3, 2, 1), 9/28/97.

120 *STOCKHOLM, SWEDEN*, SSC Satellitbild, © CNES, SPOT Image, WorldSat International, Inc.: SPOT HRV 10m (1, 2, 3), 5/12/93.

121 *ST. PETERSBURG, RUSSIA*, Space Imaging: Landsat TM 30m (4, 5, 3), 6/8/87; *MOSCOW, RUSSIA*, © CNES, SPOT Image: SPOT HRV 10m (3, 2, 1), 6/6/95.

122 *LISBON, PORTUGAL*, © CNES, SPOT Image: SPOT HRV 10m (3, 2, 1), 7/30/97.

123 *ROME, ITALY*, EarthSat: Landsat TM 30m (3, 5, 4), 3/30/93; *VATICAN CITY*, Sovinformsputnik: Cosmos KVR-1000 2m, 8/9/94; Resurs-F KFA-1000 5m, 7/24/91.

124 *BUDAPEST, HUNGARY*, © CNES, SPOT Image: SPOT HRV 10m (3, 2, 1), 11/13/95; *VENICE, ITALY*, © CNES, SPOT Image: SPOT HRV 20m (3, 2, 1), 3/30/94.

125 *ATHENS, GREECE*, © CNES, SPOT Image: SPOT HRV 20m (3, 2, 1), 8/27/87.

ASIA

126-127 *MOUNT FUJI AND TERRAIN*, Shashin Kagaku Co., Ltd., GSI: Landsat TM 30m (3, 2 and 4, 1), 10/28/93, 11/4/93, 4/22/94, 11/4/94.

IMAGERY CREDITS

128-129 *ASIA*, NASA/JPL/CalTech/CAG, NGS: NOAA AVHRR 1km (2, 2, 1), 1990-94.

132-133 *GREAT WALL*, NASA/JPL/CalTech: space shuttle *Endeavor* SIR-C/X-SAR 25m (L-band HH, L-band HV, C-band HV), 4/10/94.

132 *UBAR*, NASA/JPL/CalTech: Landsat TM 30m (7, 4, 1), 1/13/86.

133 *SILK ROAD*, EarthSat: Resurs KFA-1000 5m (panchromatic), 11/13/86; *ANGKOR*, CRISP, © CNES, SPOT Image: SPOT HRV 20m (3, 2, 1), 12/12/96.

134 *MECCA*, ERIM International, Inc.: Landsat TM 30m (4, 3, 2), 1/24/86; *THE OLD CITY OF JERUSALEM*, Aeropan Aerial Photography: AZTECH Aircraft RMK TOP Zeiss Camera 0.2m, 2/16/97; *GANGES*, NRSA: IRS-1A LISS-II 36m (2, 3, 4), 2/4/89.

135 *THE HOLY LAND*, ROHR Productions, Ltd., EarthSat, © CNES, SPOT Image: Landsat TM 30m (3, 2, 1), 1/18/87; SPOT HRV 10m (panchromatic), 4/2/92–4/8/94.

136 *MOUNT EVEREST*, Swissphoto Vermessung, AG: Learjet Wild RC20 1:35,000, 12/20/84; *TIBET*, DLR, NASA/JSC: space shuttle *Endeavor* Linhof Camera (natural color), 10/10/94.

136-137 *THE HIMALAYA* (bottom), WorldSat International, Inc., Jim Knighton, NOAA: NOAA AVHRR 1km, 1991-94.

137 *THE HIMALAYA* (top), Scripps Institution of Oceanography, NOAA/NESDIS/NODC: GEOSAT, ERS-1, GTOPO30 Radar altimeter 3km, 1985-86, 1994-95.

138 *IRAN*, University of Munich, DLR, NASA/JSC: space shuttle *Columbia* German Spacelab D2 Mission MOMS-O2 4.5m, 4/26/93; Landsat TM 30m (7, 4, 1), 6/6/90.

139 *GOBI*, Space Imaging: Landsat TM 30m (7, 4, 2), 6/25/92.

140 *MOUNT PINATUBO*, RESTEC, NASDA: MOS-1, 1b MESSR 50m (3, 4, 2), 11/25/89, 7/5/91; *PINATUBO'S GLOBAL ASH*, NOAA/NESDIS/ORA: NOAA AVHRR 4km (color-coded aerosol optical thickness), May 1991, July 1991, August 1991.

141 *RUSSIAN VOLCANOES*, NASA/JPL/CalTech: space shuttle *Endeavor* SIR-C/X-SAR 25m (L-band HH, L-band HV, C-band HV), 10/25/94; *LAKE TOBA*, CRISP, © CNES, SPOT Image: SPOT HRV 20m (3, 2, 1), 7/29/96.

142 *ARAL SEA, 1976*, GEOSPACE, WorldSat International, Inc.: Landsat MSS 80m (6, 5, 4), December 1976; *ARAL SEA, 1997*, WorldSat International, Inc., SSC Satellitbild, SOVZOND: Resurs-01-3 MSU-SK 160m (1, 2, 4), October 1997.

143 *TASHKENT*, Space Imaging: Landsat TM 30m (7, 4, 2), 4/9/89.

144 *UNITED ARAB EMIRATES (U.A.E.), 1972*, USGS/Headquarters: Landsat MSS 80m (1, 2, 4), 11/11/72; *UNITED ARAB EMIRATES, 1990*, USGS/Headquarters: Landsat TM 30m (2, 4, 7), 8/28/90; *SAUDI ARABIAN OASIS*, © CNES, SPOT Image: SPOT HRV 20m (3, 2, 1), 5/17/92.

145 *KUWAITI FIRES*, USGS/EROS Data Center: Landsat TM 30m (7, 4, 2), 2/22/91.

146 *MEKONG RIVER DELTA*, CRISP, ESA: ERS-2 SAR 25m (bands 5/4/96, 6/9/96, 7/14/96).

147 *KATHMANDU VALLEY*, IFG: Aero Commander 680 FL RMKA Zeiss Camera 1:4,000 (natural color), 2/2/78; *BANGLADESH*, EarthSat: Landsat TM 30m (2, 4, 7), 1/10/89–1/21/90.

148 *PEARL RIVER DELTA* and *HONG KONG INTERNATIONAL AIRPORT* (top), Geocarto International Centre, RSGS: Landsat TM 30m (5, 4, 3), 12/10/88, 12/19/88; *HONG KONG INTERNATIONAL AIRPORT* (bottom), © CNES, SPOT Image: SPOT HRV 10m (3, 2, 1), 1/29/97.

149 *SINGAPORE*, CRISP, © CNES, SPOT Image: SPOT HRV 20m (3, 2, 1), 1/25/97, 6/19/97; *AIRPORT EXPANSION* (left to right), CRISP, © CNES, SPOT Image: SPOT HRV 20m (3, 2, 1), 6/19/86, 3/4/91, 5/3/97.

150 *BAGHDAD, IRAQ*, Space Imaging: Landsat TM 30m (7, 4, 2), 3/16/91.

151 *MUMBAI, INDIA*, EarthSat, © CNES, SPOT Image: SPOT HRV 20m (1, 2, 3), 9/30/94; *BANGKOK, THAILAND*, CRISP, © CNES, SPOT Image: SPOT HRV 20m (3, 2, 1), 5/28/97.

152 *BEIJING, CHINA*, Geocarto International Centre, RSGS: Landsat TM 30m (5, 4, 3), 4/9/95.

153 *SEOUL, SOUTH KOREA*, Space Imaging: Landsat TM 30m (4, 5, 3), 5/1/89; *TOKYO, JAPAN*, Geographical Survey Institute's Ministry of Construction: 250m DEM and land-use data.

AFRICA

154-155 *THE SAHARA*, © CNES, SPOT Image: SPOT HRV 20m (3, 2, 1), 9/28/88.

156-157 *AFRICA*, NASA/JPL/CalTech/CAG, NGS: NOAA AVHRR 1km (2, 2, 1), 1990-94.

160 *NILE DELTA*, EarthSat: Landsat MSS 80m (3, 2, 1), 1972, 1990; *PYRAMIDS OF GIZA*, Sovinformsputnik: Cosmos KVR-1000 2m, 2/27/91.

161 *LOWER NILE*, ESA: ERS-1 land SAR 30m (C-band), water ATSR 1km (sea surface temperature), 1992, 1995.

162 *KILIMANJARO*, © CNES, SPOT Image: SPOT HRV 20m (3, 2, 1), 2/7/94; *AFAR TRIANGLE*, GEOSPACE, Space Imaging: Landsat TM 30m (3, 2, 1), 3/9/85.

163 *NGORONGORO CRATER*, EarthSat: Landsat MSS 80m (4, 5, 7), 1/25/76.

164 *MAURITANIA*, © CNES, SPOT Image: SPOT HRV 20m (3, 2, 1), 10/6/93.

164-165 *ALGERIA, TUNISIA, AND LIBYA*, EarthSat: Landsat MSS 80m (4, 5, 7), 2/18/76.

165 *LIBYA*, EarthSat: Landsat MSS 80m (4, 5, 7), 2/19/75.

166 *ANCIENT SAHARA RIVER SYSTEMS*, USGS/Flagstaff: Landsat MSS 80m (5, 4, blue simulation), 11/25/75, 1/18/76; space shuttle *Columbia* SIR-A 40m (L-band), 11/14/81; *LIBYA*, IFG: Landsat MSS 80m (7, 5, 4), 1/29/76.

167 *OKAVANGO DELTA*, GEOSPACE: Landsat TM 30m (3, 2, 1), 9/13/84; *KALAHARI DESERT*, © CNES, SPOT Image: SPOT HRV 20m (3, 2, 1), 4/7/86.

168 *GRAN CANARIA*, © CNES, SPOT Image: SPOT HRV 10m (3, 2, 1), 11/29/93; *MAYOTTE, COMORO ISLANDS*, © CNES, SPOT Image: SPOT HRV 20m (3, 2, 1), 1994.

169 *MADAGASCAR*, USGS/Headquarters, ANGAP, USAID: Landsat MSS 80m (1, 2, 4), TM 30m, 1973-1995.

170 *TSETSE FLIES*, GEOSPACE, Space Imaging: Landsat TM 30m (2, 3, 4), 1/16/86.

171 *SAHARA DUST*, NASA/Langley Research Center: space shuttle *Discovery* Lidar In-space Technology Experiment (LITE) horizontal 740m x vertical 30m, 9/18/94; *ATLAS MOUNTAINS*, EarthSat: Landsat MSS 80m (7, 5, 4), 11/3/72.

172 *LAKE TURKANA*, USGS/EROS Data Center: Landsat MSS 80m (4, 2, 1), 2/1/73, 1/1/79, 1/12/89.

173 *EAST AFRICAN RIFT SYSTEM*, NASA/JPL/CalTech/CAG, NGS: NOAA AVHRR 1km (2, 2, 1), 1990-94.

174 *REFUGEE CAMPS, 1994* and *REFUGEE CAMPS, 1996*, UNHCR Environmental Database, I-MAGE

Consult (Namur, Belgium), ESA, © Eurimage: Landsat TM 30m (4, 5, 3), 8/3/94, 7/7/96.

175 *VIRUNGA MOUNTAINS* (left), Rutgers Center for Remote Sensing and Spatial Analysis, NASA/JPL/CalTech, EarthSat: space shuttle *Endeavor* SIR-C/X-SAR 25m (L-band HH, L-band HV, C-band HH), 10/4/94; (right) NASA/JPL/CalTech: space shuttle *Endeavor* SIR-C/X-SAR 25m (L-band HH, L-band HV, C-band HH), 4/13/94; *AGRICULTURAL FIRES*, ESA, CEOS, IGBP, NASA, NOAA, USGS, Ikonia processing by ESA/ESRIN: NOAA AVHRR 1km, 1993.

176 *CASABLANCA, MOROCCO*, EarthSat: Landsat MSS 80m (4, 5, 7), 10/21/78; *TRIPOLI, LIBYA*, © CNES, SPOT Image: SPOT HRV 20m (3, 2, 1), 4/2/93.

177 *ALGIERS, ALGERIA*, © CNES, SPOT Image: SPOT HRV 20m (3, 2, 1), 7/5/88; *CAIRO, EGYPT*, GEOSPACE: Landsat TM 30m (3, 2, 1), 7/2/84.

178 *CAPE TOWN, SOUTH AFRICA*, ISTAR, © CNES, SPOT Image: SPOT HRV 20m (3, 2, 1), 5/6/96.

179 *KINSHASA, DEM. REP. OF THE CONGO*, © Eurimage, SAC: Landsat TM 30m (3, 2, 1), 4/11/97; *NAIROBI, KENYA*, © Eurimage, SAC: Landsat TM 30m (4, 2, 1), 1/30/95.

AUSTRALIA AND NEW ZEALAND

180-181 *GREAT BARRIER REEF*, GEOIMAGE Pty., Ltd.: Landsat TM 30m (land 7, 4, 1; water 3, 2, 1), 9/17/89.

182-183 *AUSTRALIA*, NASA/JPL/CalTech/CAG, NGS: NOAA AVHRR 1km (2, 2, 1), 1990-94.

186 *SHARK BAY AND DENHAM SOUND*, DOLA: Landsat TM 30m (land 4, 3, 2; water 3, 2, 1), 8/30/86.

187 *GIBSON DESERT*, © CNES, SPOT Image: SPOT HRV 20m (3, 2, 1), 3/12/86; *TASMANIA*, GEOIMAGE Pty., Ltd.: Landsat MSS 50m (4, 2, 1), September 1985–May 1991.

188 *FIRE FOOTPRINT, 1980*, CSIRO: Landsat MSS 50m (7, 5, 4), 12/14/80.

189 *FIRE SCARS*, DOLA, ACRES: Landsat TM 30m (7, 4, 1), 9/22/94, 9/29/94; *LOOKING BACK, 1988*, CSIRO: Landsat MSS 50m (7, 5, 4), 2/25/88.

190-191 *STIRLING RANGE NATIONAL PARK*, CSIRO: Landsat MSS 50m (7, 5, 4), 2/13/88.

191 *ULURU (AYERS ROCK)*, VirtuoZo Systems International, NTDLPE, Vexcel Imaging Corp.: Airborne Zeiss Camera 1:30,000 planimetric aerial (top) and DEM (bottom) from aerial photograph, 10/14/82.

192 *PERTH*, DOLA, ACRES, © CNES, SPOT Image, Space Imaging: Landsat TM 30m (7, 4, 2), 1/25/96; SPOT HRV 10m (panchromatic), 1/15/95; *SYDNEY*, ACRES, © CNES, SPOT Image, Space Imaging: Landsat TM 30m (5, 4, 3), August 1995; SPOT HRV 10m (panchromatic), July 1995.

193 *CANBERRA*, ACRES: Landsat TM 30m (7, 4, 1), September 1990; *MELBOURNE*, ACRES: Landsat TM 30m (4, 5, 1), 12/14/88, 1/24/89.

194 *NEW ZEALAND*, NASA/JPL/CalTech/CAG, NGS: NOAA AVHRR 1km (2, 2, 1), 1990-94.

195 *MOUNT COOK*, Landcare Research New Zealand, Ltd., © CNES, SPOT Image: SPOT HRV 20m (3, 2, 1), 2/23/87; *MOUNT RUAPEHU*, Landcare Research New Zealand, Ltd., NOAA: NOAA AVHRR 1km (1, 2, 4), 6/17/96.

196 *MOUNT TARANAKI*, Landcare Research New Zealand, Ltd., NASDA/MITI: JERS-1 SAR 18m (L-band), 11/5/93.

197 *WELLINGTON*, Landcare Research New Zealand, Ltd., © CNES, SPOT Image, DEM data courtesy of DoSLI: SPOT HRV 20m (3, 2, 1), 4/7/86, 4/24/89; *CHRISTCHURCH*, Landcare Research New Zealand, Ltd., NASA: Landsat MSS 80m, 1970s.

ANTARCTICA

198-199 *JAMES ROSS ISLAND*, © CNES, SPOT Image: SPOT HRV 20m (3, 2, 1), 3/23/89.

200-201 *ANTARCTICA*, NASA/JPL/CalTech/CAG, NGS: NOAA AVHRR 1km (2, 2, 1), 1990-94.

204 *1997 RADAR MOSAIC*, Byrd Polar Research Center, RADARSAT International, CSA, Alaska SAR Facility: RADARSAT-1 SAR 25m (C-band), September–October 1997; *1994-95 RADAR MOSAIC*, University of Bristol: ERS-1 Radar altimeter 5km x 350m, April 1994–March 1995.

205 *LAMBERT GLACIER*, ACRES: Landsat TM 30m (4, 3, 2), March 1989; *EREBUS VOLCANO*, Byrd Polar Research Center, RADARSAT International, CSA, Alaska SAR Facility: RADARSAT-1 SAR 25m (C-band), 10/4/97.

206-207 *FILCHNER ICE SHELF*, USGS/Headquarters/EROS Data Center/Woods Hole: Landsat MSS 80m (7, 4), 11/11/73 (left) and 11/10/86 (right); *SOUTH ATLANTIC SEA ICE*, NASA/JPL/CalTech: space shuttle *Endeavor* SIR-C/X-SAR 25m (C-band HH, L-band HV, L-band HH), 10/3/94.

207 *ANTARCTIC SEA ICE*, NASA/GSFC: U.S. Air Force DMSP SSM/I 54km (wavelengths 1.55cm, 1.35cm, 0.81cm), 2/15/95 (left) and 9/15/95 (right).

208 *McMURDO SOUND*, USGS/Flagstaff: Landsat MSS 75m (7, 5, 4), 1973-75.

209 *OZONE HOLE*, NASA/GSFC: Earth Probe TOMS 1.25 degrees longitude, 1 degree latitude (120-440 Dobson units), 10/1/97; *SOUTH POLE*, Byrd Polar Research Center, RADARSAT International, CSA, Alaska SAR Facility: RADARSAT-1 SAR 25m (C-band), 9/14/97.

THE FUTURE

210 *NORTH AMERICA*, WorldSat International, Inc., NOAA: NOAA AVHRR 1km, 1991-94; *IKONOS*, Space Imaging.

211 *WHITE HOUSE*, VARGIS, LLC: Piper Navajo Chieftain Wild RC30 Aerial Film Camera 1m, 3/25/95.

ACKNOWLEDGMENTS

222 *SOUTHERN HEMISPHERE*, WorldSat International, Inc., NOAA: NOAA AVHRR 1km, 1996.

88–89; effects of El Niño on 9; physical map 74–75; political map 76–77; population 17, 90; tectonic forces 82–83, 86
South Australia, Australia 186
South China Sea 148, **148**
South Island, New Zealand 195, **195**, 197, **197**
South Pole 21, **23**, 186, 199, 204; station 209, **209**; *see also* Antarctica
Southwest N.P., Tasmania, Australia 187, **187**
Southeast Asia: Buddhists 134; fires 142; population 127; temple complexes 132
Southern Alps, New Zealand 181, 195, **195**, 197, **197**
Southern Oscillation *see* El Niño/Southern Oscillation (ENSO) phenomenon
Soviet Union 11; irrigation 142
Space junk 11, **11**
Spaceborne Imaging Radar (SIR-C) imagery: Russia 141, **141**
Spain 104, **104**, 106, **106**, 110, 171, 176; oil spill 116, **116**; *see also* Iberian Peninsula, Europe
Spatial resolution 14, **14**, 211
Special Sensor Microwave Imager (SSM/I): rainfall measurements 32, **32**
Spectral resolution 14, **14**, 211
Sputnik 1 (satellite) 10
Sri Lanka 141
Star dunes 164, **164–165**, 166, **166**
Stirling Range N.P., Western Australia, Australia **190–191**, 191
Stockholm, Sweden 120, **120**
Subduction 86; *see also* Earthquakes; Faults; Tectonic forces
Sudan: sleeping sickness 170
Suleiman the Magnificent, Sultan (Ottoman Empire) 134
Sumatra (island), Indonesia 141, **141**
Sun-synchronous orbits 10, 12, **12**
Superior, Lake, Canada-U.S. 55, **55**
Suruga Bay, Japan 127, **127**, 153, **153**
Susquehanna River, U.S. **52–53**, 53
Swan River, Western Australia, Australia 192, **192**
Sweden 109, **109**, 113, **113**, 120, **120**
Switzerland 98–99, 99, 106, 107, **107**
Sydney, New South Wales, Australia 192, **192**
Synthetic Aperture Radar (SAR) imagery 13; Egypt 161, **161**; New Zealand 196, **196**
Syr Darya River, Central Asia 142, **143**
Syria 135, **135**; Muslims 134

T

Table Bay, Cape Town, South Africa 178, **178**

Table Mt., Cape Province, South Africa 178, **178**
Tagus River, Portugal 122, **122**
Taklimakan Desert, Xinjiang Province, China 133, 136, 139
Tanganyika, Lake, East Africa 173, **173**
Tanzania 162, **162–163**, 173–174, **173–174**
Taranaki, Mt., North Island, New Zealand 196, **196**
Tashkent, Uzbekistan 142, **143**
Tasmania, Australia 186, 187, **187**
Tassili-n-Ajjer, Algeria **154–155**, 155
Tectonic forces 28, 34; Africa 162, 169, 171–173; Asia 136–137, 140; Europe 99, 108, 110; global plate map 28–29; South America 82–83, 86
Tel Aviv-Yafo, Israel 135, **135**
Telescope Peak, Death Valley, Calif. 50, **50–51**
Television and Infrared Observation Satellite (TIROS) 10, 10–11, 32
Tempelhof Airport, Berlin, Germany 119, **119**
Temporal resolution 14, **14**, 211
Tepuis 82–83, **82–83**
Terracing 147, **147**
Thailand 146, 151, **151**
Thailand, Gulf of 151, **151**
Thames River, England 118, **118**
Thane, India 151, **151**
Thematic Mapper (TM) imagery 123, **123**; Adriatic Sea 117, **117**; Argentina 91, **91**, 97, **97**; Australia 192–193, **192–193**; Bangladesh 147, **147**; Brazil **80–81**, 81, 90–91, **90–91**, 94–95, **94–95**; California 50, **51**, 60, **61**; Canada 56; creation of 12, **12**; Democratic Republic of the Congo 179, **179**; Egypt 177, **177**; Europe **98–99**, 99, 106, **106**; Israel 135, **135**; Italy 110, **110**; Jordan **105**; Kenya 179, **179**; Lebanon 135; Mali 170, **170**; Massachusetts **12**; Paraguay 91, **91**; Peru 90, **90**; Russia 15, **15**; Tanzania 162, **163**; United Arab Emirates 144, **144**; Uruguay 97, **97**; Utah 65, **65**; Uzbekistan 142, **143**; Washington, D.C. 71, **71**; *see also* Landsat Thematic Mapper (TM) imagery
Thermal Infrared Multispectral Scanner (TIMS) imagery 50, **50**; crater 54, **54**
3-D imagery: Africa 175, **175**, 178, **178**; Australia 191, **191**; California 66, **66**; Europe 107, **107**; France 106, **106**; Greenland 49; ice field 56, **56**; Italy 110, **110**, 123, **123**; Japan 153, **153**; Mexico 54, **54**, 71, **71**; South America 86, **86**; Spain 106, **106**; Venezuela 92, **92**
Tian Shan (mountains), China-Kyrgyzstan 127
Tiber River, Italy 122, 123, **123**

Tibet: Buddhists 134
Tibet, Plateau of 136–137, **136–137**, 139
Tierra del Fuego (archipelago), South America 84, **84–85**, 85
Tigris River, Turkey-Iraq 132, 150, **150**
TIROS *see* Television and Infrared Observation Satellite (TIROS)
Titicaca, Lake, Bolivia-Peru 78, **78**
Toba, Lake, Sumatra (island), Indonesia 141, **141**
Tokositna River, Alaska 49
Tokyo, Japan **126**, 127, 153, **153**
Tokyo Bay, Japan **126–127**, 127, 153, **153**
Tongariro N.P., North Island, New Zealand 195, **195**
TOPEX/Poseidon radar altimeter satellite imagery 37, **36–37**
Tornadoes 58
Torrens, Lake, South Australia, Australia 186
Tower Bridge, London, England 118, **118**
Trade winds: effects on sea level 36
Trans-Alaska Pipeline, Alaska 64, 65
Transantarctic Mts., Antarctica 204, **204**
Tripoli, Libya 176, **176**, 177
Tropical Rainfall Measuring Mission satellite 33
Tsetse flies 170
Tsunamis 34
Tuareg people 164
Tunisia: sand dunes 164, **164–165**
Tupungato, Mt., Argentina-Chile 86
Turkana, Lake, Kenya 172, **172**
Turkey 104, **105**, 106, 110, 135; Greek ruins 132; Muslims 134; *see also* Tigris River
Turneffe Islands, Belize 56, **57**
Tutsi people 174
Twelve Apostles (mountains), South Africa 178, **178**
Tyrrhenian Sea 123, **123**

U

Ubar (ancient city), Oman 132, **132**
Ubari Sand Sea, Africa 166, **166**
Uhuru Peak, Kilimanjaro, Tanzania 162, **162**
Ukraine 114, **115**
Uluan Peninsula, Samosir Island, Sumatra (island), Indonesia 141, **141**
Uluru (Ayers Rock), Northern Territory, Australia 191, **191**
United Arab Emirates (U.A.E.) 144, **144**
United Kingdom: tensions with Argentina 85
United Nations (U.N.) 21, 39
United Nations High Commissioner for Refugees (UNHCR) 174
United States 40; borders 62–63, **62–63**; contiguous

40–41, 41, 46, **46–47**, 62; intelligence imagery 11, **11**; weather 41, 58; *see also* Arizona; California; Colorado River; Delaware; Florida; Great Lakes; Louisiana; Maryland; Massachusetts; Mississippi River; Montana; New England; New Mexico; New York, New York; North Carolina; Pacific Northwest (region); St. Lawrence River; Utah; Virginia
Ural Mts., Russia 104, 136
Uruguay 97, **97**
Uruguay River, South America 97, **97**
U.S. Capitol, Washington, D.C. 11, **11**
U.S. Department of Defense: elevation databases 18, 32
U.S. Geological Survey: MSS imagery 208, **208**
U.S. Navy 208
Ushuaia, Argentina 84, 85
Utah: lake 65, **65**
Uttar Pradesh, India 134
Uzbekistan 142, **142–143**

V

V-2 rocket 10
Valdez, Alaska 65
Valparaíso, Chile 96
Vancouver, British Columbia, Canada 66, **66**
Vatican City 122, **123**
Vatnajökull Glacier, Iceland 108, **108**
Vaux, Calvert 69
Venezuela 82–83, **82–83**, 92, **92**
Venice, Italy 124, **124**
Vesuvius, Mt., Italy 110, **110**
Victoria, Australia 186, **187**, 188, 193, **193**
Vietnam: irrigation 146, **146**
Vinson Massif (peak), Antarctica 204
Virginia 14, **14**, 52, 53, 71, **71**
Virunga Mts., Africa 175, **175**
Volcanoes 28, 34; Africa 162, **162**, 168, **168**, 173, **173**; Antarctica 205, **205**; Asia 126, 140, 141, **141**; Europe 99, 108; New Zealand 196, **196**; North America **4–5**, 5, 60, **60**, 71, **71**; South America 78, **79**, 87, **87**
Volgograd, Russia: petrochemical complex fire 114, **114**

W

Wadden Zee, Netherlands **112**, 113
Wairarapa Falls, North Island, New Zealand 197
Waldecker, Burkhart 160
Wales 98
Washington: volcanoes **4–5**, 5, 60, **60**
Washington, D.C. 52, 53, 71, **71**, 210, **211**; U.S. Capitol 11, **11**
Washington, George 71
Water: pollution 116, 121;

shortages 144, 146, 166
Waves: global 24, **25**
Weather satellites 10, 10–11, 32–33
Weddell Sea, Antarctica **198–199**, 199, 204
Wellington, New Zealand 197, **197**
West Bengal, India 134
West Falkland Island, South Atlantic Ocean 85, **85**
West Indies 40, *see also* Caribbean Sea
Western Australia, Australia **186–187**, 186–189, **190–192**, 191–192
Western Desert, Egypt 160
Westminster Abbey, London, England 118, **118**
White House, Washington, D.C. 71, **71**, 211
White Sands, New Mexico 10
Will, George 66
Wind speed: global 24, **25**
Winkel Tripel Projection 18–20
Winslow, Arizona 54
World Heritage Sites (UNESCO): Australia 187, **187**; New Zealand 195, **195**
World War II 10, 35, 119, 124, 153
World Wide Web *see* Internet
WorldSat imagery: volcano 60, **60**
Wright, Wilbur: first aerial photo taken by 10

X

Xingu River, Brazil 81, **81**
Xinjiang Uygar Autonomous Region, China 133, 136, 139, **139**

Y

Yamuna River, India 134, **134**
Yangtze River, China 127, 136
Yellow River, China 127, 132, 136
Yellow Sea 132
Yerba Buena Island, California 66, **67**
Yokohama, Honshu (island), Japan 126, 127, 153, **153**
Yucatán, Mexico 54, **54**

Z

Zagros Mts., Iran-Iraq 138, 139
Zaire: refugees 174; *see also* Democratic Republic of the Congo
Zuider Zee, Netherlands **112**, 113

LIBRARY OF CONGRESS CIP DATA

National Geographic Society (U.S.). Book Division.
National Geographic satellite atlas of the world.
p. cm.
Includes index.
ISBN 0-7922-7216-1 (reg) ISBN 0-7922-7217-x (dlx)
1. Earth—Remote-sensing images. I. Title.
G1046.A43 N3 1998 <G&M>
912—DC21
98-24760
CIP
MAPS

ACKNOWLEDGMENTS

In addition to the many groups and organizations named on pages 212-213, the National Geographic Book Division and National Geographic Maps wish to extend a special thanks to the individuals listed below for their generous assistance during the preparation of this atlas.

Aeropan Aerial Photography CARLOS KATZMAN
Alaska SAR Facility (ASF) JOANNE GROVES, DONNA SANDBERG
Australian Centre for Remote Sensing (ACRES) JIM MOLLISON
Byrd Polar Research Center KENNETH C. JEZEK
Canada Centre for Remote Sensing (CCRS) CHRISTINE W. LANGHAM
Centre for Remote Imaging, Sensing, and Processing (CRISP) LIM HOCK
CSIRO Office of Space Science and Applications SUSAN CAMPBELL, DEAN GRAETZ
Department of Land Administration (DOLA) PETER SANDERS
EarthData International of Maryland, LLC CHRIS BARNARD, DAVID WHITE
Earth Satellite Corporation (EARTHSAT) BYRON R. LOUBERT, MAX MILLER
ERIM International, Inc. LARRY E. REED
Eurimage, S.p.A. CHRIS PHILLIPS
European Space Agency (ESA) WENDY SLATER
Geocarto International Centre KAM NIN AU
Geographical Survey Institute (GSI) YOSHIKAZU FUKUSHIMA
GEOIMAGE Pty. Ltd. BOB WALKER
GEOSPACE Beckel-Satellitenbilddaten, GmbH LOTHAR BECKEL
German Aerospace Center (DLR) STEFAN W. DECH, WOLFGANG METT, ACHIM ROTH
Hammon, Jensen, Wallen, and Associates, Inc. (HJW) ALAN H. AMBACHER
Imagerie Stéréo Appliquée au Relief (ISTAR) CHRISTOPHE LANCHON
Infocarto, S.A. JULIA YAGUE
Institute for Applied Geosciences (IFG) WILLI MEIER
Instituto de Ingeniería GUSTAVO RUIZ
Instituto Nacional de Pesquisas Espaciais (INPE) PAULO ROBERTO MARTINI
Istituto Nazionale di Geofisica (ING) FABRIZIA BUONGIORNO, LAURA COLINI
Landcare Research New Zealand, Ltd. STELLA E. BELLISS
Lunar and Planetary Institute VIRGIL L. SHARPTON
M-SAT Corporation, Rockville, Maryland JEAN-YVES CARTOUX
NASA/Ames Research Center BRUCE COFFLAND
NASA/Goddard Institute for Space Studies (GISS) WILLIAM B. ROSSOW
NASA/Goddard Space Flight Center (GSFC) ANTONIO J. BUSALACCHI, JR.,
    DONALD J. CAVALIERI, GENE C. FELDMAN, DOROTHY K. HALL, A. FRITZ HASLER,
    ALEX KEKESI, CHESTER J. KOBLINSKY, CLAIRE L. PARKINSON, HAL F. PIERCE,
    GREGORY W. SHIRAH, BARBARA SUMMEY, JOEL SUSSKIND, COMPTON J. TUCKER
NASA/JPL/CALTECH ELSA ABBOTT, MICHAEL J. ABRAMS, RONALD G. BLOM,
    NEVIN A. BRYANT, MOUSTAFA CHAHINE, ROBERT E. CRIPPEN, THOMAS G. FARR,
    TONY FREEMAN, ROBERT O. GREEN, MARY HARDIN, KEVIN HUSSEY,
    ANNE B. KAHLE, WILLIAM C. PATZERT, JEFF PLAUT, ERIC J. RIGNOT
NASA/Langley Research Center SYED ISMAIL, KATHLEEN POWELL, DAVID WINKER
NASA/Marshall Space Flight Center (MSFC) STEVEN J. GOODMAN, KEVIN DRISCOLL,
    TOM SEVER
NOAA/National Weather Service (NWS) CRAIG BAUER, RAY MOORE
*NOAA/NESDIS/Cooperative Institute for Meteorological Satellite Studies at
    University of Wisconsin–Madison* GARY S. WADE
NOAA/NESDIS/Headquarters JANE A. D'AGUANNO, PATRICIA W. VIETS
NOAA/NESDIS/National Climatic Data Center (NCDC) RICHARD S. CRAM,
    AXEL GRAUMANN, RALPH E. MEIGGS
NOAA/NESDIS/National Geophysical Data Center (NGDC) KIMBERLY BAUGH,
    CHRIS ELVIDGE, PETER W. SLOSS
NOAA/NESDIS/National Oceanographic Data Center (NODC) WALTER H. F. SMITH
NOAA/NESDIS/Office of Research and Applications (ORA) RALPH FERRARO,
    PAUL P. PELLEGRINO, LARRY L. STOWE
National Remote Sensing Agency (NRSA) R. JOSEPH AROKIADAS, D. KAVERIDEVI
National Remote Sensing Centre, Ltd. (NRSC) JOHN J. SHANNON
RADARSAT International (RSI) CORY ASPDEN
Remote Sensing Technology Center of Japan (RESTEC) TADAHIRO WATANABE
ROHR Productions, Ltd. RICHARD L. W. CLEAVE
Rutherford Appleton Laboratory (RAL) NIGEL R. HOUGHTON
Scripps Institution of Oceanography DAVID T. SANDWELL
Shashin Kagaku Co., Ltd. MASAO TANAKA
Sovinformsputnik Y. DENISOV, M. FOMTCHENKO
Space Imaging MARK E. BRENDER, HOWARD BURDICK, E. DREW CASSIDY,
    CARL GRAY, MARY GREENE, JEFFREY K. HARRIS, LINDA LIDOV, JOHN T. NEER,
    AMY OPPERMAN

SPOT Image Corporation ISABELLE GUIDOLIN-JARA, TED NANZ,
    CLARK A. NELSON, RENÉE SAUNDERS
Swedish Space Corporation (SSC) CHRISTER ANDERSSON, MATS ERIKSON,
    JÖRGEN HARTNOR
Swissphoto Vermessung, AG MANUELA SCHMIDHAUSER
Systems for World Surveillance, Inc. (SWS) STEPHEN W. STETSON
United Nations High Commissioner for Refugees (UNHCR)
    JEAN-YVES BOUCHARDY
United States Senate JOHN GLENN
United States Senate Committee on Governmental Affairs SEBASTIAN O'KELLY
Universidad de Alcalá, Madrid EMILIO CHUVIECO, JOSÉ SANCHO
University of Bristol JONATHAN L. BAMBER
University of California Santa Barbara, Remote Sensing Research Unit
    JOHN E. ESTES, KAREN D. KLINE
University of Miami OTIS B. BROWN, ROBERT H. EVANS
University of Munich MICHAELA FREI
University of New Hampshire BARRETT N. ROCK
University of Wisconsin–Madison THOMAS M. LILLESAND
U.S. Naval Space Command DAVID C. LYON, GARY WAGNER, TERESA WATKINS
USGS/EROS Data Center RONALD E. BECK, THOMAS R. LOVELAND,
    ROSE TYRRELL
USGS/Flagstaff PAT S. CHAVEZ, JR., JO-ANN ISBRECHT, BAERBEL K. LUCCHITTA,
    GERALD G. SCHABER (retired)
USGS/Headquarters JANE G. FERRIGNO, PAUL P. HEARN, JR.,
    JEAN-CLAUDE THOMAS
USGS/Woods Hole RICHARD S. WILLIAMS, JR.
VARGIS, LLC DAN BROOKS, ALYONA RIAZANTSEVA, GREG TILLEY
Vexcel Imaging Corporation HEINZ LIPPMANN
VirtuoZo Systems International GRAEME BROOKE
WorldSat International, Inc. SCOTT GOWAN, EMERY MILLER, ROBERT D. STACEY

Composition for this book by the National Geographic Society Book Division. Color separations by the National Geographic Society Pre-press Services and Digital Color Image, Pennsauken, New Jersey. Printed and bound by Cayfosa Industria Gráfica, Barcelona, Spain.

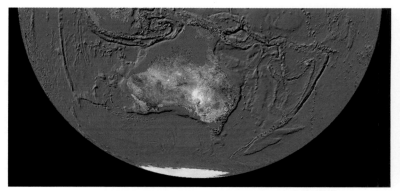

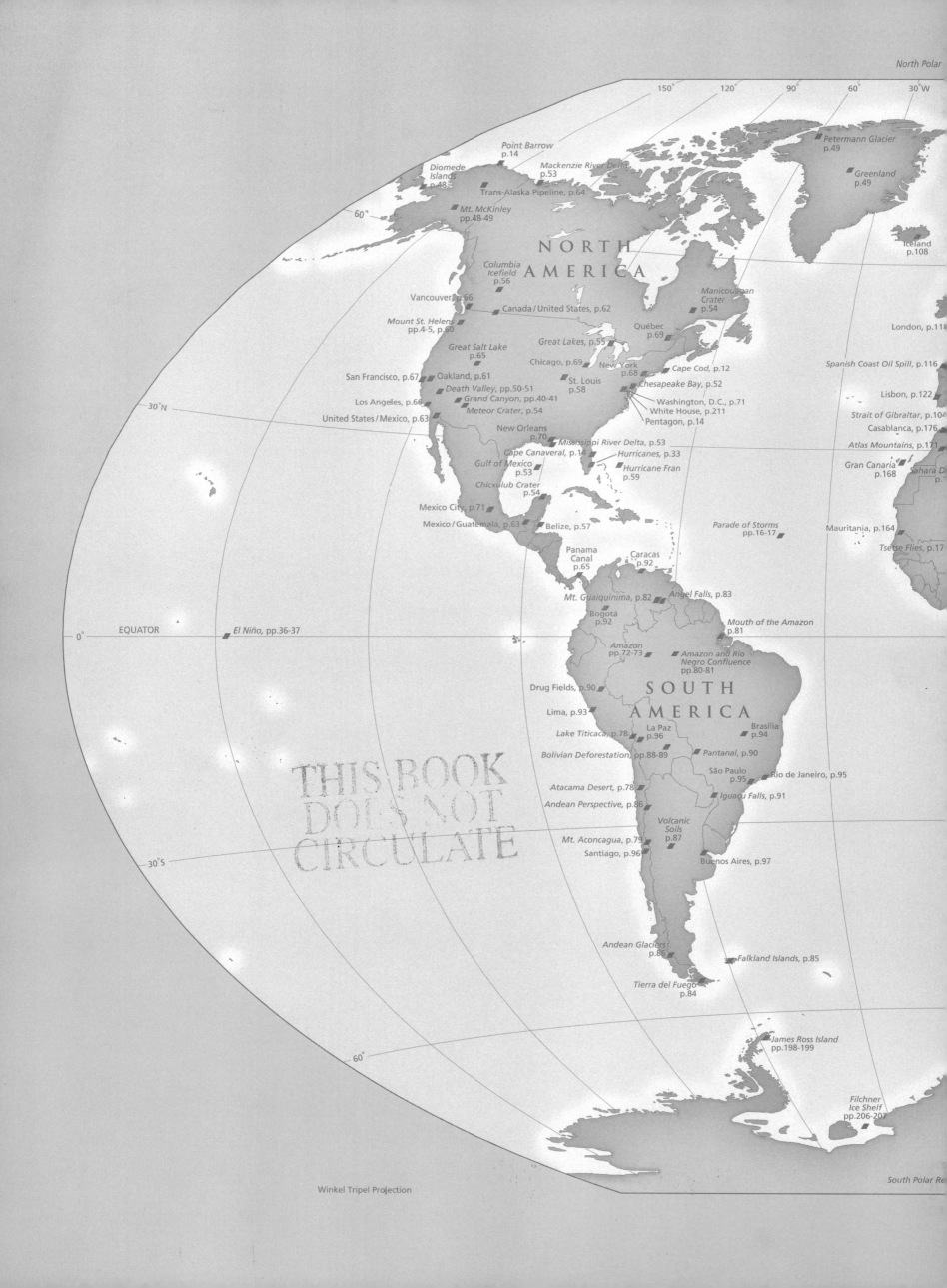

North Polar

150° 120° 90° 60° 30°W

Point Barrow
p.14

Diomede
Islands
p.48

Mackenzie River Delta
p.53

Petermann Glacier
p.49

Trans-Alaska Pipeline, p.64

Greenland
p.49

60°

Mt. McKinley
pp.48-49

NORTH
AMERICA

Iceland
p.108

Columbia
Icefield
p.56

Vancouver, p.66

Canada / United States, p.62

Manicouagan
Crater
p.54

Mount St. Helens
pp.4-5, p.60

Québec
p.69

London, p.118

Great Salt Lake
p.65

Great Lakes, p.55

Chicago, p.69

Spanish Coast Oil Spill, p.116

San Francisco, p.67

Oakland, p.61

New York
p.68

Cape Cod, p.12

Lisbon, p.122

Death Valley, pp.50-51

St. Louis
p.58

Chesapeake Bay, p.52

30°N

Los Angeles, p.66

Grand Canyon, pp.40-41

Washington, D.C., p.71

Strait of Gibraltar, p.104

United States / Mexico, p.63

Meteor Crater, p.54

White House, p.211

Casablanca, p.176

Pentagon, p.14

Atlas Mountains, p.171

New Orleans
p.70

Mississippi River Delta, p.53

Gran Canaria
p.168

Cape Canaveral, p.14

Hurricanes, p.33

Sahara D
p.1

Gulf of Mexico
p.53

Hurricane Fran
p.59

Chicxulub Crater
p.54

Mexico City, p.71

Parade of Storms
pp.16-17

Mauritania, p.164

Mexico / Guatemala, p.63

Belize, p.57

Tsetse Flies, p.17

Panama
Canal
p.65

Caracas
p.92

Mt. Guaiquinima, p.82

Angel Falls, p.83

Bogotá
p.92

Mouth of the Amazon
p.81

EQUATOR

0°

El Niño, pp.36-37

Amazon
pp.72-73

Amazon and Rio
Negro Confluence
pp.80-81

SOUTH
AMERICA

Drug Fields, p.90

Lima, p.93

La Paz
p.96

Brasília
p.94

Lake Titicaca, p.78

Pantanal, p.90

Bolivian Deforestation, pp.88-89

THIS BOOK
DOES NOT
CIRCULATE

São Paulo
p.95

Rio de Janeiro, p.95

Atacama Desert, p.78

Iguaçu Falls, p.91

Andean Perspective, p.86

Volcanic
Soils
p.87

Mt. Aconcagua, p.79

30°S

Santiago, p.96

Buenos Aires, p.97

Andean Glaciers
p.86

Falkland Islands, p.85

Tierra del Fuego
p.84

60°

James Ross Island
pp.198-199

Filchner
Ice Shelf
pp.206-207

South Polar Re